Parents and Teachers

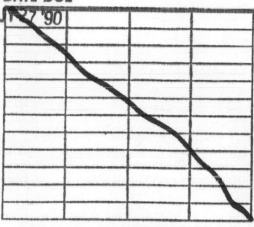

Parents and Teachers:
A Resource Book for Home,
School, and Community Relations

Doreen J. Croft

De Anza College

Wadsworth Publishing Company, Inc.
Belmont, California

Education and Family Studies Editor: Roger Peterson
Production Editor: Connie Martin
Designer: Nancy Benedict
Illustrator: Martha Weston

Printed in the United States of America
1 2 3 4 5 6 7 8 9 10—83 82 81 80 79

Library of Congress Cataloging in Publication Data

Croft, Doreen J.
    Parents and teachers.

    Includes bibliographies and index.
    1. Home and school. 2. Parent-teacher
relationships.
3. Parent-teacher conferences. I. Title.
LC225.C72   371.1'03   78–11130
ISBN 0–534–00610–8

This book is lovingly dedicated
to the memory of my mom and dad,
whose positive influences are
hopefully reflected in these pages.

Parents must make room in their hearts and
then in their house and then in their schedule for
their children. No poor parent is too poor to do that,
and no middle-class parent is too busy

Jesse Jackson

Contents

3. Guidance for Parents 97

Appendix of Resources 169

Preface

This book was written to fulfill a need for a practical guide and resource for home, school, and community relations. More so than ever before, teachers must involve parents more completely in school life. It is my hope that this book will assist teachers in this important process.

Many changes in the field of early education have taken place since I first started teaching. But collaboration between the home and school had been going on long before I entered the picture and, I am sure, will continue long after I'm gone. This ongoing relationship has not been without problems and controversy, but to those of us who have been involved, there appears to be a common core of materials, ideas, and workable guides that have resulted from and survived the many years of cooperative involvement between parents and teachers.

I have gathered together these materials, some of which have a modern emphasis, some of which are familiar to old-timers in the field of parent-teacher relations. Since I started teaching nursery school more than twenty-five years ago I have, like most of my colleagues, saved, collected, hoarded, and squirreled away handouts, teaching guides, helpful hints, and what-have-you for the day when they "might come in handy." My work with parents and teachers has forced me to sort out, sift through, and evaluate these materials, and present them in a more organized and systematic format. This book is the result.

Although some of the pages will seem familiar, many others are the result of my direct experiences with families from a wide variety of cultural and socioeconomic backgrounds. The age span to which I am exposed goes from infancy to senior citizens. I am indeed fortunate to have such a rich background for learning.

This book is divided into four parts. Part 1 discusses the importance of sensitive communications, individual differences, and protocol. Part 2 deals with specific kinds of parent-teacher meetings and activities. Part 3 provides teachers with some guidelines for answering some of the typical questions that many parents believe teachers should be able to answer. No formula answers are provided. Parents, their children, and their situations differ, and these suggestions are offered merely as a starting point for further reading for both teachers and parents. In the Appendix of Resources, a compilation of checklists, parent and teacher evaluation forms, referral agencies, and planning schedules is offered. The suggestions are based on my experience and that of teachers and parents with whom I have worked. They are "food for thought" for your imagination and creativity.

I sincerely hope the materials and experiences presented here will be useful.

Acknowledgments

Writing a book can be a lonely task. I used to wonder how a person could be so self-disciplined as to spend hundreds of hours confined to a typewriter and a room cluttered with piles of resource materials. I find it is fatal to dwell on such matters before starting, but now that the book is complete, I rejoice in having reached the end of the tunnel. I can now luxuriate in contemplating the details of my journey.

My many lonely hours of writing were made infinitely more bearable by my good friend and editor Roger Peterson. From the moment I conceived the idea of this book to the present, Roger has been of invaluable assistance—providing suggestions, sending materials, helping with the outline, summarizing reviews, and generally being supportive. I think he also did some prodding, but he was so charming and diplomatic that I welcomed it. Roger's talented editing and writing skills, combined with his extensive knowledge of the field of education, have convinced me that he should write a book of his own.

The first draft of this manuscript was prepared by the De Anza College word-processing department. I am deeply indebted to Dick Weismann for the many hours he spent agonizing over my poorly typed, hand-corrected, confusing drafts of the first stages of this book. He spent many hours after his regular working day to help me make my deadlines. Dick's professionalism sets a high standard for others to follow.

The original art has been revised and part opening drawings have been added, but the first manuscript required the rendering of patterns and cartoons. I am indebted to Kathy Mitchell for working under great time pressure and to her husband Tim for his help in preparing the material. Margaret Jackson of De Anza College's graphics department provided her usual creativity and skill to design the original manuscript cover.

During the last few weeks of writing, when all of the elements seemed too disorganized to pull together in order to make the deadline, two people came to my rescue. Cynthia Henderson, a library assistant and college student, took time from her busy schedule of classes to research some titles. My elder daughter, Karen Croft, applied her skills as a research assistant in the psychology department at Stanford University to make suggestions and help with editing. She spent the better part of a weekend compiling and annotating the list of referral agencies in the appendix. She did a very professional job, and I'm proud of her!

During the early stages of writing, my younger daughter, Colleen Croft, provided positive reinforcement in the form of praise and encouragement. She helped me set short-term goals and checked up on me for progress reports. My early education techniques have not been wasted.

My students in the Home, School, Community class suffered through the trial renditions of this book with tolerance and good humor. Their observations and suggestions contributed much to the final revised manuscript. They have suggested that my indebtedness to them be reflected in their grades.

My colleague, sometime coauthor, and best friend Robert Hess brought me articles and research materials to help give a broader perspective to the book. He lent encouragement and support at crucial times, and the great dinners he prepared for me when I was too tired to cook cannot be adequately acknowledged here.

Lastly, I want to express my appreciation to the manuscript reviewers whom Wadsworth provided: Joyce Huggins of Fresno State University, Mary Knox Weir of Long Beach City College, Kay Pasley Tudor of Washington State University, Marie Van Schuyver of Northeastern Oklahoma State University, Mary Shepard Cook of Florida Junior College, and Sheryl Fullerton, Wadsworth's pre-production editor. Their contributions helped make this a better book.

Although the task of writing can be lonely, I have been warmed by the knowledge that these people cared enough to lend support above and beyond the ordinary. I want them to know I shall be forever grateful.

Parents and Teachers

Part 1
Working and Communicating with Parents

Introduction

How do you suppose your parents learned how to be parents? Do certain insights on effective parenting go along naturally with becoming a mother or father? Does a person know automatically on giving birth what is best for a baby?

It is likely that your parents and their parents before them learned how to raise children by watching the adults around them. They got their ideas about feeding, discipline, sex, manners, and generally raising a child through their daily living experiences. They developed habits such as eating certain foods and sleeping certain hours and generally behaving and believing in certain ways because of the habits and beliefs of their parents. And so it goes—on and on from one generation to another. Parents influence their children, and the children grow up, become parents, and influence their children.

However, each generation gradually discards and revises some of the outmoded parenting methods, and beliefs become modified and changed. Sometimes these changes result in "better parents"; other times, results are less than positive. Ideas about discipline, for example, have changed radically from your grandparents' time to ours. Because of child-rearing experts and researchers, many parents have been influenced to try new ways of parenting—ways quite different from the way they were raised.

Today's parents have many more choices to make than their parents before them. We are bombarded with media messages, hundreds of books by "experts" telling us how to raise a healthier, happier, more intelligent child. We are hit with statistics bewailing the sad state of our society, and much of the blame is assigned to parents.

Our new technology in science, education, psychology, and communication has a profound influence on each of us and affects how we feel about people and things. Our attitudes are often shaped by people we don't even know or see. The choices given to us are more numerous and confusing than those offered our grandparents. Through modern technology the pace of our lives has increased dramatically over previous generations, and often, this modernization has made "commonsense" child rearing useless and outmoded.

All this change often results in confusion, apathy, and unhappiness. "New" approaches to living, child rearing, marriage relationships, and education are being examined. Parents and teachers often feel compelled to adopt more modern techniques without the advantages of having older and wiser adults share helpful hints with them about whether or not these techniques will work. We are increasingly pressed to explore new ways to live and work without help or guidance from others.

Where and to whom do parents turn for guidance? Many turn to teachers. This kind of collaboration between home and school has become increasingly more important in recent years. There is recognition that the alliance formed by parents and teachers to reinforce common goals for children is indeed a powerful influence. Each aspect of the parent-teacher relationship enhances and strengthens the total cooperative effort. Teachers provide educational expertise, objectivity, and of course, many affective elements unique to a child-teacher relationship. The parents, by virtue of being parents, add knowledge about the child that can be acquired only through the intimacy, love, and caring existing between parent and child. Together, the combination is unbeatable.

The following section covers communication, team teaching, working with nontraditional families, and generally expanding the areas of interaction between parents and teachers.

1

Reasons for Being Concerned about Parents

Today, teachers are so overworked writing reports, attending meetings, keeping records, and planning curriculum materials that they feel they hardly have any time to devote to the children they are supposed to be teaching. So why be concerned about parents—an involvement that undoubtedly will require even more of the teacher's time?

Life used to be much simpler for parents and teachers—at least where decisions and choices were concerned. Roles and responsibilities were more clear-cut. Parents and the church were to teach values, morals, ethics, and proper behavior; teachers were to teach reading, writing, and arithmetic. If children misbehaved in school, the teacher or principal punished them and then reported the incident to the parents, who were ultimately responsible for "straightening their child out."

The Changing Family

Our families and schools have undergone more changes in the last decade than in fifty years of our grandparents' time. Today, our roles are no longer as clearly defined.

When our parents were young, there were usually more family members in the home to teach children "how to behave." For example, in the 1920s more than half the households had at least one other adult—grandparent, aunt, uncle—besides the two parents. In the 1950s that figure dropped to 10 percent, and today it is more like 4 percent. That means that most of the teaching of values and "proper behavior" rests with Mom and Dad.

Today, however, more often than not, Mom is out working. In 1975, 54 percent of mothers with school-age children (six to seventeen years of age) were in the labor force. Thirty-nine percent of mothers with preschoolers (children under six) were working—more than three times as many as in 1948. An even more astounding statistic shows that nearly one out of every three mothers of an infant (children under three years of age) is working.

Not only is mother out of the house and away from her young child, but in more and more cases, one of the parents—usually the father—is missing completely. One out of six children under eighteen years of age lives with only one parent. In 1974, 13 percent of all infants under three—nearly one million babies—lived with only one parent.[1]

In addition to the increasing numbers of single-parent families, there are families formed through remarriages, resulting in six million children living with stepparents.

What are the implications of all these statistics for parents and teachers of today? In what ways does the changing family scene affect us and how are we expected to deal with these changes?

Obviously, today's parent has a much more complex task of raising a young child. Most young people no longer have an extended family of

---

1. Urie Bronfenbrenner, "The American Family in Decline," excerpted from *Current Magazine*, January 1977, p. 41.

grandparents, cousins, brothers and sisters, and parents to rely on for baby-sitting and just plain old commonsense advice. The mother or father now has to make important decisions about teaching values and reinforcing them all alone. Certainly there are books and resource organizations, but those aren't the same as a caring relative. Many of today's parental anxieties stem from this feeling of being alone and being overwhelmed with the responsibility for making decisions. Our institutions seem to be of little help. The church, the school, and the larger society seem to be in conflict as to what is good and bad. There are no clear-cut models of what a child should grow up to be like—at least none that everyone agrees on and supports consistently.

Some of the most significant changes affecting the lives of parents are: (1) the increasing number of divorces, leaving only one parent to raise the children; (2) occupational mobility—having to move in order to keep or find a job; (3) the breakdown of friendly, stable neighborhoods; (4) school districts that require children to leave their neighborhoods to attend; (5) separate patterns of social life for different age groups; and (6) the delegation of child care to institutions.[2]

Increasing needs to work in order to provide food and shelter place a dilemma on the parent of today. Less and less time is spent with children—less teaching at home, less guidance, less loving and nurturing. When a mother or father has to spend most of his or her waking hours working to earn enough to pay for just the basic needs of a family, there is little time or energy left to spend with children. In addition, many working parents are too tired by the end of a day to attend classes or educational seminars to discuss child-rearing practices. The Russell Sage Foundation reports that some mothers devote as little as fifteen minutes a day to actual communication with their preschoolers.[3] Many families no longer sit down to eat together, or share in a family project, or simply converse. Parents rely on television to baby-sit their children, and the children themselves have gotten into the habit of sitting impassively in front of the TV and tuning out anything the rest of the family may have to communicate. In a very real sense, parents are being pushed out of the traditional family roles by social and economic forces beyond their control.

With so many forces working against the nuclear family, it is no wonder that child abuse, family abandonment, suicide, and delinquency are on the rise.

2. Kenneth L. Woodward and Phyllis Malamud, "The Parent Gap," *Newsweek*, September 22, 1975, p. 50.
3. Ibid., p. 55.

Parents of today's children often need somewhere to turn for help. According to the General Mills survey of American families, parents report they are most likely to turn to teachers for advice rather than family agencies, social workers, or other such support services.[4] The challenge of meeting this responsibility relies heavily upon good parent-teacher relationships.

Reasons for Parent Involvement

In addition to the changing needs of today's families, the teacher must be familiar with some of the reasons leading to greater parent involvement in the schools.

During the 1960s, when civil rights became a major issue in the country, schools, along with other publicly supported institutions, were criticized for being unresponsive to the needs of the people they served. Political pressures and greater awareness among citizen groups were sufficient to bring about programs mandating more community control. The rationale was that schools would be more responsive to the needs of low-income, minority children if parents were actually involved in the classrooms and in decision-making roles. Since many teachers are from a middle-class culture, the argument was that they tended to be insensitive to people who are different.

Another important factor contributing to the support of parents was the failure of early-intervention programs to maintain the initial gains experienced by children. Follow Through programs such as Bereiter-Engelmann's model of pattern-drill lessons and Caldwell's omnibus day care demonstrated impressive cognitive gains, only to have these gains decline. In order to maintain the child's learning success, parents were necessary to sustain the school's accomplishments.[5]

Results of the surveys of both parent participation and nonparticipation programs concluded, according to Bronfenbrenner, "the involvement of the child's family as an active participant is critical to the success of any intervention program."[6]

4. Yankelovich, Skelly and White, Inc., *Raising Children in a Changing Society*, The General Mills American Family Report, 1976—77.

5. Alice S. Honig, *Parent Involvement in Early Childhood Education* (Washington, D.C.: National Association for the Education of Young Children, 1975).

6. Urie Bronfenbrenner, *Is Early Intervention Effective: A Report on Longitudinal Evaluations of Pre-school Programs*, vol. 2 (Washington, D.C.: Office of Child Development, U.S. Dept. of HEW, 1974), p. 55.

An evaluation of parent involvement programs carried out by Goodson and Hess points to three assumptions underlying parent programs:[7]

1. Home deficit. Homes in low-income environments often do not provide proper stimulation for success in school.

2. Early years are important. Research has been interpreted by some programs to indicate that a child's intellectual potential is predictable by age four.[8] Thus, it is assumed that successful intervention should take place during the preschool years.

3. Family effects. The impact of the family is not overcome by later schooling. Research indicates that the family has the major impact on the educational outcome of its children.[9]

The recognition of the importance of parents in the educational process started with the early years but has now spread to elementary as well as high school programs. Some states require parent representation on boards as well as the classroom in order to qualify for funding. The impressive programs of Rev. Jesse Jackson aimed at the teen-age student recognize the importance of parent involvement through the use of contracts to commit the family to be responsible for, and supportive of, effective study by the student.

Putting aside social changes and funding mandates, perhaps one of the most important reasons for working with parents is satisfaction. Both parents and teachers who have established cooperative working relations report that such teamwork is so satisfying and rewarding that they would never choose to go back to the closed classroom.

As one teacher put it, "I feel a sense of elation and pride when I see the power we have in creating optimal learning experiences for the children and ourselves. I am convinced that the only way to be effective in educating young people is through collaboration of parents and teachers."

There is much to be said for teaching in an environment in which there is a true sense of cooperation and support between the school and family. The strength and unity established through common goals can only be of benefit to our children and the future of our society.

7. Barbara Dillon Goodson and Robert D. Hess, "Parents as Teachers of Young Children: An Evaluative Review of Some Contemporary Concepts and Programs" (Palo Alto: Stanford University, 1975).

8. B. S. Bloom, *Stability and Change in Human Characteristics* (New York: John Wiley & Sons, Inc., 1964).

9. J. S. Coleman et al., *Equality of Educational Opportunity* (Washington, D.C.: U.S. Office of Education, 1966); Robert D. Hess, "Parental Behavior and Children's School Achievement, Implications for Head Start," in *Critical Issues in Research Related to Disadvantaged Children* (Princeton, N.J.: 1969); Educational Testing Service, C. Jencks, *Inequality: A Re-assessment of the Effect of Family and Schooling in America* (New York: Basic Books, 1972); Goodson and Hess, *Parents as Teachers of Young Children.*

2

The Art of Communicating with Parents

The quality of teacher-parent involvement relies heavily upon the skills of the teacher. Some schools may be fortunate enough to have a group of sophisticated parents who are experienced in carrying on cooperative programs, but generally, planning and guidance for parent participation rest on the shoulders of the teacher.

The new and inexperienced teacher undoubtedly has to spend more time and energy preparing for the program. The children and immediate curriculum needs demand most of a teacher's time. The added demand of parent involvement can be most unwelcome to a teacher who is pressed for time.

Parents who were interviewed about the positive and negative aspects of working with new teachers responded that inexperienced teachers seemed to be more eager, willing, and often more patient than their more experienced counterparts. The new teachers appeared to be more willing to work harder at preparations and to take time from their personal lives for job-related tasks. Parents at one school gave the example of the student teachers spending endless hours preparing for special learning projects and field trips, staying late, and taking work home.

On the other hand, parents report that most new teachers appear to be easily intimidated. This is not surprising, considering their lack of experience, but parents complain that new teachers will often avoid real problems because they don't know what to do. "They're too easy with the children." "They're too nice." "They let both children and adults get away with 'improper' behavior and demands."

Another complaint is that new teachers tend to rely heavily on "textbook answers" to problems rather than on responses based on direct experience with the individual child. Perhaps this can be interpreted to mean the parent wants a more affective, caring kind of counsel based on the extended-family sort of interaction as opposed to the clinical, professional approach.

Whether or not the teacher is experienced, it is clear that in order to be effective with parents and children, one must learn to face the discomfort of being new to a situation, of dealing with strong feelings, and of making mistakes. Avoiding parents is no longer a viable choice for the teacher of young children. Working with parents can be a teacher's most meaningful professional and personal growth experience.

Some Teachers Report What It Is Like to Work with Parents

A young student teacher who went straight from college training school to work in a co-op reports:

When I first started teaching in a co-op nursery school I saw the parents as a kind of blur of faces, each one wearing a schedule for the day pasted on a toilet paper roll around her neck. They all looked alike to me, and I expected they all had about the same ideas as I did for their children and the school.

As I became more comfortable with my new job, I became less self-conscious and was able to see that each parent had a definite personality. Now that I look back, I can see I spent a lot of my energies trying to understand and please the parents without being misunderstood or intimidated by them. Working with parents is very demanding, exhausting, and satisfying.

A male teacher in a primary K–3 class reports a different kind of experience with parents:

I took pride in the reputation I had for running a creative open classroom in our primary school. I was popular with the kids and their parents, and I made it a point to invite fathers and mothers in to share their skills and interests with the children. But that kind of relationship was quite different from the kind in which parents actually become my "boss" in a sense. A couple of years ago our school decided to apply for public funds to support our classrooms. Our open classes and interest in team teaching seemed to qualify us easily to receive extra monies. We also felt the guidelines for parent involvement were in harmony with our philosophy.

I don't mean to be critical of parents, but I did find that I had to go through some uncomfortable periods and a great deal of uncertainty as a result of "real" parent participation. Having an occasional parent assistant is quite a different matter from working with a parent-controlled board that determines curriculum policies affecting the way I teach.

It has taken two years of close communication, adjustment, and a lot of hard work to achieve the classroom we have today, and it is infinitely superior to the class I ran alone. I still hate the tons of paper work and extra time I have to devote to matters away from the children, but there's nothing to compare with the satisfaction of working with parents toward our common goals.

Most teachers are not sufficiently trained or experienced to deal with parent groups in close settings. Those who are successful often report that they had to learn from experience. Most parent groups realize that the teacher who takes charge of a parent-oriented program must be mature, if not in years, certainly in experience. How then is a newly graduated teacher to cope? Must she simply leave all her learning to experience and a gradual maturing through years of work? Or can she prepare in some way to be knowledgeable about the important aspects of parent involvement and parent education?

When "experienced" teachers were interviewed and asked these questions, most felt that though experience certainly helps, there were many things they wish they had been told or had read about before they started work with parents. Each felt that he or she could share those personal experiences with new teachers to help prepare the less experienced for the work they would be doing with parents.

Some Typical Parents

First, it is useful to know what parents are all about. What is their frame of reference? Who are they? What do they want? How can you determine some general kinds of expectations about them and their relationship to you? Let's take a look at some typical parents.

When eight-year-old Billy A. brought a notice home from school announcing the need for volunteers to serve on a task force to write a proposal for state funding, both his father and mother agreed to help with the project. Mr. and Mrs. A. had moved to the suburbs when Billy was born because they wanted their child to attend good schools and grow up in a residential neighborhood. They felt the best way to ensure their investment was to work actively in supporting the causes and institutions that would enhance their goals. Mr. A.'s income as an account executive provided a comfortable living for his family, so Mrs. A. had the time to serve on volunteer committees. She was eager to be involved in a project directly affecting her son's education and hoped the task force proposal would result in an opportunity for her to work in Billy's classroom.

Steve W. is the father of four-year-old Melanie and six-year-old David. The family was abandoned by the mother, who moved to another state to live with a friend. Divorce proceedings are underway, and Steve intends to seek custody of both children. He wants the best care possible for his two children, but he also needs a center that will provide services during the hours he is at work. He has the added requirements of finding a place that will be close enough to his son's elementary school where he attends first grade. Steve could not afford to hire a full-time sitter, so he had to leave his children at the neighborhood center. He makes special efforts to attend all parent meetings and participation programs. He has to drive ninety miles round trip each day to work, so he rarely has time in the morning to speak with the teachers, but he appreciates any notes or informal comments they may want to make about his children. He reports that he doesn't want to remarry just to have a built-in baby-sitter, but he would certainly welcome the assistance of a woman around the house.

Susan M.'s son was born out of wedlock. Susan chose not to get married and also chose not to have an abortion. Her parents did not approve of her decisions, so Susan and her 2½-year-old Ronnie live alone in a small two-room apartment partially paid for by welfare. She works at an electronics assembly plant and earns just enough to make payments on her car and buy food and clothing for Ronnie and herself. Ronnie goes to a federally funded child care center near Susan's work, but when he is sick, she has to leave him with a sitter. Sometimes she can get one of her neighbors in the apartment building to care for Ronnie, but other times she has to call in sick in order to stay home with Ronnie herself. Susan is spending her free time working with the center and local city officials to try to develop some programs for sick child care in private homes to serve people like herself. So far, no money has become available to serve such a need.

Some Things Parents Have in Common

Each of these parents represents some typical situations facing today's teacher. Although their lives are quite different, they have some things in common:

1. Parents look to the school and depend heavily upon its staff to maintain the health and emotional well-being of their children.

2. Their training and ideas about raising children may be quite different from the teacher's.

3. They probably feel some sense of guilt or ambivalence about leaving their children in an institution (i.e., day care center, public school).

4. They worry about their children.

5. They hope the teachers will relate to their children in a warm and caring way.

6. They are happy to provide input into decision making if they are convinced of the importance of their involvement.

7. Their ideas about the kind of role the teacher should fill are colored by their past experiences with teachers.

8. Their own roles and responsibilities as parents may not be clear to them or to the teacher.

9. Because parents come from different backgrounds and have differing needs, the teacher has to be flexible in methods used to communicate with them.

10. Parents expect teachers to have the expertise to help them raise their children.

11. The advice of teachers is more likely to be respected if parents are convinced that the teacher truly cares about the child.

12. Parents are a teacher's most important resource in reinforcing what the school wants the children to learn.

How to Communicate with Parents

Knowing some of the things parents have in common can help a teacher plan a program of involvement and communication. Today's teacher has many constraints to overcome in working with busy parents. Even when both father and mother are in the family, the hectic pace of living leaves little time for many adults to attend meetings or work as assistants in a school or center. Yet, when parents are truly interested and feel they are genuinely needed, they can be the most loyal supporters of any school program. The wise teacher learns how to communicate with parents to involve them in meaningful ways.

Communication is the first and most important step in parent involvement. Unless the teacher can convince the parent that his or her child will benefit directly through parent involvement, efforts at working together are less likely to succeed. Also, parents have to be "turned on" and excited about being part of the school. Having parent participation because "it's good for the children" or because the teacher says this should be done is not nearly as effective as working with the parent who knows his or her contribution is essential to the quality of the program.

There are various methods a teacher can use to communicate the genuine need for parent participation:

1. Providing facts based on responsible research studies indicating the value of parent involvement can be convincing to some parents. These should be included in short, easy-to-understand summaries in a newsletter.

2. Appreciation and recognition for contributions of time and talent often serve as reinforcers for further parent involvement. Even the smallest act of a parent should be appropriately recognized. Sometimes we forget how good it makes a person feel to be genuinely appreciated.

3. Making general announcements about specific needs, such as needing volunteers for certain field trips, can interest some parents who may have time for occasional work.

4. Asking specific people to do specific tasks can be surprisingly successful. "I notice you printed your emergency identification card so clearly. I wonder if you would be willing to print some of the notices for us from time to time?"

5. Provide "escape hatches" for parents who do not like to work with children or do not have time to be at the school. Involvement should not mean only working with children at the school. It should be made clear that parents can be involved in many other ways, such as working on materials at home, helping with special trips or school events, working on the school yard on weekends, making phone calls, addressing letters, etc. Lists of needed help should be made available to all parents, stressing the need for cooperation, even if it seems insignificant.

6. Persistence in continuing with communication pays, even if the teacher sometimes feels the communication is all one-way. Most parents read the notes that are pinned to their child's jacket. They may not respond to these notes as wholeheartedly as the teacher would like, but each note increases their awareness of what the school is doing.

7. Using the children to get the parents to school may seem a bit unfair, but many teachers report success at involving parents through projects that their children have become excited about.

8. Use every opportunity to build trust and open communication. Sometimes a few words at the door when a parent drops a child off is sufficient to open up more important discussions later on. A smile, a comforting phrase, a positive comment—all go a long way in building good feelings about the school. Parents are less reluctant to "bother" a teacher if they know the teacher is accepting and receptive.

9. Phone parents during the evening or at other times when they are least likely to be busy. Share some positive anecdote with them about their child, or let them know about some interesting incident that occurred during the day. If they have no phone, send a short friendly note home.

10. When parents are required to work at the school, praise them for those things they have done well and encourage them to try new things.

11. Never criticize or correct a parent in front of others.

12. Be sensitive to all parents. Some may require more of your attention, but others who are less demanding of your time also appreciate having you notice them.

13. Plan an environment that allows parents to be "experts." If materials and equipment are set up in such a way that parents have to ask the teacher every time they need to find something or every time they want to supervise a particular task, parents will feel less confident about their own abilities.

14. Identify genuine needs of the program as opposed to "busy work." Parents are more likely to be involved in helping to meet genuine needs.

15. It is easier to involve parents when meetings are held in familiar settings close to their homes.

16. The program in which parents are expected to participate must be built around the immediate concerns and lives of the families.

17. Teachers need to interpret clearly to parents the goals of the program and show how parent involvement can be of real help.

18. Direct solicitation by an enthusiastic staff member is more effective than impersonal notices and announcements.

19. Don't be afraid to try unconventional methods of recruiting parents.

20. Rely on well-established neighborhood groups and institutions like churches and other schools to help bridge the gap between a new program and the home.

Some parents who work in a school are there because they want to be; others, because they have to be. Although the teacher is wise to recognize the different motivations of each group, the techniques used in communications need not be so different. It does, however, help to recognize and verbalize some of the feelings and frustrations the latter group may need to ventilate.

The Importance of Expressing Feelings

One of the most important aspects of communication between parents and teachers is that it allows for honest expression of feelings and ideas. This requires a nonthreatening environment and one in which everyone feels safe. The responsibility for creating such an environment rests with the teacher. An ability to identify with others is a real asset in creating a setting conducive to good discussion. The leader must be alert to both the verbal and nonverbal responses of the group and use that feedback to establish limits and to guide the discussion. One-way communication in which one person dominates the conversation is never as satisfying as communication in which all members of the group have an opportunity to contribute. The group leader has to sense by watching the total group just when it is time to steer the topic toward another person or subject. Injecting a question or comment like 'I wonder if some of the others in this group feel the same way?" or "Has anyone had a similar experience?" or "I'd like to hear from someone who has a different perspective" can help prevent one person from dominating the discussion.

A nonthreatening environment means that all people feel free to say what is on their mind without fear of being judged or condemned. People may disagree with one another, but the leader must make it clear from the start that all opinions are valued. The leader does not have to agree with all opinions, but he or she must be careful to encourage people with differing viewpoints to speak. In addition, the leader "protects" speakers from attack by others in the group. There is a difference between people expressing different viewpoints and people criticizing or rejecting others for saying what they believe. The leader must make this clear and be firm about interfering when necessary. The same guidelines are applicable even when the communication is between two people.

Teachers do more than simply moderate or establish ground rules for discussion groups. Most of the communication carried on by the teacher is on a one-to-one basis. Such communication requires special skill in receiving (listening) as well as sending (communicating) messages. Practice with another staff member can be useful in learning how to "hear" what the other person is saying. One such exercise requires that two people sit facing each other. One talks first while the other listens attentively. Attentive listening means attending to what the other person is saying by looking at him directly, paying full attention with the body as well as the eyes and ears. Active listening means making every effort to hear and understand what the other person is really communicating by asking questions to clarify and by restating what you think the other person said. Very few people experience the luxury of having someone listen attentively to what they are saying. Most people communicate as though they do not expect the receiver to be interested in attending to what they are saying. Such active listening can be learned by anyone. Both parents and teachers would benefit from practicing the art of active listening. Teachers who are successful counselors and who are trusted by parents are good listeners.

But, you ask, what happens when Mary's mother tells you not to let Mary play with those "nasty little boys," or Harry's father says to keep Harry out of the doll corner? How do you communicate with parents when you disagree with them? It is helpful to visualize disagreements as barriers between two people. A statement can be made in such a way as to create a barrier. The same information can be gotten across in ways that create smaller barriers. Teachers need to be very sensitive to ways in which barriers to communication are created. Parents may create tremendous barriers, but teachers needn't build more on top of them. In fact, teachers can break some of them down by their attitude in receiving what the parents have to say. The creation of barriers in any communication takes at least two people. If one person refuses to acknowledge them, they are diminished in size and potential threat.

When Harry's father tells you he wants you to keep Harry out of the doll corner, you can get defensive about your program and try to justify the appropriateness of letting little boys engage in dramatic play. Or, you can consciously listen to Harry's father and encourage him to express some more of the feelings underlying his request. "Would you like me to try to get Harry to play outdoors more?" might encourage him to provide details for you to build upon. Just visualize those barriers going up when people converse, and try to rephrase a statement or ask a question in a nonthreatening way while you collect more information that will help you better understand the underlying reasons for the statements. Perhaps Harry's father is worried because his son is not like other boys he has seen; or maybe he's disappointed in Harry for some reason unknown to you. It is possible that he himself had some identification problems as a youngster, and he is afraid that Harry will have the same problems. In any event, there are reasons, sometimes unknown to the parent, for stated concerns. Try to understand them rather than change them.

You may find that you still disagree with Harry's father after a discussion, but your responses will be based on a greater appreciation of his needs. A supportive teacher is sensitive and empathetic. This does not mean you give up on your own convictions, but it does mean you express them within a context that includes the other person's perspective.

Sometimes the real reason for a complaint is not clear, even to the parent. One teacher tells the following story about his attempts at communication with a mother:

Every morning Daniel S.'s mother would come up to me and ask; "How's Daniel doing in school?" to which I would answer, "Just fine." Then she would comment very nicely that he wasn't doing any art and she knew he liked art. I would remind her that sometimes children like to do new and different things at school and Daniel certainly seemed to be enjoying other activities.

The next day Mrs. S. would do the same thing: "How is Daniel doing in school?" Then the concerns about art again. I finally promised that I would try to interest Daniel in art.

That day I took Daniel to the easel and said, "Daniel, your mom says you like to do art at home. Show me what you can do here." Daniel said he didn't feel like painting and ran outside to play. My feeling was that Daniel seemed to be well adjusted and it really didn't matter if he didn't do any art. But I knew I would have to face his mother.

After a few more sessions of the same kind of communication I finally took Daniel to the easel and said, "Daniel, I want you to paint something. Your mom wants you to paint something. Here, (handing him the brush) paint something!" Daniel painted something and ran off to play.

That afternoon I proudly handed Mrs. S. her son's painting and instead of showing pleasure at Daniel's art work, she said, "Daniel can do better than this. He makes detailed pictures at home. This is just a scribble."

I patiently remarked that Daniel had so many creative things to do at school and so many friends to play with that he probably didn't want to spend as much time at solitary activities as he did at home. She continued to comment about the good work he turned out at home, ignoring what I said.

Mrs. S. continued with her daily "And how is Daniel doing in school" preface to the usual dissatisfied commentary about his poor art work. I found myself trying to avoid her.

I thought a lot about Mrs. S. and spoke to the other staff members about her unrealistic demands. She had not approached any of them, but they suggested that I try to find out if something else might be bothering her. They thought that maybe her criticisms might only be a symptom of a deeper concern. That suggestion got me off my angry attitude and started me thinking about really communicating with her.

The next day she found me on the playground and stood around watching Daniel until she saw an opportunity to approach me:

"How is Daniel doing?"

"Well, how do you think he's doing?" I asked.

"He doesn't concentrate on his activities here at school the way he does at home," she replied. "He isn't performing up to his usual standards. I think you should help him settle down more instead of just running from one activity to another."

I took a deep breath. I was not going to lecture or be defensive. I took a big risk and decided to be completely honest.

"Mrs. S." I said, looking her full in the face, "I really feel frustrated. We've talked about Daniel and his adjustment here at school and somehow I feel we aren't getting down to the things that really concern us."

She looked surprised. "Why, what do you mean?"

"Well, I feel honestly that Daniel is doing very well. He's one of our best-adjusted children. He enjoys the activities, he participates well, he's popular with his classmates, and I feel he is very happy and progressing beautifully for a boy his age. I also feel you are not happy with something about him or the school or maybe yourself."

I put my hand on her arm and asked quietly, "Is there something else besides Daniel that's bothering you?"

Mrs. S. looked directly at me for a full two seconds and then burst into tears!

"My husband may have cancer," she sobbed. "He's been going to the hospital for tests and we're pretty certain he will have to undergo chemotherapy. My mother died of cancer and I'm scared to death."

I was so surprised to get such a dramatic reaction to my risky efforts at communicating that I didn't quite know what to do. I mumbled something about being sorry and knowing that things would all work out, but I was thinking that all those annoying efforts of hers to let me know of her problems could have been avoided if she had only been direct. But then maybe even she wasn't aware of what she was doing. I shudder to think how our relationship could have continued on an unsatisfactory basis had I not expressed my feelings. My perceptions of Mrs. S. and of Daniel changed dramatically, and we never had any more complaints about his poor performance at school.

Of course, my supervisor and I talked at great length and often with Mrs. S. about her fears and she was able to see how her behavior toward me was a reflection of those fears. We are good friends now and our communication is direct, honest, and very satisfying. Daniel is doing great at art too!

Advice from Experienced Teachers

Not all efforts at communicating are as dramatic as this teacher's, but each incident can and should be a learning experience. When asked to reflect upon their own experiences in communicating with parents, some teachers had the following advice to offer:

1. There's usually a hidden meaning to a question like "How's my child doing at school?" A response like "Just fine" is not going to suffice.

The parent may want more details about the child's day or may want an opening to express some idea or concern. The concern need not be serious, but the overture is a cue that the parent wants to talk.

2. A busy teacher can easily forget that each parent is an individual and needs attention in the same way each child needs attention. Just a friendly comment in passing or a nod and smile—some bit of recognition—is important communication.

3. Teachers should never overreact to seemingly hostile or threatening comments and questions. Defending your expertise as a teacher takes on less importance as you grow in confidence.

4. Try not to be too harsh with parents who appear to be doing and saying all the "wrong things" to their children. Most teachers side with the "poor little kids" who have "misguided parents." Teachers tend to be very disapproving of those who do not meet their own high professional standards. There's usually a good reason for a parent's behavior. You don't have to approve of the behavior, but at least try to understand it.

5. Attitudes are not easily changed. Giving up on a parent for being "hopeless" or feeling that you have failed because you were not able to convince a parent that your way was better is naive.

6. What a teacher does is often more important than what he or she says. A genuine appreciation of both child and parents just the way they are can do much toward establishing a basis for good communication.

7. Work on being nondefensive. Don't throw up barriers to parents' questions and comments, even when you suspect they are meant to be critical.

8. Parents' concerns are natural. Don't intimidate them or make them feel they shouldn't express these concerns, no matter how trivial they may seem. A sensitive teacher will even voice some of them to make it possible for parents to feel their worries are normal.

9. Parents want to know what you are doing and understand why you do those things. Teachers sometimes become impatient with others who do not immediately accept their philosophy of child rearing.

10. Be clear about your beliefs and learn how to communicate those beliefs to others. "Do you let the children just play all day, or do you teach them something?" is a challenge to the teacher to do some real thinking about her philosophy.

11. A parent's seemingly intrusive question may be an indirect way of wanting to get better acquainted with you and the program. A seemingly hostile remark may be a cue that the parent wants help or more attention.

12. Don't hide your feelings behind a "clinical, professional" mask. Parents need to know you are human, and they should get feedback from you if you are puzzled, angry, hurt, or uncertain. Sometimes they are not aware of the effects of their remarks. You need not make them feel guilty for upsetting you, but honest feedback is necessary for improving communication.

13. Do not hesitate to call on more experienced people for help. Teachers sometimes feel they are expected to know all the answers. It is far more important to make the proper referral or simply avoid a definitive response. There are no quick and simple answers to complex problems.

14. Resist answering a problem question by suggesting a simple solution. It will be ineffective at best.

15. Effective communication between parent and teacher means the child is also included in the relationship. A young child's strongest ties to adults are his family and teachers. The most important learning takes place in a supportive and cooperative relationship through the parent-teacher-child relationship.

16. Learn to absorb feelings of anger, hostility, and frustration from parents as well as children. More often than not, these feelings need to be ventilated, and you may be one of the only plausible recipients. Opportunities for adult interaction are often very limited for many parents, and the school may be one of the few places they have to release their feelings.

17. Teachers should take every opportunity to learn from parents. Exchanging information is much more useful than a report by the teacher.

18. Expand your own horizons. Take an interest in a wide variety of things and in many different kinds of people. A broad background of experience improves your communicating abilities.

19. Parent-teacher communications are more likely to be successful if they are based on the common goal of the child's welfare. Identify and agree on some things you both want for the child before you start talking about problems. It is possible that each person is operating under the mistaken assumption that others share the same goals.

20. Sometimes the best thing to do is to defer discussion until a time when both people can be more receptive or when there are fewer distractions. Although some very meaningful and important exchanges take place when the child is being dropped off or picked up, the teacher needs to recognize when a discussion requires a more formal setting. "I feel your situation deserves more time than I can take right now" or "I want to give my undivided attention to what you just brought up. Can you plan to set aside some time today so we can talk?" are comments that are tactful and appropriate in many instances.

3

Parents in the Classroom

For many adults, parent participation is only as familiar as PTA membership or an occasional day of assisting a teacher as a room mother. Until government-funded programs like Head Start mandated parent involvement, most adults left the teaching to the "experts."

Today, parents are considered the experts who know more about their children and who are the most effective agents in getting children to learn. The school, also, is no longer a formal, remote institution where parents fear to tread. It has become an agency where various forms of social services are coordinated and made available to families.

These changes have wrought much confusion in redefining roles and expectations of parents and teachers and of the home and school. Although there are some model early childhood programs exemplifying the exciting cooperation of parents and teachers, there are many more that are still struggling to organize around new and sometimes frustrating criteria.

Training programs for parent involvement, teacher-parent collaboration, and team teaching have not kept up with the needs of the field. In most instances, teachers were already ensconced in their classrooms teaching according to a routine that did not include parents as decision makers. Even when programs were available, retraining to learn new ways of working meant extra time and effort when little was to be had after a busy day of work. Parents also were reluctant to make the effort since the pay for aides did not justify the added expense of finding baby-sitters or the cost of providing transportation to return to school. Besides, teachers and parents felt they had enough expertise and common sense to know how to teach their children.

The co-op nursery schools and early education facilities that had been accustomed to "open classrooms" and cooperative teaching teams probably made the smoothest transition to parent-run organizations. The elementary schools, with their closed classrooms and one teacher to each class, often found the adjustment to having more than one teacher a bit more confusing.

Some K–3 teachers reported that they loved the extra help that parents and volunteers provided. Others complained bitterly about the added responsibility of having to train parents who were too opinionated. Just about all the teachers involved in any funded parent participation program felt the added paper work was a burden detracting from the amount of time they had to interact with children.

Parent Programs Differ in Focus

Today, there exist many forms of parent-teacher programs. A clear understanding of the type and goals of each program is essential to success. According to Goodson and Hess, "programs that involve parents are concerned with changing the parents in some way their knowledge, behavior, attitudes, or some combination of the three. The extent to which changing the parents is given priority varies greatly from one type of program to another."[10]

Researchers differentiate among four focuses which help to identify priorities in parent involvement programs. Each is not exclusive, and programs often combine several goals. It is helpful, however, for parents and teachers to be aware of the common goals or focus identified with their particular program. The four focuses are:

1. Parents as policy makers—based on the assumption that parents should have a greater degree of control over the programs affecting their children.

2. Parents as more effective teachers of their children—based on research showing that parents are crucial in their children's learning and parents should be made aware of their potential capabilities.

3. Parents as supporting resources for the school—based on the assumption that increased home support and involvement in education will improve the child's motivation to learn. The goal is to reduce the distance between home and school.

4. Parents as "better" parents—implies that some parents lack knowledge about such things as child development principles, nutrition, etc.,

10. Goodson and Hess, "Parents as Teachers of Young Children," p. 3.

and the goal is to provide parents with more knowledge so they will change or improve their child-rearing practices. In this case, parents become another set of students.[11]

Guide for Training Parents as Teacher Aides

Whatever the focus of your program, some general guidelines should be followed in training parents as aides. The following procedures were developed by teachers and parents suggesting a practical sequence of activities to help parents learn their new duties in the classroom. A systematic procedure allowing plenty of time for less experienced helpers to become oriented to program duties is a good investment. Too often, a haphazard schedule leaves parents and volunteers confused and uncertain. Following a carefully planned routine helps to build confidence and avoid misunderstanding.

1. *General Orientation at the School*
   Background information, business forms, brochure
   Informal welcome and get-acquainted time
   Tour of the school and facilities
   Refreshments and questions

2. *Small Group Meetings*
   Discussion of individual feelings and expectations
   (Discussion groups can be led by experienced parent aides already teaching in the school)
   Clarification of roles and duties

3. *Practice Observations and Visits by Parent Trainees*
   Individual or small group observations of classroom procedures
   Discussion and questions after class

4. *New Parent Aides Assist in Classroom*
   Following of assigned daily routine with supervisor (can be another parent)
   Assessment and discussion after class

5. *Group Meeting of All Teacher Aides*
   After everyone has had at least one opportunity to assist in the classroom, discussion of experiences
   Reassessment and clarification of duties and roles

11. Goodson and Hess, "Parents as Teachers of Young Children," p. 3.

6. *Revision of Work Schedules as Needed*
Increasing or decreasing of responsibilities of parent-teacher team according to team assessments

Meetings and individual conferences can take place any time within this framework, but the teacher should be careful not to overwhelm the new parent aide with too much information, too many rules and regulations, and too many things to remember. Take things one step at a time.

Many questions will be directed at discipline problems and specific children. Assure parents they are not expected to know everything at first. Individual children and problem situations should be discussed in detail as the parent becomes more comfortable with his or her work situation.

For the first few weeks of school, concentrate on the parent's successful adaptation to the work schedule. Feedback, evaluations, and in-service training should continue throughout the parent's involvement.

Orientation Brochure

In addition to the general orientation and opportunity to ask questions about the school, parents appreciate having this information in printed form so they can refer to it from time to time.

One co-op school designed an inexpensive brochure that was humorously illustrated by one of the parents. One illustration shows a mother and child quivering and quaking outside the classroom door with the caption "What Am I Doing Here?" The commentary points out that parents are often afraid at first but reassures the parent that the teachers are friendly and "regardless of past experience, school is a good place to be." Another page deals with the meaning of parent participation outlining the hours each person is expected to work and the reasons for meetings, etc. One illustration heading "What to Wear?" shows a mother with high heels, dangly earrings, and lacy dress sitting in the sandbox with a child. Suggestions for appropriate clothing are offered.

The brochure goes on to cover discipline, suggestions about how to talk with a child, and other details regarding such things as illness, absences, rules for coffee breaks, smoking, health checkups, field trips, and hiring substitutes.

Even when questions about the daily routine are answered, parents like to have something they can hold onto so they can refer back to the rules and information to reassure themselves. The humorous touch is useful in communicating the importance of not taking the task of parent involvement too seriously.

Serving the Needs of Parents

Just as young children thrive best under optimal conditions, parents are likely to do their best in an environment planned to meet their needs. Some considerations include:

1. *A special place* where parents can meet or chat, such as a conference room, a coffee corner, a space set aside for the specific purpose of allowing parents to congregate. It should be easily accessible to the children's classroom.

2. *Bulletin board* where parents can readily see notices that are of interest. These might include up-to-date information about school regulations, announcements of parent meetings and workshops, daily center activities, reports on school meetings and policies, and information about educational opportunities.

3. *Parent handbook* with information about the history of the school, how the organization is set up with job descriptions and responsibilities of each member of the administration, eligibility requirements, and funding information. Another section should include rules and regulations affecting the parents, such as holidays, the hours the school is open, routine information relating to illness, health requirements, permission slips, and phone numbers to call.

4. *Free materials* such as newsletters, recipes, brochures, bulletins, information fact sheets, and educational materials. Parents are interested in information about such topics as tax laws, insurance, birth control, diet, and dealing with legal and emotional problems. If these materials are interestingly displayed and easily accessible, parents will make good use of them.[12]

5. *Lending library* of latest books and magazines with articles about child development, family concerns, and related topics. The library might also

---

12. Some popular titles prepared by teachers are: "How You Can Help Your Child Learn Faster and Better"; "Is Your Child Ready for Kindergarten?"; "Games Parents Can Play with Their Children"; "The Alphabet" (a printed brochure of upper and lower case letters); "What Is a Parent Conference?"; "Local Field Trips."

include toys and children's books and records that families can check out to use at home.

6. *Suggestion box* for those who are reluctant to voice their complaints or comments about various aspects of the program.

7. *Clothing and food exchange* where outworn children's clothing or lost and found items can be made available to families in the school. Also, people who grow their own fruits and vegetables appreciate having the opportunity to trade surplus foods.

Ways to Help Parents Learn Good Teaching Methods

There are many direct and indirect ways to help parents learn techniques that will make them more effective in the classroom and at home. Some of these techniques are modeled by the teacher because parents pick up teaching styles by watching another more experienced person in the classroom. Your tone of voice, the way you phrase a question, the manner in which you redirect a child—all these and other skills are imitated by the parent when he or she sees how effectively you manage the children.

In addition to modeling, another effective method is to post suggestions in a simple format for adults to read in different areas of the classroom. These lists can incorporate suggestions for good teaching techniques in the art area, book corner, and even at home. The following pages contain several examples of suggestions designed for parent assistants.

Suggestions for the Art Area

1. Place art materials on low shelves so children can learn independence through self-help.

2. Encourage the children to help each other.

3. Give children plenty of time to explore. Don't rush them by asking if they are finished.

4. Do not ask children what they are making or painting.

5. Show appreciation for children's art products.

6. Get down to the children's eye level when talking with them.

Another poster might be placed in the storybook corner to encourage language:

Suggestions for the Book Corner

1. Language skills are essential to school success.

2. Children who verbalize well tend to become good readers.

3. Encourage verbalization in young children by getting them to help you name objects.

4. Stop to talk with the children about the story you are reading.

5. Ask questions that encourage a narrative response. (What children did, where did they do it, what happened, etc.)

6. Shy children are more likely to respond if you engage them in talking about topics that interest them rather than focusing on themselves.

7. Attend to what the child is saying. Be interested.

Parents are more likely to reinforce the teacher if both agree on long-term goals. Some schools place suggestion or information sheets in a special rack where parents can help themselves. One such information sheet might be:

Teaching Values

1. Your child develops a sense of values by watching you.

2. Treat others with respect and consideration.

3. Recognize and praise the good behavior of your child and his or her friends.

4. Encourage curiosity, independent thinking, and problem solving.

5. Encourage self-expression.

6. Be consistent in approving or disapproving of certain behavior.

7. When you discipline your child, let him know it is his behavior, not him, of which you disapprove.

8. Give reasons for your decisions.

9. Keep the promises you make to your child.

10. Your home and school are the laboratories where your child learns values by observation, by imitation, and by reward and punishment.

11. Approval or positive reinforcement is more effective than punishment in teaching values.

12. Show your child that you love him.

Parents welcome specific suggestions telling them how they can help their children do well in school. The following are examples of the kinds of lists parents can take home.

How You Can Help Your Child
Learn Faster and Better

Does your child know his own age? His birthdate?

Does your child know the shapes of things—a circle, square, triangle, oval, rectangle?

Can your child identify colors—red, yellow, blue, green, orange, purple, black, brown?

Does your child know what it means to go up, down, around, behind, inside, and outside?

You can help your child learn these and other useful school-related skills at home. Here is how:

1. Teach your child naturally around daily routines:
   "Get *two brown* socks."
   "Put the spoon on the *right* side of the *round* bowl."
   "*Count* how many steps there are when you go *up* the stairs."

2. Show interest in your child's learning.

3. Praise your child often.

4. Give full attention with your eyes and ears when you are teaching your child.

5. Teach only one concept at a time. Be sure your child understands before you go on to something new.

6. Limit teaching times to short periods of about ten to fifteen minutes.

7. Reinforce what you teach by calling attention to the same concepts in the child's environment.

8. Work at a time when the child is rested and there are no distractions.

9. Stop before the child loses interest.

10. Avoid criticizing or scolding the child. Correct mistakes but do not make your child feel he is a failure or that you are disappointed in him.

11. Start each lesson with something familiar; end each lesson with a success.

12. Make the teaching-learning experience a special time when both you and your child can enjoy each other. Relax and have fun together.

How to Select Good Toys
That Are Safe for Your Child

Toys are good if:

They can be used in many different ways. For example, a set of building blocks can be manipulated and used to build many different kinds of structures. Blocks require children to use their hands, body, and imagination. They give children an opportunity to use their large and small muscles and their creative skill. Blocks can become buildings, trains, airplanes, hiding places, etc. A mechanical toy, on the other hand, does not require much creativity, physical involvement, or imagination. Think about these things the next time you buy toys for your child.

They are simply constructed and built of sturdy materials. Toys with lots of moving, interrelated parts are more likely to come apart. Simple, well-constructed toys will last longer. A sturdy, simply designed doll house can be used in more ways and stand more abuse than a doll house that has lots of cute gadgets that will not withstand wear and tear. Doors and drawers should work smoothly; wheels should not stick. Construction materials should be durable.

They encourage imagination and creativity. Toys that are versatile, allowing a wide range of imaginative play, will intrigue children and keep them involved much longer than toys that can be used in only one way. Materials such as sand, clay, and play dough lend themselves to creative play.

They encourage cooperative play. Housekeeping equipment is a good example of toys that allow children to act out their family life experiences with one another. Through such insights, parents and teachers can help children socialize more effectively.

They are safe. Corners should be rounded on such things as furniture and wooden toys so as to prevent injuries. Nails and screws should be sunk. Run your fingers around metal toys to check for sharp edges. Check the quality of painted equipment to determine the likelihood of chipping. Separate parts should be securely attached. Avoid dolls and stuffed animals with eyes that can easily be pulled off. Are materials likely to cause allergies? Can parts of the toy, if detached, be easily swallowed?

Write to the following for additional information:

Metropolitan Life's Health and Welfare Division
1 Madison Avenue
New York, N.Y. 10010
("Your Child's Safety" pamphlet)

U.S. Consumer Product Safety Commission
Washington, D.C. 20207
(800) 638-2666 (toll free)
(Pamphlets and films on toy safety and other related topics)

Office of Child Development
U.S. Department of Health, Education and Welfare
Children's Bureau
Washington, D.C. 20201
("Safe Toys for Your Child,"
Children's Bureau publication #473-1971)

Help Your Child Learn to Read

Before children can learn to read, they must develop many other skills such as listening, observing, speaking, and coordination. Long before they read, they are acquiring these important skills and you can help by doing the following:

1. *Talk with your child.* Listening to words, responding to conversations, and learning self-expression are essential before a child can read.

2. *Listen to your child.* Encourage verbalization by paying attention to your child's words and ideas.

3. *Read to your child.* Your interest in books will help your child develop an appreciation for good literature and reading.

4. *Make up stories with your child.* Encourage the imaginative use of words, and experience the delight of sharing stories together.

5. *Visit the library often.* Enjoy browsing through books in the library. In most libraries, young children can get their own library cards when they can print their names.

6. *Play learning games with your child.* Select games that require guessing, rhyming, listening, following simple rules, and learning directions.

7. *Help your child be aware of surroundings.* Call attention to signs, posters, and details of the environment.

8. *Help your child develop coordination.* Teach your child to use small muscles in doing such things as sewing, cutting, pasting; encourage large-muscle activities like jumping, running, swimming, and playing ball.

9. *Teach your child how to use resources.* Show your child how to look up answers to questions. Use encyclopedias, dictionaries, almanacs, etc.

10. *Broaden your child's background of experiences.* Take your child on field trips to the zoo, museum, farm, and community agencies such as the post office, police department, and the fire department. Go look at boats, trains, airplanes. Encourage curiosity for new things.

Visitors to a school learn much about the basic philosophy of the program through observation and referring to posted lists such as the following:

What Makes a Good School for Young Children?

1. Are there plenty of materials available for children to use?

2. Are the materials and equipment in good condition?

3. Is the ratio of adults to children no more than 10:1 (lower if the children are younger than four or five)?

4. Do children seem comfortable and busily engaged in a variety of activities?

5. Is it neither too noisy nor too quiet?

6. Do the teachers make allowances for children who are different?

7. Are projects planned that engage children in cooperative participation?

8. Are there plenty of opportunities for both indoor and outdoor play?

9. Are the children interacting socially?

10. Are the adults in the school friendly, calm, and alert?

11. Are there areas for quiet, solitary play?

12. Are the supervisory duties well coordinated among the staff?

Other more detailed observations about definite areas and personal interactions can be added to this list. Such a guide can be helpful not only to visitors who are considering your school but to the parents who are already participating.

Some Essentials for Success in Parent-Teacher Classrooms

In assessing the ingredients that make for success in parent teacher classrooms, the following characteristics seem to be evident:

1. *Early recognition, understanding, and acceptance of the concerns and expectations each person brings into the classroom.* This seems to be one of the first and most important "hindsights" reported by teachers and parents alike. Adults should not be expected to be able to work together without knowing what each person thinks about his or her role and how that role fits into a larger picture. But more than simply defining who is to do what in an orientation session, each person must have an opportunity to recognize and express whatever concerns or reservations he or she may have about the job of teaching. Many parents remarked that they were unaware of their fears associated with a school. Even though many had done well in school during their youth, they admitted they were accustomed to a more formal setting where the "teacher was law" and you never talked back or questioned him or her. The teacher was the authority and the parent and child were the subordinates. Teachers, too, sometimes felt the importance of their roles was diminished and wanted to remain in charge and be the important one in the child's eyes. These honest, human feelings cannot remain unexpressed if a program requiring close cooperation between parent and teacher is to succeed. Too often, the initial planning of such a joint venture jumps immediately from an orientation designed around schedules and physical setup to establishing common goals. Yet, the most important groundwork upon which a successful teaching relationship is to be established has not even been explored. If an educational program requiring parent-teacher participation is to be effective, time must be allocated very early in the planning stages to explore, discuss, and share feelings and expectations of the adults involved.

2. *Carefully planned training sessions.* Parents, volunteers, and other teaching assistants complain that they often feel helpless because they don't know the rules and are not sure how they are expected to handle difficult situations. Either the teacher or a training specialist should be responsible for the detailed planning and systematic presentation of training sessions for teaching aides. Printed instructions, step-by-step follow-through on routines, practice sessions with immediate feedback and evaluation, and time for questions and discussions are essential to a successful team teaching experience. Teachers and administrators who have only enough time for a cursory explanation or who expect the parents to know the right things to do will probably complain that parent participation doesn't work. In order to incorporate well-planned training sessions into the program, administrators and teachers need to request sufficient funds in their proposals to enable teachers and other trainers to have planning time and release time to do an adequate job. This important aspect of any proposal is often overlooked, and the teacher is burdened with yet another task to squeeze into an already full schedule.

3. *Clear rules.* Teacher aides report that they feel most comfortable operating within a well-defined set of rules. They want to know exactly what the school expects of them ("Arrive no later than 8:45," "Do not leave your assigned area," "All injuries must be reported immediately to the head teacher"). They also appreciate a supervisor who is firm with them about following the rules. Some admit that they test the teacher in the same way their children test them.

4. *Goals that are agreed upon by both parents and teachers.* Even when goals seem obvious to one or the other ("Of course the children should learn good manners!"), they should be identified and discussed. Clearly defined and verbalized goals are more likely to be carried out. Parents and teachers benefit by having a list of goals available to look at and think about. Specific objectives leading to those goals ("The five-year-old will learn his address and be able to repeat it upon request") help the adults measure their own teaching effectiveness and progress. In addition, well-defined goals are good reminders that serve to establish a clearer framework for the parents and teachers. A short-term objective is more easily tested or measured than a long-term goal that may not be evident until some future time.

5. *Careful instructions about the options that are available to parents and teachers during the decision-making process.* The democratic procedure is to be desired, but meetings often get bogged down unnecessarily because the participants are operating from different perspectives, inadequate information, and lack of understanding. If a policy decision is to be made by a parent-teacher board, the decision makers should be carefully instructed by a knowledgeable person familiar with all the ramifications of the possible outcomes of decisions. Voting for a large expenditure without full knowledge of where the money is coming from or in what ways the group might be affected through such an obligation can seriously affect the success of a cooperative effort. Sometimes decisions are made at the administrative level and parent groups "rubber stamp" these decisions without knowing about other options. In many instances the parents do well to rely on more expert judgment, but to be truly effective, a parent-teacher group should be involved at all levels of decision making.

6. *Genuine commitment, inordinate amounts of patience, perseverance, and a good sense of humor.* Working closely together can be stressful. The teacher may feel she is being observed and evaluated by the parent, and the parent may suspect that she is not satisfying the high standards of the teacher. Each must be so committed that he or she is willing to accept responsibility for making mistakes, for looking foolish, and for being less than a model. Each must also be willing to accept the faults of the other. In looking back on their experiences, both parents and teachers agree that there seems to be a tendency to take the task of educating young children so seriously that adults forget to relax and laugh once in a while. Children learn attitudes through modeling. Laughter and the obvious enjoyment of what one is doing can be contagious and may be one of the most worthwhile things teachers, parents, and children can learn in school.

7. *A curriculum planned around an atmosphere of mutual cooperation and dependence.* Although the head teacher will have more responsibilities for planning, the parent aide should be an essential part of the program. The smooth and successful functioning of various aspects of the program should depend on each person carrying out important tasks. This interdependence among adults (and children too) creates a cohesiveness essential to the successful operation of a cooperative venture.

8. *Time to talk.* Different groups find different ways to schedule quiet, undisturbed periods of time to talk. Successful teaching teams usually find a way to get together, formally or informally, to give each other feedback about their work. Many report that the informal get-together with their coworkers is essential to job satisfaction. They look forward to the exchange of information, to another person's assessment, and most important, to the opportunity to let their hair down and simply "replay" some of their more frustrating or satisfying moments. Many lasting friendships have been built around the teacher-parent cooperative.

(See the Appendix for examples of orientation materials, training information, teaching suggestions, and parent-teacher questionnaires.)

4

Families with Special Needs

Most teachers have not had specific training to work with single-parent families, with minority children, with low-income, bilingual, handicapped, or migrant families. Some may have had more personal experiences in a variety of settings, but the sensitivity, understanding, flexibility, and insightfulness needed by a teacher under special circumstances are characteristics that are difficult, if not impossible, to teach in a college classroom. How then does a teacher prepare for work with families who have special needs? What do you do with the bilingual family, with children who are accustomed to a culture quite different from your own? What about the children who are poor? Or the child who has no mother or father? Are there "rules" a teacher can use as a guide? How can a teacher avoid making mistakes in unfamiliar situations?

The changing character of today's family creates many "special" needs. For the first time in American history a majority of mothers with school-age children now work outside the home. In 1975, 39 percent of mothers of children under six were working and nearly one in three mothers with infants—children under three—was in the work force.

The teacher will be working with an increasingly large number of single-parent families. Three of the main contributors to the rise of one-parent homes have been divorces, illegitimate births, and desertions. Nearly 40 percent of all marriages now end in divorce; the number of children from divorced families is twice that of a decade ago.[13]

Children with special needs will also include adopted children, children born out of wedlock, and those living with unmarried couples. Fathers with custody also present a group with special needs, as do families created out of remarriages.

In addition to the changing family scene, other special needs are created by children who are physically or mentally handicapped—many of whom are being cared for in regular schools and centers. The emphasis on mainstreaming—integrating the child with special needs with "normal" children—has received public attention and additional school aid in funding grants. The teacher has to be informed and aware of the concerns of families whose children are unlike the majority group.

13. Urie Bronfenbrenner, "The American Family in Decline." *Current Magazine*, January 1977, p. 41.

A word of caution: A family that is different or has special needs is not necessarily a "disadvantaged" family. Oftentimes, children who are handicapped in some way—whether physically or because of ethnic origin—are often brighter and more resourceful and bring a richer background of experiences to the school than their peers. It is easy for teachers with limited experiences to "feel sorry" for a child who is different in some way and to relate to that child and his or her family in a condescending manner. It is always more useful to focus and build on the strengths of the child and family.

Another group of people needing special help are teen-age parents and their young children. The Planned Parenthood Federation of America reports that more than one million adolescent girls become pregnant each year, resulting in more than 600,000 births.[14] A five-year study undertaken at the Dr. Solomon Carter Fuller Community Mental Health Center in Boston indicates that teen-age girls are often so poor at mothering that their children are unable to form human attachments and show early aggressive behavior. These adolescent parents need help in developing the capacity to nurture and in learning effective ways to care for their children.

Physical handicaps such as crippling defects or visual and auditory impairments generally require the assistance and referral resource of a doctor. The teacher can usually refer to the physician or therapist who is treating or working with the child and family for recommendations and suggestions that can be implemented in the classroom. Additional resources and referral agencies are listed at the end of this section as well as in the Appendix.

Perhaps the most common category of children with special needs in the school are those labeled as "learning disabled." This ambiguous and confusing label has been attached to a variety of conditions in an attempt to offset the negative connotations of such descriptions as "retarded," "autistic," "stutterer," or "problem child." As a result, many educators and parents are confused about the actual conditions of the child's disability.

Learning disability can refer to any of the following: brain damage, autism, aphasia, dyslexia, hyperactive, minimal brain dysfunction, problem learner, reading disability, underachiever, and many more. Statistics released by the Association for Children With Learning Disabilities indicate that between six and ten million preadolescents in this country are thought to have some form of learning disability.

14. *San Francisco Chronicle*, December 19, 1977, p. 2.

A child who exhibits such symptoms as easy frustration, short attention span, frequent headaches, allergies, lack of coordination, and many other such behaviors may be suspected of learning disability. Teachers need to be familiar with diagnosis and treatment of such conditions and make proper referrals. (See Hyperkinesis in Part 3 and the Appendix of Resources.)

Families with special needs no longer comprise a small minority of our school population. Over nine million school-age children in the United States are non-Anglo and consequently differ from the culturally and racially dominant majority. About five million of these children speak some language other than English. Most of the bilingual, multicultural families live in ghettos, on reservations, or in barrios. They have a school dropout rate as high as 60 percent.

In spite of the melting pot tradition of the United States, our educational systems have perpetuated a white, Anglo-Saxon, Protestant ideal. This monocultural standard ignored diversity among its students; success in school demanded conformity to the majority standards. These standards were not necessarily bad, but students learned that in order to enter the mainstream of society, they had to strip themselves of their cultural differences or pay the high emotional price of being in conflict with their teachers and peer groups. Those who were most vulnerable to alienation were the visibly different children—the blacks, Asians, American Indians, Chicanos, Puerto Ricans, Filipinos. Other minorities such as the Italian, Irish, German, and Polish often denied their own cultural heritage, changed their names, and cut their family ties in order to increase their chances for success.

In 1974, the Bilingual Education Act mandated that the educational system provide instruction in the native language of the children of limited English speaking ability. Today teacher training colleges are offering more programs to prepare teachers in bilingual, multicultural education, but much more needs to be done. Individual states have to pass legislation in support of bilingual, multicultural education. Some are supportive of the philosophy but do not have the funds to establish sound programs. Of the 1.6 million Mexican-American children in schools, only 70,000 or about 4 percent are being reached by bilingual programs. Many schools and teachers do not know what to do and others continue with teaching methods that suggest bilingualism is an obstacle to success.

Many bilingual, multicultural families are middle class, but many more are socioeconomically disadvantaged. The problems associated with being visibly different are further aggravated by poverty. Poor people have to spend more time than others in seeking jobs, finding a place to live they can afford, getting to and from their work, and stretching what little money they have to support a family. Poor people are also intimidated by the mystifying maze of red tape and dehumanizing experience of completing complex forms to qualify for public assistance. Those with a poor command of English are exposed to even more frustrations. It is no wonder that families with special needs are often too exhausted emotionally to have much patience or strength to concentrate on their children.

A teacher who has experienced adversity may be more sensitive to the needs of disadvantaged families, but everyone is capable of learning to be more empathetic. One way is to gather as much factual information as possible and then imagine yourself in that same situation.

An Asian Family

An example can provide us with some guidelines. Mrs. Chung is a recent immigrant from Taiwan. She and her two children have just joined her husband who has been living in the U.S. for about a year. The family speaks no English. John, the seven-year-old, is starting in a special first grade class in public school. Ginny, the three-year-old, is enrolled in the child care center while Mrs. Chung works part-time in a "sewing factory" where many women like herself stitch dresses and other wearing apparel for local fashion designers. Her pay is relatively low with no fringe benefits, but she considers herself fortunate to have employment at all since she cannot speak English. Without knowing any more than this about Mrs. Chung, jot down some of the concerns you think she might have. What does she want for her children? What does she want or expect from you, the teacher?

How do you think Mrs. Chung will answer these questions:

1. When Ginny grows up, what kind of adult do you want her to be? What kind of job should she have? Where do you want her to live? What kind of friends do you want her to have? Do you want her to speak mostly Chinese or English? Should she marry a Chinese?

2. What do you think we should be teaching Ginny in school?

3. What are the most important things we can teach her that you can't?

4. What things do you teach her at home that you want us to reinforce?

5. What values do you want your child to retain even if this means she will be different from the American culture?

Now let's take a look at Mrs. Chung's answers:

1. When Ginny grows up I definitely want her to go to college. It would be very good if she would be a doctor or a highly paid professional. I would like her to stay in Chinatown to be near me so she can help me translate. Her friends can be of any race but they should all be of the best moral upbringing. She should speak both Chinese and English fluently and definitely marry a Chinese. Otherwise, I would not be able to converse with my son-in-law. Besides, I do not approve of interracial marriages.

2. Discipline should be taught in the schools. Also, teach her to be respectful. Her brother attended schools in Hong Kong and he has learned to be respectful. Also, I want Ginny to learn how to sew. Clothes are too expensive to buy.

3. I lack the skill to teach Ginny how to read and write in English. It is very important that you teach her English, but it is equally important that you help her learn more about the Chinese culture and language. I do not want her to give up her heritage. I want her to understand and love her own culture.

4. I try to teach her to be polite. She also must learn there is a time and place for everything. My husband and I both have to work long hours and we need the children to help clean up and do things around the house. Good manners are important.

5. The Chinese culture, of course. We want our children to show respect for their family and always to love and support their family. We don't want them to be disrespectful or dishonest. We want them to value education, to celebrate Chinese holidays, to speak the language, and to be proud of their ethnic heritage. They should retain the virtue of patience. We are not used to American values, but sometimes Americanized children seem to have too much freedom. When they grow up, Americans leave their parents, and this is not good. However, American children are very strong and they are independent in thinking and doing what they want. They are not intimidated easily. There is much we can learn to value from American society, but I feel it is important to teach my children the traditional virtues of the Chinese—loyalty, filial piety, honesty, love, brotherhood, and peace.

(See the Appendix for some examples of questionnaires used in a Chinese children's center. These can be adapted for use in other bilingual, bicultural programs.)

Not all Chinese mothers feel the same way as Mrs. Chung regarding American schools and teachers. However, it is useful to read individual interviews in order to develop a different perspective about some general concerns.

Migrant Children

One language specialist who deals with migrant children reports that as a migrant child herself, she feels teachers need to "lift the masks from the faces" of these children if they hope to teach them.[15]

Some of the "masks" of migrants are:

1. Periodic tuning out or daydreaming. This may be the result of the child's conditioned response to living in an atmosphere of noise, discord, and confusion.

2. The mask of nonverbal behavior, probably a product of a nonverbal environment. The parents are too busy, too depressed, or too uneducated to appreciate the importance of sitting down and carrying on extended conversation. Children who hear only monosyllables are unlikely to become very verbal themselves.

3. The mask of hostility or belligerence has a social and economic origin. Poverty teaches "survival of the fittest." One study done by the author on a group of five- and six-year-old migrant children asked what they would do if a child smaller than themselves started a fight with them. Ninety-eight percent answered, "I'd kill him." Hostility may also stem from an educational setting of failure and rejection. Children who are made to feel stupid and unwanted are likely to respond in angry and hostile ways.

4. The mask of blank stares may be caused by poor communication. Inattentiveness in a classroom is often interpreted to mean poor motivation, when in reality the teacher's instructional methods are geared to patterns of middle-class speech.

5. The mask of ignorance may be due to the ways we determine intelligence. Intelligence tests are standardized on middle-class white populations; children who are different are penalized. For example, children received no points for the following answers:

15. Ida Brownlee Bragdon, "How to Help Migrant Children," *Today's Education,* January-February 1976, p. 57.

Vocabulary	Response
Cushion	Something you sleep on
Spade (heard as space)	Like when you leave some room in the bed
Sword (heard as sewed)	Fix my clothes when they tore up

(In some dialects, s-w-o-r-d is pronounced SWord. The w is heard.)

Studies show that when test results indicate a child is moronic, the teacher treats that child as a moron.[16] Also, the use of nonstandard English can give the false impression of ignorance.

Suggestions for Working with Families with Special Needs

The teacher of today's young children will inevitably be faced with the challenge of working with some family having special needs. That may be a single-parent family, a low-income or ethnic minority family, or someone who is physically or emotionally handicapped. Whatever the situation, there are no easy rules to follow. However, the teacher who is willing to expend some extra effort to get more information, usually from the families themselves, and who is sincere in wanting to be more sensitive to the feelings and concerns of others will find the task a rewarding one.

What Are Some of the Things a Teacher Can Do?

1. Observe and listen. Watch for cues and relate to behavior that is familiar to you (separation anxiety, shyness, aggressiveness, etc.).

2. Be patient. Parents and children from different sociocultural backgrounds may not want to deal with problems in the same way as others in the school.

3. Be supportive. Encourage parents to express their feelings. Show them the ways you can reinforce their values.

16. Bragdon, "How to Help Migrant Children."

4. Build in successful experiences. Enable each child and parent to complete tasks responsibly and successfully.

5. Use plenty of praise to reinforce their efforts.

6. Be aware that it takes time to build confidence in you and the school.

7. Don't push your knowledge and educational background on parents.

8. Don't relate to poor and different families out of a sense of pity for them. They need compassion and guidance to develop their abilities, not have someone feel sorry for them.

9. Make rules and expectations clear. Keep them simple and few, and follow up with supportive suggestions.

10. Communicate your feelings honestly. "I feel helpless when José won't respond. Can we talk about it?"

11. Admit your own lack of knowledge. "I don't know much about Viet Nam. Tell me about the schools there."

12. Accept the language of the child. Provide coordinated training to enable him to learn standard English while still retaining his native tongue.

13. Adapt parent programs to involve special needs of all families.

14. Parent involvement includes doing many things other than attending meetings. Let your parents help devise nontraditional parent involvement techniques.

15. Incorporate the results of questionnaires and surveys into the curriculum where possible, but be careful not to build in failure or disappointment from false expectations.

16. Identify mutual goals and start from where the family is at that moment.

17. Programs and plans are more likely to succeed if they are developed around the immediate needs of the families (e.g., where to shop, how to save money, immigration procedures, birth control, medicine).

18. Use complete sentences in talking with children, and encourage them and their parents to talk in complete sentences. Build discussion topics around their experiences.

19. Don't be misled by standardized intelligence test scores. Use your own experience with the children to assess their educability.

20. Instill a sense of cultural pride and self-worth through activities that encourage social interaction among all groups in the school. Parents and children learn from each other. Minority groups also have their prejudices and misconceptions about others.

Some Generalizations about Families with Special Needs

The following generalizations are usually acknowledged by experienced teachers:

1. Most children want to please the teacher. In many cultures families are taught to honor and respect the authority of adults. Children from these cultures tend to be obedient. The teacher needs to be especially sensitive to the well-behaved child who is less likely to show unhappiness or frustration than the more outspoken youngster. Quiet children who show little emotion still value the praise and acceptance of the teacher.

2. The "different" child is not deficient. Being clear about this makes a big difference in the methods you use with the child.

3. There is a wide range of differences in attitudes among ethnic groups. Don't generalize from one person to another just because they share the same cultural or ethnic heritage.

4. The socioeconomic status rather than ethnic background of a family may account for greater differences between families. That is, the values of an upper-class wealthy black may differ more from a poor lower-class black than from a white person.

5. The teaching strategies of such families may be quite different from yours. Approaches to problem solving should be observed, compared, and brought into harmony and consistency where possible.

6. The child who comes from a different background almost certainly has to learn to deal with more inconsistency in life. There will be more discontinuity to cope with because his or her home environment is different from the school environment. This lack of continuity can be a factor in early academic failure.

7. Many children from low-income homes learn responsibility at a very early age. By the age of nine or ten, many migrant children care for younger children while parents work. By the age of twelve, they are often contributing to the family income by their work in the fields or doing other needed tasks.

8. Children from culturally different families often express themselves differently at home from the way they do at school. They learn quickly that their usual means of communicating and behaving are different from those of the majority. The teacher must be careful not to belittle them or make them feel ashamed.

9. Children who are different from the majority are likely to be more perceptive and sensitive to reading visual cues, facial expressions, and body language. They are often quite sophisticated in being able to "size up" a situation or "read" people.

10. In spite of the many obstacles to their involvement, families with special needs still value the advantages of an education. For many, the school may be the only route out of poverty or the ghetto or the prejudice against handicaps.

11 There may be good reasons for children retaining behavior inconsistent with the expectations of the school. Their beliefs, values, and coping strategies may be essential to survival in the life they live at home.

12. Parents with special needs are more likely to be involved in a program at school if they can see some immediate benefit to them and if they feel respected and needed.

(See the Appendix for referral agencies and information about other special needs such as alcoholism, child abuse, learning disabilities, etc.)

5

Home Visits and Conferences

"Guess what?! Mrs. Johnson came to my house last night," boasts Jennifer loudly to her friends at school.

"She came to my house too," says Benjie.

Angela listens to her peers bragging about this special experience, looks shyly at Mrs. Johnson, and asks, "Are you coming to my house, Mrs. J?"

"Yes, I'll be coming to visit you sometime soon, Angela."

"Why?"

Why, indeed. Why does Mrs. J. make home visits? Teachers often are not clear about the real purposes of their visits. Is it because home visits are mandated by the school? Or has Mrs. J. been told that a good teacher should visit the child's home? Or is she simply curious to know more about each child in his or her own environment?

These are all good reasons, but let's look at home visits from the perspective of the individuals concerned. It is likely that the teacher, the parent, and the child will agree (maybe for different reasons) that home visits are good.

It is usually very clear from children's responses that they feel important and enjoy the special kind of relationship they share with the teacher when they can spend time together in the child's home. Looking at those things that are special to a child, such as his or her bedroom and favorite toys, helps to build better understanding of where that child is coming from. A teacher gets a more complete picture of each child visited. The child, on the other hand, feels a sense of importance in being able to assume a role of host or hostess to the teacher. Often a child reacts to such a meeting with shyness, tears, or "acting up," but the fact remains that such a visit is very special. The positive aspects generally outweigh the negative ones, especially if the intent of the teacher is supportive and clear to the family.

But what about the parents? Is the pending visit of a teacher the signal to clean house, bake cookies, put aside other important matters to make a good impression? Do parents silently grit their teeth and "put up with" the annual visit because it is expected of them? Do they secretly wish the teacher wouldn't come? Or are they eager to welcome their visitors? No doubt, there are varying degrees of ambivalence among parents. Just as there are some people who are casual and gregarious, there will be those who are cautious, tentative, and anxious about having an important visitor in their home.

Why Home Visits?

First, it is important to clarify for yourself just why it is you want to visit a child's home. You may very well decide in certain circumstances that no matter what the books or funding agencies say, your common sense tells you that a home visit is not the thing to do. Fine! The important thing is to be clear about why you make a particular decision.

Teachers are often pressured by the administration or by research studies to do things they themselves are not certain about. Certainly, it is useful in most cases to know as much as you can about the children with whom you work. There are many ways to gain additional information— home visits being one of them.

If, however, you and the parents and child are uncomfortable, you need to reassess your goals and methods. It may be significant to learn that parents are ashamed of their homes, or that children get too nervous and anxious having you there, or that you really hate the task of having to put in more time. If any of these are so, then why do it? Why build yourself up for failure or, at best, a negative experience?

Home visits are time-consuming. Parents and children do have to expend energy to prepare for your visit. You do have to put other important tasks aside to take time from your work at school to get to the child's home. If this is a burdensome chore, it becomes apparent to all involved. But before you decide that home visits probably aren't worth all the trouble, let's take a look at the positive side.

A Teacher's Experience

Linda, a teacher in a city in the Midwest, reported the following:

I have to admit I wasn't keen on going out to visit Roberto's home. They live in a neighborhood I've never dared to go into because I've heard so many stories about getting ripped off. I had already set up visits on two separate occasions, and both times when I got there no one was home. After the second time I figured Roberto's mom didn't really want to see me. When I reminded her of our appointments, she always apologized and had some excuse about having to be out for an emergency, but she didn't offer to make another date.

I let it drop for awhile, but it bothered me because Roberto is such a great kid and he would ask me when I was coming to visit him. I also wanted very much to meet the rest of his family—his dad has never come to school—and Roberto speaks often of his grandpa, who lives with them. There was one other important thing on my mind. Roberto is very eager to learn how to read and often sits in the story corner for long periods of time looking at books and obviously trying to make out what the words say. Sometimes he will ask me to show him how to read. I'll read a story to him and he practically has it memorized the next time we look at it together. When we talk about what he does at home he tells me he watches TV all day long. On weekends he turns the TV on first thing in the morning and watches it until he has to go to bed. Evidently the family has no books or magazines or newspapers in the house. I'm not sure what I thought I could do by going to see for myself, but Roberto's such a neat kid and he wanted me to visit him so much that it became a challenge to me.

Well, one day he left his sweater at school, and I decided that was my opportunity to drop it off. The family doesn't have a phone, so I couldn't have called them to let them know I was coming. When I got to the door,

Roberto was already inviting me in. His grandpa and about six other people were sitting and eating in the tiny living room. His mom came out from the kitchen and seemed surprised and embarrassed to see me. I apologized for dropping over but felt Roberto might need his sweater. All this time he was tugging at me to come in, but his mother obviously was not as enthusiastic.

She finally asked me in, and I wasn't about to refuse after all this time. I know we were all uncomfortable, especially the friends and relatives who had been noisily conversing in their native tongue. No introductions were made so I asked Roberto to show me his baby sister he spoke about so often at school. He took me into a bedroom which he shared with his sister. It was cluttered with toys—many of them broken—some half empty packages of potato chips, some empty cans of soda, and candy wrappers strewn around the floor. Some mothers I know would have been making all kinds of excuses for the condition of the house, but Roberto's mother simply followed us in. Roberto, in his youthful innocence, was unaware of the mess. He was genuinely pleased to have me in his home.

Several times I felt the urge to make a hasty retreat, but I made myself continue to chat with Roberto and his mom in the bedroom. I was aware of subdued conversation in the living room while the TV continued to blare its commercials. I admired the baby and some of Roberto's treasures, and on my way out I decided to introduce myself to Grandpa. I also talked with each of the other people, telling them who I was and asking who they were (cousins, neighbors). They seemed to relax and were friendly. I told them "Roberto is very smart in school and he likes to read a lot." I gave him a big hug and told them Roberto was very well liked by his schoolmates. They seemed pleased. Grandpa laughingly said in his broken English, "You teach him read, write for help me. I no can read." "Don't worry," I heard myself saying reassuringly, "Roberto will learn how to read and write. He's a very smart boy and he will help you."

Roberto offered me his half-finished bowl of food and said, "Teacher, we're having menudo.[17] Here, eat mine." I refused gently but invited Roberto's mother to come to school and teach us how to cook menudo. She laughed and said no one in our school would want to eat it. I assured her we would (the other teachers had better not let me down!). I know I intruded, but I still felt good when I left.

Driving back to my own relatively uncluttered apartment in the 'better' part of town, I found myself eager to remember and assess everything that had taken place at Roberto's—what I had said and how I interacted

17. Menudo is a soup made of corn seasonings and tripe (the lining of a steer's stomach).

with the people. I couldn't isolate any instance that made my home visit a great success, but the total experience was a very positive one for me, even though it was not the kind of visit I had planned. I wondered how the others felt about me, the school, and the society that I represented. Clearly Roberto would be the "bridge" between his culture and those "foreign elements" that would provide him with the necessary skills to help Grandpa. Maybe I accomplished nothing more than to see for myself what was at the other side of our "bridge," but I was exhilarated to find that it is not that forbidding and I believe I can make a difference.

A teacher's visit such as Linda's need not and should not be a unilateral kind of experience. That is, both family and teacher often operate on the expectation that the teacher is doing the family a favor by visiting the home and giving the parents some magical insights into their child. Linda's elation was in part due to her realization that she had learned from her experience.

She could hardly wait to tell Roberto how glad she was to visit him, to meet his friends and relatives, and to tell him she really liked his grandfather. She was genuinely eager to learn to cook some of the dishes Roberto's mom prepared (they smelled so good!), and she was now certain that she would be seeing more of the family. Suddenly the notion of having to "suggest" that they buy books for Roberto and not let him watch TV so much seemed less important. Not that Linda was going to forget her concerns, but they would be taken up in due time and with more appropriate strategies. For now, learning how to cook menudo had to take precedence.

Initiating Home Visits

Sometimes parents and teachers feel awkward about home visits. The parents may not want the teacher to see the condition of the house, the neighborhood, or the general living situation. In some cases, the parents may not want to be bothered with having to clean house and set aside time to entertain the teacher. The teacher, on the other hand, feels "on the spot" for intruding and may also resent having to take time from a busy schedule to visit families.

Not all situations are difficult, however, and in those where adults see the advantages of home visits, little effort is required to arrange for everyone to get together.

The instances when home visits are difficult to initiate can be a real challenge to the teacher. It always helps to know the real reasons for the reluctance of parents to have a teacher visit. Most of the time, the real reasons are not verbalized and teachers are left on their own to ponder and try to figure out how to get around the real objections by trying to assure parents that the location or cleanliness of a home is of no concern. It is difficult to overcome the judgmental aspects of a home visit.

In some cases, parents have no choice. When educational funding stipulates that home visits are required in order to qualify children for a particular program, parents must cooperate or be ineligible. This may make it easier for the teacher to get into the home, but her sensitivity to the possible discomfort of the parents and their need for reassurance is not diminished.

A group of parents and teachers were asked to role play a situation in which the parents felt uncomfortable about having the teacher visit in their home. Some of them "cancelled" their appointments, were not at home when the teacher arrived, pretended to be sick, or didn't answer the door. One aspect of the role playing had both parents and teachers give what they thought were the real reasons for parental reluctance. Both groups agreed on the following:

1. The house is a mess, and the parents do not want the teachers to see their poor housekeeping habits.

2. Parents are fearful that teachers will judge them and get bad impressions.

3. Teachers are intruding on the privacy of the parents' lives.

4. The family culture or way of life may be so different that the teacher would never understand it.

5. Parents' past experiences with home visits are all negative. If the teacher comes over, it's only because the child has been bad.

6. Parents do not see any real value in teacher visits.

7. Teachers try to change the parents and tell them how to be "better" with their children.

8. Parents are too busy to bother.

Assuming that some of these reasons are truly the underlying causes for parents' resistance to home visits, what are some of the ways a teacher can initiate some changes in attitude?

Getting acquainted on neutral territory helps to alleviate many anxieties. If the teacher can suggest or make the opportunity to meet the parent at the park or playground, or chat during a bus ride on a field trip, the parent has an opportunity to interact with, and simply get to know and trust, the teacher as a person. A teacher recalls that one family consistently cancelled out on conferences and home visits until they had gotten better acquainted with her at school. Then she only got into their home when she stopped by informally to pick up a recipe. She stayed for coffee and had a two-hour conference. Sometimes the formality of an appointment can be too anxiety provoking. A teacher who senses the discomfort of parents can work on alternative ways to have a "conference."

Establishing a firm and friendly relationship over many informal chats and get-togethers can help to ease the way for teachers. Adults as well as children need to feel a sense of trust in the teacher, and familiarity takes time. Much useful information can be gained from informal interaction, and a home visit may or may not provide much more useful information.

Parents may indeed be too busy with other children and necessary work to spend time on a home conference, especially if they do not see any real value in it. Teachers need to let parents know just why they want to visit the home and what benefits the parents will derive from such a visit. Telling the parents what you would like to talk about, some areas where you need more information, and how long you plan to stay will establish a clearer framework of interaction and help parents be better prepared.

Sometimes teachers rely on the church, neighbors, or other family members to "introduce" them into a home. If you know others who already have the trust of the family, you are more likely to be welcomed. The children attending your class, of course, can be your best allies.

Helping to establish a community cooperative baby-sitting pool can free the parents from responsibilities that might prohibit having a conference. Sometimes a small group of parents might meet in one of the homes, or in a nearby public facility, where the teacher can have conferences with each individual.

Parents are more likely to cooperate on a home visit if they can see some immediate needs being met. They may have concerns about their child or some other matter that they recognize can be alleviated by the teacher. Or the teacher may be able to help them out in some very practical way. For example, one resourceful teacher, knowing that the mother was confined to the home without the use of a car or public transportation, offered to take her and the children to a grocery store to shop. The mother was delighted to get out of the house and have help in watching her children while she bought her food. The teacher carried on an informal conference while driving, and her observations of the parent-child interaction during the shopping experience gave her many insights into the family. Another teacher learned that one of the bilingual families did not subscribe to any reading materials, so she saved newspaper and magazine articles relating to the family needs and went to the house to read them to the adults.

Being clear about the motives and reservations underlying home visits and conferences helps both teacher and parent to overcome barriers to better understanding. The teacher who is sensitive to the parent's reluctance will show understanding and empathy in reaching that parent through nonthreatening avenues of communication.

Suggestions for Parent Conferences

Although teachers may not have the same kind of experience as Linda, many home visits will not be the "traditional" kind of conference that their training might have led them to expect. There are, however, some general guidelines to follow in any kind of visit or conference:

1. Do not expect to change a parent's attitude or solve a problem in one conference. Forcing your opinion on another person when he or she disagrees or is not ready to accept it can interfere with progress. A process of discussion and mutual thinking takes time but is far more effective.

2. Be clear in your own mind about your short- and long-term goals. Short-term goals might include seeing where Johnny lives, meeting his family, letting them know you care about Johnny, and letting them see what you look like. Long-term goals might include determining how you can help Johnny be less restless in school, learning more about his culture, and establishing some common goals that both school and home can reinforce. Most teachers start with long-term goals, and failure to reach them immediately often leads to disappointment. It takes time to build trust, establish rapport, and make any noticeable change.

3. Much of the success or failure of a conference depends on the teacher. Careful planning, the pulling together of useful information about the child's school performance, and generally setting the stage for the interaction are the teacher's responsibility.

4. Stay on the subject, but be flexible enough to see when some other approach is just as important or meaningful to explore. Talking about her child may not be of interest to a mother who is having problems requiring more of her immediate energy and attention.

5. Protect the privacy of others. Sometimes families are curious about how other children or parents might be doing. They may even use this occasion to ventilate their hostilities toward another co-op parent and question you about others. Their comments are significant as a reflection of their situation, but be very careful to protect the privacy of other families. You can be misquoted, and establishing trust with the parents will be made doubly difficult.

6. Be truthful. If Johnny is tearing the school apart, you must get the parents' help in setting consistent limits. You don't have to be tactless, but you need to let the parents know about your concern. They probably are aware that Johnny is no angel; so tell them the good things about Johnny, but also let them know you are having difficulty in curbing his destructiveness. Ask the parents to think and work with you to see what all of you can do. If you disagree with them about strategy, say so and tell them why. Find some common ground and start from there.

7. Use a nonthreatening approach. What you say and how you say it makes a big difference.

8. Concentrate on hearing what the parent is saying instead of thinking about what you are going to say next. Learn to pick up and build on what you hear; encourage expression of ideas.

9. Try to plan on uninterrupted time for the conference. If you are meeting at the school, sit with the parents rather than behind your desk. If you are meeting in the home, try to arrange a time when you are least likely to be interrupted. If the child or other children insist on being with you, it might be appropriate to give them a project to keep them busy; or, you may need to change the format of your discussion to include the child.

10. Avoid giving direct advice. Sometimes parents will appear to be very helpless and be glad to relinquish the responsibility of solving problems by transferring the burden to you. It is especially important in such cases to lead the parent into some understanding of the reasons for the problem and work on mutual decisions.

11. Do not extend a conference beyond a reasonable length of time. It is helpful to start by telling the family what you want to discuss and establishing a loose structure around which the discussion can be held. When you have finished, say something like "that about covers what I wanted to share with you" and bring the meeting to a close, unless the parents have more input.

12. Be persistent. Sometimes a conference or home visit falls far short of being satisfactory. If you honestly feel that further communication would be helpful, alter your methods and try different ways to carry out your plan. One teacher made it a point to pin short, positive notes to the children whose parents were hard to reach. She was prepared to accept the less-than-satisfactory one-way communication, but she kept it up with the hope that some of the parents would respond at some future time.

13. Establish realistic expectations. Not all conferences end happily ever after. If you have taught for a while and worked with families who are in need, you probably know how vulnerable they can be to all kinds of problems. Some days their children are fortunate just to make it to school, much less have breakfast, clean clothes, or someone nice to go home to. You wonder where you can begin when it's obvious there is no end to the troubles some families can have. Your "conference" may have to be on the run or consist of notes pinned on the children or some other less than satisfactory method of communication.

14. Some problems need to be referred to other professionals. The wise teacher will recognize when situations are serious enough to recommend that the parents seek more specialized help. It is not useful for the teacher to become involved in complicated family problems requiring therapy or professional intervention.

15. Close a conference or home visit on a constructive, positive, and pleasant note with the expectation or reassurance that you and the parents will continue to communicate.

16. Limit your note taking so as not to distract from the verbal interaction. Make notes immediately after you have finished the conference.

17. Where it is not convenient or possible to carry on individual conferences, try having three or four parents meet with you at the same time. Let the parents help determine discussion topics of general interest.

Preconference Information

Parents often simply do not know what to expect in a conference. Some preconference information supplied in the following sample forms can alleviate many anxieties and help to establish more clearly the topics to be discussed. Expectations of both parents and teachers are identified, and a kind of "mental set" helps to clarify many of the unclear aspects of a conference. Parents may be fearful of teachers asking questions they cannot answer, or they may worry that they will be expected to share some personal, private information. Information based on the following forms can help to "set the stage" and relieve parents of unnecessary concern.

First Preconference Form

Dear Parents of _____:

A conference time will soon be scheduled for you and your child. In order for the teacher to plan for this three-way conference, it is important that you express your feelings, interests, and areas of concern.

Please respond to the following items and return a copy to the teacher tomorrow. One copy may be kept by you and brought to the conference. Your help will be appreciated.

What is your child's attitude toward school? _____

_____

What are his out-of-school activities and special interests? _____

_____

Does he have some physical difficulty or health problems we should know

about? _____

_____

Is there anything else you might tell us about your child which will help us better

understand him? _____

_____

Topics for the First Preconference

Follows directions	Respect of other people's property
Friendships (has friends—makes friends)	Self-confidence
Gets along well with others	Self-control
(students, teachers, and parents)	Work habits (neatness)
Punctuality	Works well with group
Respect for authority	Listens and pays attention

Art   Science
Health   Spelling
Mathematics   Social Studies
Music   Writing
P.E.   Other _____
Reading

From the above areas, select three of the items you would like to discuss during the parent-pupil-teacher conference and list them below:

1. _____

2. _____

3. _____

                          _____
                                  (Parent's Signature)

Source: From Prof. Kay Pasley Tudor, Ed.D., Washington State University.

What Is a Parent-Teacher Conference?

A parent-teacher conference is a meeting between a child's parents and teacher to discuss the child's education. It is a time to talk about any problems your child might be having, and also to learn about those areas in which your child does well. Conferences give the teachers a chance to learn about your child's life outside of school. But most of all, conferences are important to your child. They allow parents and teachers to plan and work together so your child can get the most out of his or her education.

The Group Conference Is Where It All Begins (Open House)

Early in the school year you will be invited to a group conference with the principal and teachers. Here you'll learn how the individual parent-teacher conferences will be set up and how you as a parent can participate. Also, the principal will talk about the school's program in general and answer any questions that concern parents, such as:

- How is the school day organized?
  When does school begin and end?
  What about lunch periods?

- How are the classes set up?
  How many aides? What about volunteers?

- What curriculum materials are used?
  What textbooks and workbooks?
  Other materials—films, records, labs?

- What is the school's homework policy?
  Should parents help their children with school work at home?

- What are the school's standards of behavior?
  How are they enforced?

- What are the grading policies?
  How does the school report student progress?
  Are student folders sent home? Report cards?

- How can parents become involved?
  What about advisory committees?
  Are parent volunteers used? For what?

- What special programs and services are available?
  Is there a health program? A school nurse?
  What about a bilingual program?

- What about other activities, such as field trips, assembly programs, etc?

Remember that the group conference is a time for you to discuss the school and its policies in general. Specific questions about your child should be directed to the principal or teacher at another time. At a group conference you can get to know the principal and the teachers in the school, meet and talk to other parents, and tour the school building. Also at the group conference you may be able to sign up for your first individual parent-teacher conference.

Your Individual Parent-Teacher Conference Comes Next

For each child you have in the school, you are guaranteed at least two individual parent-teacher conferences each year. The first is usually before Thanksgiving and the second is around the time of spring vacation. You will receive a written invitation to the conference or possibly you will be contacted by phone.

You may need to make some special arrangements for your conferences:

1. An evening conference if needed

2. Two conferences on the same day if you have two children at the same school

3. Someone to serve as a translator if you need one

Each conference is scheduled to be about thirty minutes long. But if you feel you haven't had enough time to discuss everything you wanted to about your child, let the teacher know. You may be able to continue the conference at that time or schedule one as a follow-up.

If at any time during the school year you want additional conferences, call the school and set up a time to meet with the teacher.

What Should You Learn from the Teacher?

During the individual conference, you should learn how your child is doing in his or her school work, what his or her attitudes are toward school, and how he or she gets along with other people. The teacher should show you examples of your child's work and discuss them with you. Also, the teacher should show you your child's results on the achievement tests given throughout the district and explain what those results mean.

Here are some questions you might want to ask the teacher:

- What is my child's behavior in school?
  How does he or she feel about school work?
  Does my child take part in class activities?
  Does my child work well with other students?
  Does he or she make friends easily?

- What are my child's work habits?
  Does he or she start and finish projects on time?
  Does my child work well alone?

- What areas does my child do well in?
  In what areas has he or she shown improvement?
  What areas need more improvement?

- Is my child grouped for instruction with other students of similar abilities?
  How is this grouping determined?
  Is individualized instruction given?
  What textbooks and workbooks are used?
  Do all the children in the class use the same ones?

- What special interests does my child have in school?
  Does he or she particularly like art, music, science, etc.?
  How have my child's interests been encouraged?
  What special programs or services are available from which my child could benefit?

When the conference is over you should have a clear idea of how your child is doing in school and, if there are any problems, what you as a parent can do to improve your child's progress.

What Should the Teacher Learn from You?

What you learn from the teacher about how your child is doing in school is important. Just as important is what the teacher learns from you about your child outside of school. This will help the teacher understand your child.
   Here are some things you might want to tell the teacher:

- How your child feels about school.
  What he or she tells you about it.
  What subjects your child likes or doesn't like.

- What your child's work habits are at home.
  How well he or she accepts responsibility.
  The size of your family.
  How well your child gets along with other family members and friends.

- What you feel your child's strong points are.
  Areas in which you see improvement.
  Where you feel your child needs to improve.
  The way in which you feel the school can most help your child.

- What your child does after school, his or her activities with friends.
  Your child's special interests or hobbies.
  Your child's involvement in activities like scouts, church groups, etc.
  How your child feels about homework and how long he or she spends doing it.
  Any problems he or she might be having with other children.

- Any health problems your child might have.
  Any emotional problems.
  Any unusual experiences, such as a death in the family, serious illness, etc.

- Any transportation and scheduling problems you might have.

At the end of the conference, the teacher should know what your child's home life is like, be aware of his or her special interests, and most importantly, have a better understanding of your child.

Source: The following pages are adapted from "The Conference Handbook: Getting the Most from Your Parent-Teacher Conference," a publication of the Alum Rock School District, funded by a grant from the National Institute of Education.

Annotated Readings

The following readings were selected to provide additional information on concerns shared by parents and teachers. Some books cover program planning; some deal with special topics likely to be discussed in parent conferences.

Breitbart, Vicki
The Day Care Book. New York: Alfred A. Knopf, 1974.
Covers such aspects of day care as starting a center, child care in other countries, and liberating children from sex roles.

Curtis, Jean
Working Mothers. New York: Doubleday and Company, Inc., 1976.
Ways to cope with problems that may arise when the mother of young children works. Detailed personal examples.

DaSilva, Benjamin, and Lucas, Richard D.
Practical School Volunteer and Teacher-Aide Programs. Englewood Cliffs, N. J.: Prentice-Hall, 1976.
How to plan activities in the classroom to incorporate the use of volunteer help in such areas as reading, math, and art.

Honig, Alice S.
Parent Involvement in Early Childhood Education. Washington, D.C.: National Association for the Education of Young Children, 1975.
Covers ways in which parents are being involved in programs, evaluation problems, why parent involvement is a hard job, and additional resources.

Hymes, James L.
Effective Home-School Relations. Sierra Madre, Calif.: Southern California Association for the Education of Young Children, 1974.
Discusses home-school relations, home visits, observations, and participation.

Lane, Mary B.
Education for Parenting. Washington, D.C.: National Association for the Education of Young Children, 1975.
Discusses state of parent-child life in America, the needs of parents, education for parenting, and alternatives.

LeMasters, E. E.
Parents in Modern America. Homewood, Illinois: The Dorsey Press, 1970.
A sociological analysis of parents in modern America. Analyzes roles of mothers, fathers, parents without partners, minority parents, and socializing influences.

Levine, James A.
Who Will Raise the Children? New Options for Fathers (and Mothers). New York: Bantam Books, 1976.
A book for men who have custody of the children, single adoptive fathers, and househusbands.

Maddox, Brenda
The Half-Parent: Living With Other People's Children. Philadelphia: Evans and Company, Inc., 1975.
An exploration of the emotional and adjustment problems and rewards of being a parent by marriage.

Mager, Robert F.
Preparing Instructional Objectives. Belmont: Fearon Publishers, 1962.
A basic guide in the preparation of objectives for the classroom.

Mason, Robert Lee.
The Emotionally Troubled Child: A Guide for Parents and Teachers in the Early Recognition of Mental and Nervous Disorders in Children. Springfield, Ill.: Thomas, 1976.

Payne, James S., et al.
Exceptional Children in Focus. Columbus, Ohio: Charles E. Merrill Publishing Company, 1974.
Covers incidents, concepts, and issues in special education. Includes speech and hearing, giftedness, and learning disabilities.

Pierce, Ruth I.
Single and Pregnant. Boston: Beacon Press, 1970.
Practical guides for the single woman who is pregnant. Discusses what to do and where to turn for help, and explores the possibilities of adoption, abortion, and other alternatives.

Rowlands, Peter
Children Apart: How Parents Can Help Young Children Cope with Being Away from the Family. Westminster, Md.: Pantheon Books, 1973.
Describes some of the difficulties that may arise when for various reasons children find themselves cut off from parental support, and discusses how to teach the child to view these instances as learning experiences that are not to be feared.

Siegal, Earnest
Special Education in the Regular Classroom. New York: The John Day Company, 1969.
Deals with mainstreaming the marginally exceptional children—emotionally disturbed, retarded, brain damaged—into the regular classroom by offering practical aids for the teacher.

Wooley, Persia
Creative Survival for Single Mothers. Millbrae, Calif.: Celestial Arts, 1975.
Suggestions to single mothers on such topics as "Keeping Your Own Balance," "How to Handle Disaster," and other related problems such as money, men, and children.

See also list of Books for Children (pp. 164–67) dealing with special problems affecting children.

Part 2
Ideas for
Parent-Teacher Meetings

Introduction

In this section, parent-teacher meetings refer to such activities as work-shops, discussion meetings, parent-staff training, and other such formal and informal get-togethers of the adults who share the responsibility for the successful operation of a school.

Parents and teachers both benefit from meetings and workshops that provide opportunities for improving teaching skills. Parents often feel isolated from educational events because of their busy work schedules, and the school can provide one of the few avenues for adult education. In addition, learning the words to a child's favorite song or how to mix finger paints can do wonders for a parent's self-confidence when it is time to assist in those activities. Many adults look forward to meetings because of the opportunities they provide to talk with people who share common concerns. The social aspects are not to be underrated, and a good re-freshment committee is essential for the success of parent-teacher meet-ings!

Most teacher training provides plenty of suggestions and practical ex-perience in planning the curriculum for the children. There are also many activity resource books available. When it comes to parent meetings, however, the teacher is expected to know enough to plan and conduct these without much help from books or special training. Many teachers report they feel least prepared to carry out discussion meetings and other such events. Yet, much of the success of a school's program hinges on parent-teacher meetings.

This section offers some tested suggestions and ideas for planning parent programs, speakers, discussion topics, special events, publicity, and fund raising. Additional ideas will grow out of meetings that more closely reflect the unique interests and needs of each group.

6

Systematic Planning of Parent Programs

In order to achieve the greatest success, programs of any kind should be carefully and systematically planned. This means that the participants specify in detail the goals they have in mind, how they plan to reach those goals, and finally, how they plan to assess whether or not they reached those goals.

This kind of procedure is known as specifying objectives. In recent years many program groups have been required to write down in detail exactly what their objectives were in order to justify their existence. Teachers and administrators have complained that the task required too many unnecessary details about goals that were obvious. However, in carrying out their specifications, they realized that the task itself was a good exercise in helping them think through just exactly what they wanted, how they intended to get what they said they wanted, and most importantly, whether or not they were successful in attaining their goals.

The following are suggestions for planning several broad areas of a parent participation program. Before attempting to carry out any particular area, a group of parents and teachers should sit down with paper and pencil and work at details associated with these and any other topics they wish to cover.

Specifying Objectives

Needs of a group are generally determined through discussions or the use of surveys and questionnaires. Parents may indicate that they feel isolated and want to get to know more people, or they may want to have more information about child rearing, or there may be some dissatisfaction with the program that needs correcting. A thorough needs assessment is an essential preliminary to the design of a program based on specific objectives.

Objectives specify in detail the goals of the program—that is, what the people involved will be able to do by the end of the program. Objectives are important because unless you know what your intended destination is, you may end up somewhere else. A simple objective might be "the parents will know the names of all the other adults in the program." Or another might be "each parent will attend at least six programs during the school year."

Guide for Planning Parent Programs*

Program Areas	Needs	Objectives	Methods	Evaluation
Information	Determine the factual information needed by teachers and parents.	Specify in detail the kinds of information desired.	What are the best ways to achieve these objectives?	Determine your success in achieving the objectives.
Social and Emotional	What kinds of social and emotional needs do parents have?	What are the desired objectives in this area?	What methods and strategies can be used to reach the stated objectives?	How successful were you in reaching your goals?
Parent Participation	What do parents and teachers hope to gain or achieve through participation?	Specify the kinds of outcomes desired.	What methods will be used to achieve your objectives?	Assess in what areas you were or were not successful.
Parent-Child Interaction	What are the needs of parents to improve their interactions with their children?	What are the desired goals by the end of the year?	What are the best ways to assure that these interactions take place?	How successfully were these objectives met?

*Adapted from "A Parent Involvement Manual for Day Care Parents and Staff," by the Community Coordinated Child Development Council of Santa Clara County, Inc., October, 1974.

Methods and strategies that are to be used in order to reach an objective should be identified. How are you going to get to where you want to be? In some cases, you may want to use lectures, discussion groups, or social activities. In the case of wanting parents to learn others' names, you might want to use a game-type activity.

Evaluation measures your degree of success in achieving your stated objectives. You can use tests to determine if children learned their numbers, or if parents really learned each other's names. Or you might use criteria checklists or objective observations to measure your success. If your goals are not reached, you are then able to look at your program and more accurately determine how and where you need to make changes. In other words, the success or failure of your efforts is not left to chance. You will be able to pinpoint just where you need to revise an objective or change to a different method. You will also be able to see clearly where you were successful and know just exactly why.

Knowing how to specify objectives is an important and useful tool to parents and teachers. Identifying goals and selecting appropriate methods to achieve goals are unavoidable in educational programs. Some may approach these tasks in an informal, unstructured way, but a program is more likely to be successful if it is approached through systematic planning based on the careful preparation of instructional objectives.[1]

7

Speakers

Programs for parents are greatly enhanced when knowledgeable speakers can be invited to share their expertise. Professionals in the community are often pleased to speak to a group of interested parents. Although some may expect a small honorarium, others are delighted with some gesture of appreciation, such as a special note from the parents or art work created by the children.

Suggestions for Guest Speakers

1. *Kindergarten teachers and educators.* Parents of five-year-olds are especially interested in knowing how to prepare their youngsters for

1. See Robert F. Mager, *Preparing Instructional Objectives* (Belmont, Calif.: Fearon Publishers, 1962).

elementary school. Speakers should be prepared to be quite specific about skills the children should have, such as knowing their full names and addresses, tying their shoes, dressing themselves, or whatever the teacher feels is important. The speaker should also be given an overview of the kind of audience in attendance—their concerns and interests and degree of involvement. Educators might be invited to speak about "getting back to the basics" of reading, writing, and arithmetic. Parents are concerned about optimum learning conditions for their children and welcome the opportunity to hear from knowledgeable people as well as express some of their own opinions.

2. *Lawyers.* Topics such as drawing up a will, legal problems of running a school, releases for field trips, forming car pools, rights of employees, and child abuse cases are all relevant. Juvenile officers are also good resources, especially in child abuse cases.

3. *Doctors, dentists, nurses.* Health care cannot be taken for granted, even among middle-to-high-income families. Parents need to be reminded about the necessity for physicals, keeping shots up to date, and dental checkups; how to care for contagious diseases; and other such problems. A professional visiting the school also affords the parent an opportunity to ask and hear questions that he or she might be reluctant to ask during a private visit because of constraints of time. The teacher or moderator should be careful to limit discussions to topics of general interest and not allow one or two people with personal problems to engage the speaker's time exclusively.

4. *Conservationists.* Local conservation centers and groups such as the Sierra Club can provide speakers and slides to inform groups about ways families can practice conservation. An understanding and awareness of the need for conserving our natural resources should be a topic for adults and children to explore. Parents can help make charts and posters for display showing such things as where our water comes from, how our air gets polluted, and what happens to trees that are cut.

5. *Television.* A heightened awareness of the effects of television commercials for food on viewers' eating habits can be an interesting and informative topic. Speakers from local schools and consumer groups should be able to provide information. PTA groups also have access to much information. Television and violence, effects of cartoons, and the value of educational programs are all good topics for discussion. Newspaper critics and early education researchers are another possible source of speakers.

6. *Psychologists and counselors.* In addition to the usual topics relating to children, such as discipline, bed wetting, etc., psychologists can offer much useful information about divorce, marital and family problems, assertiveness training, single-parent families, and other such topics related more directly to the needs of the adults. Provide the audience with a list of referral services, their locations, and costs.

7. *Economists, consumer advocates.* Adults are interested in ways they can save money, spend wisely, and find real bargains. Some very interesting presentations can be made by local consumer groups and economists on topics dealing with how to allocate time in order to accomplish tasks efficiently, and how to shop for food, clothing, household items, and so on. A display or slides showing comparative pricing, quality assessment, cooperative buying, label examination, and money management can be extremely useful to a parent-teacher group.

8. *Librarians.* Adults enjoy listening to good storytellers just as much as children. Local children's librarians delight in showing the latest and best books from their collections. Suggest they bring a large assortment of books to display, and provide a list of titles so parents can check off the ones they especially like. Children's bookstores are also often happy to send a representative to the school to tell stories and display suitable books for youngsters. Give suggestions about how to select a good book for a young child, and expose the adults to new ideas. Treat them to some stories geared to their level of interest. One group was spellbound listening to ghost stories. Another group learned to appreciate poetry and funny rhymes. Make this an opportunity to entertain and increase the adults' appreciation for literature and storytelling.

8

Films

Some excellent films are available on topics that are of interest to parents. The school may have access to films owned by the county or school district; or, there may be a budget for rental films. Some films made under public funding are available at no cost. (See the Appendix for an annotated list of films, costs, and order information.) It is always a good idea to preview films whenever possible to determine their applicability to the group and topic presented. Generally, films are most effective when used as introductions or reinforcement for a discussion topic. Most parent groups—especially those meeting in the evenings when people are tired—prefer programs that involve them actively. Therefore, films should be used judiciously.

Film Sources

1. *Local libraries.* Many films are available to people who hold library cards. There is usually a nominal fee.

2. *High schools and colleges.* Most have catalogs with annotated lists of films, their rental cost, and addresses for ordering. Some schools are willing to cooperate in helping parent groups obtain films through their audio-visual departments.

3. *Local school district offices.* Parent groups associated with school districts should have no difficulty ordering films to show at meetings. Schools might approach the district about the possibility of working out some arrangement for rentals.

4. *Commercial organizations.* Insurance companies, manufacturers, and food processors all produce films distributed free through their educational departments. (See the Appendix.)

9

How to Lead a Discussion

The success or failure of a group discussion relies heavily upon the leader. The topic must be one of general interest, the participants should feel they have learned something useful, and each person should feel he or she has had an opportunity to contribute to the discussion. The leader is expected to provide ground rules, limits, and guidance for the group. Some suggestions that might be helpful are:

1. Be prepared with some factual information about the topic to be discussed.

2. Introductory remarks should set the stage for the discussion by providing a broad general outline.

3. Rephrase and summarize long comments made by participants.

4. Allow people with diverse opinions to express themselves.

5. Be sensitive to those who are not actively participating. Do they appear interested? Are they listening?

6. Use names when referring to people or calling on them.

7. Involve others by making positive comments about them or their children.

8. Set limits for those who take up a lot of time talking about personal problems. The audience becomes hostile toward a leader who allows the discussion to get out of hand.

9. Keep the discussion focused on the topic.

10. Stay within time limits.

11. Praise the group for their contributions toward a good discussion.

12. Summarize what has been said and learned.

13. Stay relaxed, be an attentive listener, be firm when necessary, and inject a sense of humor whenever possible.

Various methods of discussion can be used throughout a school year. Vary the usual format of having one leader facing an audience by discussing some topics in groups. Leaders appointed to each group can be provided with a list of questions, comments, and suggestions so that each group can follow the same outline. Group members can rotate every twenty minutes or so to enable different people to get acquainted with one another.

Other topics can be presented by having a committee be responsible for doing research ahead of time and then presenting the topic as a panel.

Some of the topics covered in Part 3 (Guidance for Parents) might be useful for group discussions. They can be augmented with speakers, panels, and films.

The leader might refer to some of the techniques suggested in *Values Clarification: A Handbook of Practical Strategies for Teachers and Students.*[2] The exercises use strategies to involve participants to help clarify attitudes and values in their decision making.

Some Critical Incidents

The following pages provide another useful technique that can be used to engage parents in discussion. The open-ended critical incidents are often easier for parents to talk about because they are hypothetical. They are less threatening than talking about personal problems directly. The group leader can design other similar situations appropriate to the needs of the parents.

2. Sidney B. Simon et al., *Values Clarification: A Handbook of Practical Strategies for Teachers and Students* (New York: Hart Publishing Co., Inc., 1972).

Your eight-year-old reports, "No one plays with me at school. I have no friends. I don't want to go to school anymore."

How I feel about this situation:

My probable reaction:

How I think my child feels:

Likely outcome:

Your three-year-old has difficulty playing with other children. Neighbors complain about his aggressive-destructive play.

How I feel about this situation:

My probable reaction:

How I think my child feels:

Likely outcome:

Your fourteen-month-old sucks his thumb and fondles his blanket.

How I feel about this situation:

My probable reaction:

How I think my child feels:

Likely outcome:

Your four-year-old daughter is afraid to leave you. She won't even stay at a friend's house without you. She cries if you try to leave her with a sitter. Today she has been invited to a neighbor's for a birthday party. All the other children are there without their parents, but your child clings to you and cries when you start to leave.

How I feel about this situation:

My probable reaction:

How I think my child feels:

Likely outcome:

10

Special Events, Publicity, Fund Raising

Special Events

Some of the most memorable occasions for parents and teachers are those connected with special events, such as a fathers' work day, a holiday fund-raising sale, or a children's open house. These special times usually require the cooperation and planning of many people and thus afford opportunities for socializing as well as sharing the results of group efforts. Group affairs, when well planned, are important to the cohesiveness of any school. The spirit of working together toward a common goal, the sharing and socializing so important to busy families, all make the extra effort worthwhile.

Some of the special events planned by schools include a fathers' day, in which a time is set aside, either on a weekend or evening, when fathers, uncles, grandfathers, other male relatives, or friends take over the usual schedules of the mothers at a co-op nursery school or child care center. The children and teachers delight in having the opportunity to interact with the fathers, who are usually too busy to share in the child's school experiences. A mothers' day should also be planned for women who do not participate at the school. Teachers need to allow plenty of flexibility in the scheduling so that the adults can have an opportunity to feel comfortable at whatever they are doing. Sometimes the children will behave differently because of the "new teachers" in their school. It is important to build in satisfying and successful experiences for all concerned. It is also important to be certain that children without fathers or mothers or whose parents cannot attend be considered. In some cases, a friends' day or a relatives' day might be more suitable. Grandparents, older brothers and sisters, or aunts and uncles certainly should be a part of the young child's life at school.

Field Trips

Field trips for both parents and children constitute special events that are popular. These occasions enable families to share experiences, often new to the adults as well as the children. Parents report that they gain new and useful information from trips to a dairy, food processing plant, planetarium, farm, sewage treatment plant, telephone company, and other such places of interest. Field trips need not be elaborate to be educational. Most young children tire easily and become upset when overstimulated with long trips and overwhelming distractions. The most successful trips are those that are close to home and easy for the child to integrate into his present system of knowledge. Sometimes the most successful and least upsetting trips for the very young child are short walks in the neighborhood, a visit to the library, or visits with community workers.

Adults in one ghetto area especially appreciated a field trip to a downtown clothing manufacturer where they were able to buy seconds at greatly reduced prices. They requested a visit to the wholesale vegetable and fruit market another time. One group of immigrants had never seen the city hall, and others were delighted to learn how to take the local bus around town.

Field trips should be geared to the needs, interests, and level of sophistication of the parents and children. Where transportation costs are prohibitive, some of the responsibility for driving might be assumed by parent volunteers. It is extremely important to see that every driver and automobile is adequately insured and that release forms are obtained. Technically, releases are not binding and parents can still sue for negligence, but it is still good practice to obtain releases for each field trip. Teachers need not eliminate field trips just because of lack of transportation. Short walks around the neighborhood and visits to the bank, nearby park, and places of business can be fun and educational. Two of the most popular trips reported by the children at a child care center were a visit to the service station to watch the man pump up some tires which he donated to the school and a walk to the neighborhood grocery store, where the children were taken behind the scenes to watch how dairy products were loaded into the refrigerated compartments and meat prepared for display.

Other special events such as open houses or holiday parties offer opportunities to draw upon the talents of the adults. Musical entertainment, amateur theater productions, and variety shows all involve families and are fun to carry out in the school.

Children are proud to be a part of planning a special event such as an open house. One school tape-recorded the voices of the children during music time, sharing time, and at special projects. They then synchronized the tapes with slides of the children showing the different activities of the school. Children acted as hosts and hostesses to show the adults around the room. In the cognitive area children demonstrated how they learned

Child's Photo Puppet

Take a close-up picture of just the face of each child in the classroom. Enlarge if necessary to fit the upper portion of a 5" or 6" cardboard tube. Each "child" can then be dressed with scraps of material, lace, feathers, sequins, yarn, etc. Children can help the teacher glue the faces on the tubes, and the parents can dress the puppets during an evening meeting to surprise the children when they come back to school the next day.

"right and left" from a book of sketches showing the right and left hands which had been coordinated with audio-taped instructions.

Teachers should be certain to include each and every child in setting up displays. Parents and friends look forward to seeing their child's work and are disappointed if someone else's child appears to be given more prominence. In one school, the teachers took a close-up of each child, pasted the pictures on cardboard rolls, and decorated each with frilly hats. When parents came to the open house they were given the picture to take home along with some of the paintings and crafts done by their child. (See Child's Photo Puppet above.)

Open House

An open house for public relations and enrollment requires different planning. The purpose here is to "sell" the school to the public. Visitors need to be able to see the curriculum displayed, and the philosophy of the school should be apparent in the way it is set up. If the school has adequate help, it is usually best to hold the open house while school is in session, and visitors can bring their own children to participate in the program. This may mean that the open house is held over a period of days and appointments made to avoid too many visitors at one time. Some schools welcome visitors all year long. Others prefer to have a more formal day set aside for potential enrollees. Whatever the plans, it is important to see that each area of the school is clean, neat, and set up in such a way that the goals of each area are self-explanatory. Instructions and explanations posted over each activity can be very helpful to visitors and their children. A printed brochure giving tuition rates, car pool information, hours, and a general outline of the curriculum should be available to visitors.

If possible, the school should have a host or hostess to greet each visitor, a volunteer parent to show each family around, and some light refreshments for adults and children. Visiting times should be limited to about an hour. This provides sufficient time for adults and children to get an idea of what the school offers. When time limits are not clear, people may extend their visit beyond a useful time, and regular staff are pressed to supervise extra children. Insurance and liability can be a problem if responsibility for supervision is not made clear.

Publicity

Press releases sent to local newspapers and radio and TV stations are effective means of publicizing a school. In some cities the news media hold workshops for people who want to learn procedures to follow in order to get publicity. A public relations committee of parents should be part of every school. Even when there is a waiting list, public relations matters should still be carried on consistently. The reputation of a program is built over a long period of time, often by word of mouth and through continued efforts to let the public know of the worthwhile things the school is doing for young children and their families. Advertising in the yellow pages is not enough.

Newspapers and TV stations welcome good feature stories. Where there are several schools competing in the same area, be sensitive to the possibility that the local papers may be criticized by their subscribers and advertisers if they give more publicity to one school over another.

Topics of interest to the general public with clever news or feature angles are more likely to be published. Some papers like to take their own pictures, but if someone at the school can provide good black-and-white glossy photos, the papers may be more likely to accept the article for publication. Some ideas other schools have found successful are:

1. Show a sequence in which children plant wheat, harvest it, grind the wheat into flour, and use the flour to make bread. Wheat can be planted in planter boxes once a week several weeks apart to show various stages of growth. An old-fashioned butter churn in the background during bread baking makes a good picture.

2. Cooking projects such as making peanut butter by shelling and grinding peanuts, shelling peas and steaming them for a snack, churning butter, making ice cream, or planting vegetables and using them for soup all lend themselves to a good story about teaching children good nutrition. Many children do not have the opportunity to see how foods are grown and prepared in their natural state. They are accustomed to food coming out of frozen packages, jars, and cans.

3. Science projects showing eggs hatching, silk worms spinning cocoons, snakes feeding, and bunnies being born all make interesting features.

4. Special equipment designed and built by parents is good for publicizing the school. Parents are attracted to custom built equipment in contrast to the usual commercial playground materials.

5. Community workers visiting the school make for good public relations. Local doctors, dentists, nurses, policemen, firemen, and postmen also enjoy the publicity. The likelihood of attracting more community workers is enhanced when visits are publicized.

6. Special articles about adoptive families, children with special needs, contemporary social concerns (such as single parents), and how the school is helping to ease those problems make interesting reading. The staff should have their research done in advance and much of the information typed to submit to the newspaper. Of course, the families involved must agree to the publicity.

7. Every school has something unique about it. Perhaps it is the unusual equipment, the animals, or the kind of population it serves. In cases where there is a good ethnic mix, publicity can be given to special events such as Chinese New Year, Japanese Obon festival, and Cinco de Mayo. One school carried on an intercultural exchange of toys and books with schools in other countries because one of the parents was an airline pilot who was able to contact children's centers during his stopovers.

Fund Raising

Raising money can be a tiresome chore or the highlight of the school year. The very existence of some programs depends heavily on fund raising; other programs are not quite so dependent on outside help but find that extra money is needed if the school is to provide scholarships, extra help, materials for special projects, a building fund, or transportation money for field trips.

Even if a school is fortunate enough to be self-supporting, there may come a time when special needs require that the staff, parents, and children get together to raise some money. It is hard work but lots of fun.

Schools that have been successful in fund raising report they have found the following ideas very useful:

1. Bazaars. Antique and boutique items made or donated by families and local merchants are one possibility. Other sections of the bazaar can include a flea market, a book stall with new books on consignment or used books donated by libraries, a bake sale, flower and garden materials with cuttings donated by families and nurseries, a fresh fruit and vegetable stand, homemade ice cream or frozen yogurt, barbecued food, a white elephant sale, used clothing, and a raffle.

2. International foods sale. Special finger foods from different cultures, main dishes that can be frozen for future use, desserts, hors d'oeuvres, and holiday cookies and candies are always popular sale items.

3. Wine tasting. Some wineries or liquor stores will supply a good selection of wine along with cheese and bread for a nominal fee. An art show and sale might be combined with wine tasting.

4. Holiday sale. Parents are always interested in buying suitable gifts for their children during the holidays. One school provided child care during certain hours of the day in order to allow parents to work together to make salable items such as:

    a. Wooden table toys (with help from the local adult education class in woodworking).

    b. Dramatic play clothes, such as dance tutus, Superman and Wonder Woman capes, dance scarves, and child-size dress-ups. A very popular item is a "star wand" made of a satin star stuffed with old stockings or foam attached to the end of a dowel. The star can be decorated with sequins and lace, and glitter can be glued onto the wand.

    c. Books. A collection of favorite food recipes donated by the families and teaching staff with a silk-screened cover or recipes for art materials used in the school are popular items.

d. Storytelling materials, such as finger puppets and pop-up puppets boxed in colorful holiday wrap.

e. Homemade flannel boards including several suitable flannel board stories or rhymes and accompanying cut out characters.

f. Silk-screened T-shirts—both adult and child sizes with the name of the school or some other unique design.

g. Tote bags and back packs in large and small sizes for adults and children, made of sailcloth or water-repellent material.

h. Quilting and patchwork, such as small pillows with embroidered or appliqued pillow cases.

i. Cigar boxes covered with Contac paper, each containing some cognitive activity such as sorting buttons by color, shape, size, number of holes, etc. Instructions for proper use can be taped to the inside cover.[3]

j. School supplies. Sell commonly used school supplies such as powdered tempera, newsprint, scissors, crayons, paper punches, jars of finger paint, construction paper, etc. These can be purchased in large quantities at the school's regular discount prices and sold for a slight profit.

k. Finger play kit. Attach Velcro to tips of gloves, and make finger play characters with Velcro on the back of each to attach to the gloves. Package appropriate characters with each finger play printed on a 3" × 5" card. (See patterns on pages 89–94.)

11

Workshops

Just as young children learn best through active involvement, their parents and teachers also derive satisfactory experiences through workshops. The most successful workshops are those that are planned by both parents and teachers to cover areas that the adults really want to know more about.

If the teacher or supervisor decides unilaterally that the parents ought to know more about some topic—music and creative dance, for

---

3. See Doreen J. Croft and Robert D. Hess, *An Activities Handbook for Teachers of Young Children* (Boston: Houghton Mifflin Co., 1975), section on language-motivating experiences, for more ideas.

example—and proceeds to make plans and arrangements without consulting parents, the workshop is less likely to be as enthusiastically attended as one that comes about as the result of parent request or interest.

Parents with expertise in certain fields are often overlooked, and the school should make every effort to tap the resources that are readily available through their enrollment. Sometimes parents who are unskilled may be very good at organizing and planning activities.

The following suggestions from parent participation schools should be helpful in planning workshops:

1. Involve as many people as possible in planning and carrying out the workshop.

2. Provide a list of possible subjects to cover and have adults indicate those topics which are of greatest interest to them.

3. Plan carefully to be sure the workshop runs smoothly.

4. Provide for successful experiences so that the adults will not feel embarrassed or intimidated. (Parents attending a creative movement workshop complained that they felt awkward because the teacher made them dance without any direction or help.)

5. Provide plenty of materials.

6. Tell the participants what the outcome should be. ("You will make three finger puppets to take home." "I would like you to learn two finger plays and one story." "When the workshop is over, you should have five recipes for art materials that you can prepare at home.")

7. Results of the parents' efforts should be useful things they can take home with them.

8. Workshops should cover a wide range of topics and need not be directly related to the child.

9. Keep activities simple and easy to understand.

10. Have printed materials for recipes, patterns, songs, and so on prepared in advance and available to the parents.

11. Allow enough time for socializing since the workshop may be one of the few times parents have an opportunity to chat together.

12. Provide baby-sitting for all children in the family if possible.

Teachers and parents report that the most successful workshops are those that are planned around food. More people are likely to attend if the school can provide food and care for the whole family. Potluck dinners and baby-sitting require more detailed planning by the teacher and staff, but many families simply do not have the time or inclination to go out to meetings after a day at work. The teacher also needs to keep in mind that the cost of food may be a factor. If there is a special fund at the school, or if there are ways to raise money for suppers, these resources should be tapped in order to make participation easier for low-income families.

To encourage better attendance at parent meetings, drawings can be held for such prizes as special school toys, children's books, surprise kits of art materials, desserts, or casseroles. The parent board of one school made Christmas decorations to award as door prizes during an evening meeting.

Suggestions for Workshops

1. *Consumer education.* Have a parent committee and/or consumer education people from the community set up a display of various foods, clothing, toys, and other consumer products to provide samples for parents to examine. For example, pros and cons of fire retardant clothing should be of interest. Also, buying the most nutritious foods for the least money by learning to do comparative pricing, or examining toys and learning how to judge their safety are interesting and informative.

2. *Foods.* Most schools have parents who are good cooks. Families from different ethnic backgrounds sometimes need only an invitation to demonstrate the preparation of a native dish. Each participant could bring an ingredient, or the school might take up a collection to help pay the cost to insure that enough of each food could be prepared for ample amounts for tasting.

3. *Nutrition for children.* Buying and preparing foods that are enticing to children but still provide good nutrition can present problems to many parents. Helpful hints from home economists and nutritionists are useful. With an increase in hyperactivity, parents have been interested in the Feingold diet, which avoids all additives, food coloring, and preservatives. A guest workshop leader from the Feingold Association could provide much helpful information, even for parents who do not have hyperactive children. Parents are also interested in the cooking projects the school offers to the children. Recipes for nutritious foods that have been popular with the children can be shared and prepared by the adults at a cooking workshop. Parents might add to these recipes and plan a cookbook to raise money for future projects.

4. *Weight loss.* The popularity of articles and books on weight loss indicates a real interest in the subject. Good resources to draw upon for workshops would be health food stores, consumer counselors for grocery stores, doctors who specialize in weight loss, nutritionists associated with local colleges and high schools, and parents who have tried various diets. Be careful to have responsible people who are not trying to sell a particular program or who will profit from sales of products that promise dramatic weight loss. Avoid fad diets; stress good nutrition.

5. *Art.* Parents report that their children are intrigued with the kinds of art activities offered in the nursery schools and child care centers. Often this is the first time the young child has been exposed to such a variety of art materials. A workshop in the arts for parents has a lot of popular appeal because it teaches the adults how to mix paints and play dough and prepare lovely art activities for the child at home and it enables the adult to have some fun and experience in playing with the materials. Finger painting and other such art activities provide an emotional release as well as a good outlet for creative expression. A well-planned art workshop gives the adult "permission" to experience play activities and an opportunity to gain further insight into the art experiences of their children as well.

Plan to offer between three and six art activities. Some should already be familiar to the parents through the work of their children—for example, easel painting, collage, and play dough. Others should be new or somewhat unfamiliar—or at least not often used at home—such as finger painting or collecting and ironing leaves and shaved crayons between waxed paper. Sand painting or designing with colored soap squeezed out of cookie presses can also be fun.

It is important to remember to keep activities simple, easy to plan, and interesting for the adults. Recipes for all activities should be available, and parents should have the opportunity to practice mixing paints, preparing play dough, and learning how to plan similar activities at home. A list of helpful hints about materials needed and how to set up the activity to allow maximum involvement and minimum disruption is also useful. For example, the recipe for finger painting should include suggestions for proper setup such as having plastic or paper on the floor, aprons or old shirts for the children, a basin of water nearby, spatulas for scraping paint, and sponges and towels for clean up.

It is important for the parents to understand that much of the success of any art project depends upon careful planning. If the right materials are available, the environment is properly arranged, and the child is not overwhelmed with too many distractions or bored with too few stimuli, the chances for success are enhanced. Have a representative sample of children's art on display.

6. *Music and dance.* Parents often ask about the songs they hear their children singing. A workshop providing adults with words and music to the tunes children have learned or will be learning would be appreciated. Also, a simple guitar class teaching two or three chords to accompany any number of children's songs can be a worthwhile activity for parents. Arrangements can be made with a local music store to rent the guitars or autoharps.

A display of records and demonstrations of how they are used to encourage creative movement, singing, listening to stories, and various other group activities would be useful for those who want to add to their own record collections. Adults who are skilled at doing creative movement activities can demonstrate the use of records, tapes, and instruments to encourage children's movement. Catalogs and other sources for purchasing music materials should be available. Parents who assist in the daily program benefit from a workshop that provides them with the opportunity to learn and practice songs and dance activities to use with the children. With proper resources, many parents will go on to learn new songs to add to the existing repertoire of the teacher.

7. *Communication.* Have a panel of parents do research on such topics as parent effectiveness, sensitivity training, and clarifying values. They can present their findings and lead the group in some examples of the techniques. In some communities, family counseling facilities, therapists, the local library, and school administrators can provide names of reliable professionals who can demonstrate some useful techniques to parents who are interested in improving communications with their children, spouses, and coworkers.

8. *Projects.* Areas of the school such as science, woodworking, and cognitive activities adapt well to the making of materials that parents can use at home with their children. A workshop that promises both fathers and mothers the opportunity to make something they can take home is usually very well attended. For example, areas could be set up to teach how to make terrariums for plants and animals with suggestions for their care. Other activities might include making cardboard furniture or putting together a good carpentry kit with suggestions on the kinds of equipment to purchase and selection of different kinds of wood scraps. Another popular activity is making equipment to encourage cognitive tasks such as sorting, counting, serialization, and other Piaget-related activities.

Some useful books for workshop projects are:

Caney, Steven
Toy Book. New York: Workman Publishing Co., 1972.
Simple-to-make toys suitable for children three to eight years old. Ideas include discovery toys such as water lens, movie wheel, sun goggles; games, action toys, building toys, pretend toys, and design toys are also included.

Croft, Doreen J., and Hess, Robert D.,
An Activities Handbook for Teachers of Young Children. Boston: Houghton Mifflin Co., 1975.
Recipes and learning tasks appropriate for children three to eight years old. Science, premath and language sections provide ideas and designs for such activities as sensory perception, thunder experiment, auditory perception, conceptualization, number conservation, and forms. The cooking and art sections have recipes for a large variety of art activities and healthful foods children can prepare.

Lorton, Mary Baratta
Workjobs. Menlo Park, Calif.: Addison Wesley Publishing Co., 1972.
Includes learning tasks for young children through the manipulation of materials and activities such as sorting buttons, working with sound boxes, and various games using common materials.

Marzollo, Jean, and Lloyd, Janice
Learning Through Play. New York: Harper & Row, 1972.
Activities to enhance prereading problem solving, self-esteem, and creativity through games, riddles, art, and other simple-to-make projects.

9. *Storytelling and finger plays.* Parents and teaching assistants profit from suggestions on how to read or tell a story effectively. Demonstrate some good methods and give them an opportunity to practice these techniques. Stress the following:

a. Hold the book at the child's eye level.
b. Learn how to read upside down and move the book from side to side so all children can see the pictures.
c. Select books with pictures large enough to be seen by the whole group.
d. Use eye contact to maintain control of the group.
e. Practice using the voice to emphasize, to hold attention, and to create interest.
f. When doing a flannel board, keep story line simple.

g. Keep flannel board figures out of children's sight to avoid distractions.

h. Practice using finger puppets and hand puppets to tell stories during a transition time.

To help parents use finger plays effectively, make dittos of a dozen or so popular finger plays. These should be simple and self-explanatory. Go over each one with the parents. Repeat each one slowly to be sure everyone has learned it. Allow time for parents to memorize a few and to take turns leading the group. Patterns for finger puppets and props are given on the following pages.

Boris is a useful prop for the parent who wants to engage children in language development. Boris' teeth chatter when his head is shaken, and the adult can "interpret" Boris' comments to the children.

Glove and Finger Play Puppets

Attach small pieces of Velcro to each of the fingers on a pair of gloves. Attach similar size pieces of Velcro to the backs of each of the finger play characters described. Each set can be packaged along with the words to the finger play printed out on a 3"x5" card.

Attach Velcro to back of felt cutout

Attach Velcro strips to gloves

Three Little Witches

One little, two little,
    three little witches
Fly over haystacks,
    fly over ditches.
Slow down the moon
    without any hitches.
Hi, ho. Halloween's here!

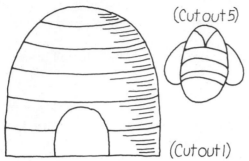

Beehive

Here is the beehive.
   Where are the bees?
Hidden away where nobody sees.
Watch and you'll see them
     come out of the hive,
One, two, three, four, five.
Buzz-z-zzz

(Cut out 5)

(Cut out 1)

Five Kittens

This kitten said, "I smell a mouse."
This kitten said, "Let's hunt through the house."
This kitten said, "Let's pretend we're asleep."
This kitten said, "Let's go creepity-creep."
This kitten said, "Meow, Meow!
    I saw him run into his hole right now."

(Cut out 5)

Squirrel in a Tree

This is the squirrel that lives in a tree;
This is the tree that he climbs;
This is the nut that he takes from me,
As I sit very still sometimes.

(Cut out 1)

(Cut out 1)

Cut out
these 2
pieces and
glue
together
to form
tree

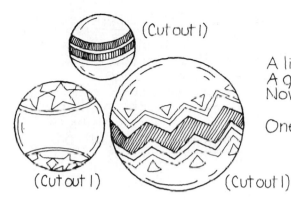

(Cut out 1)

(Cut out 1)

(Cut out 1)

Make a Ball

A little ball, a larger ball,
A great big ball I see.
Now let us count the
    balls we've made,
One, Two, three!

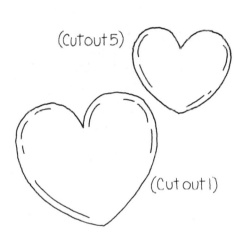

(Cut out 5)

(Cut out 1)

How Many Valentines?

Valentines, valentines,
How many do you see?
Valentines, valentines,
Count them with me:
    One for Father
    One for Mother
    One for Grandma too;
    One for Sister
    One for Brother,
    And here is one for YOU!

Ten Little Candles

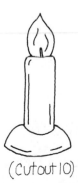

(Cut out 10)

Ten little candles on a chocolate cake,
"Wh! Wh!" Now there are eight!
Eight little candles on a candlestick,
"Wh! Wh!" "Now there are six!
Six little candles, and not one more,
"Wh! Wh!" "Now there are four!
Four little candles, looking at you,
"Wh! Wh!" "Now there are two!
Two little candles standing in the sun,
"Wh! Wh!" "Now there are none!

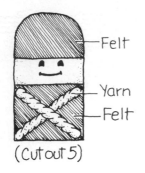

(Cutout 5)

Five Little Soldiers

Five little soldiers
Standing in a row.
Four stood straight,
One stood so.
Along came the captain
And what do you think?
Up jumped the fifth one
Quick as a wink!

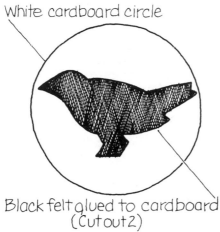

White cardboard circle

Black felt glued to cardboard
(Cutout 2)

Two Little Blackbirds

Two little blackbirds
Sitting on a hill.
One named Jack,
One named Jill.
Fly away Jack,
Fly away Jill.
Come back Jack!
Come back Jill!

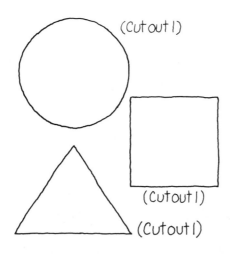

(Cutout 1)

(Cutout 1)

(Cutout 1)

Draw a Circle

Draw a circle, draw a circle
Round as can be;
Draw a circle, draw a circle
Just for me.
Draw a square, draw a square
Shaped like a door;
Draw a square, draw a square
With corners four.
Draw a triangle, draw a triangle
With corners three;
Draw a triangle, draw a triangle
Just for me.

Felt Finger
Puppets

Cut and sew together different size pieces of felt to make a family or group of finger puppets. Clothing such as dresses and vests can be stitched separately and slipped over the basic puppet. Attach hair and other head ornaments as desired. Eyes, nose, and mouth can be embroidered, marked with a pen, or glued.

←— Basic Puppet

Stitch both pieces together and turn inside out.

Boris

Cut a 5" piece from a heavy cardboard tube. Attach another 1½" piece at one spot to form the back of the neck. Use a good strong cloth tape because Boris' head and mouth should be able to open and shut by simply shaking the body back and forth. Reinforce the tube with cloth or other material to make the body and head more sturdy. Boris is dressed with suede cloth, his hair and beard are scraps of fur, his glasses are wire, and his teeth are small beads.

(Cardboard base)

Apply cloth tape here and inside tube.

Annotated Readings

The following books provide a basis for parent workshop or discussion topics. These same resources are also useful for parent guidance.

Beck, Joan
How To Raise a Brighter Child. The Case for Early Learning. New York: Pocket Books, 1975.

Suggests ways in which parents can encourage curiosity and creativity in children up to age 6.

Belton, Sandra, and Sparks, Christine Terborgh
Activities to Help Children Learn at Home. Washington, D.C.: Human Service Press, 1972.
A collection of activities that can be used at home to encourage language development, science, art, and related experiences.

Caldwell, Bettye, et al.
Home Teaching Activities. Little Rock, Ark.: Center for Early Development in Education, 1972.
Mimeographed booklet contains activities to be used with simple home materials, covering eight to twenty-four month age range.

Lehane, Stephen
Help Your Baby Learn. Englewood Cliffs, N.J.: Prentice-Hall, Inc., 1976.
One hundred Piaget based activities designed to be used with babies in the first two years.

Munnion, Catherine, and Grender, Iris, eds.
The Open Home, Early Learning Made Easy for Parents and Children. New York: St. Martin's Press, 1976.
Teaches the parent how to help children learn and explore.

Pantell, Robert H., et al.
Taking Care of Your Child: A Parent's Guide to Medical Care. Palo Alto, Calif.: Addison-Wesley Publishing Co., 1977.
Charts and descriptions of childhood diseases help parents to determine proper course of action to take.

Simon, Sidney B., et al.
Values Clarification. New York: Hart Publishing Company, Inc., 1972.
A useful book for the discussion leader in using strategies to clarify personal values.

Vaughan, Gerard
A Pictorial Guide to Common Illnesses. London: Arcade Publishing Ltd., 1970.
A large colorfully illustrated book describing how to look for and identify childhood illnesses with a special index to emergencies.

Part 3
Guidance for Parents

Introduction

During your career as a teacher, you're certain to hear comments such as these:

"All my child does is play. When is he going to do something worthwhile?"

"We've tried everything but he still insists on sucking his thumb!"

"What do you do about a child who bites?"

"She has tantrums when she can't have her way!"

"What do you suggest I tell my child about death?"

"When is a good time to start toilet training?"

"He won't share."

"We did everything the books suggested, but she's still jealous of her new baby brother!"

Parents turn to teachers for answers to such concerns. They rely heavily on the professional expertise of the teacher to guide them in dealing with their children's behavior problems. As their children's teacher, you will want to make helpful suggestions, provide workable solutions, and make appropriate referrals.

This section is devoted to some of the most common parent concerns. Many of the problems are familiar to the teacher, and offering some of the proposed suggestions can be sufficient to alleviate parental anxieties. However, the materials presented are in no way intended to be formula answers applicable to all situations, and the teacher must be cautioned to recognize when seemingly superficial problems are a reflection of deeper, more serious situations. In such cases, referrals should be made to trained professionals and reliable agencies. (Refer to the Appendix.) Parents also should be encouraged to read related materials.

Topics are arranged alphabetically for ease of reference. As you gain more firsthand experiences in these and other areas, you will find it useful to make notes incorporating your own suggestions. Further readings and additional related resources, some for children, are included in the Appendix of Resources.

12

Aggressiveness (See also Hyperkinesis)

"Billy deliberately pushed Margie off her trike, and as I was comforting her, he threw sand in David's eyes and kicked Jonathan! I just don't understand why he's so aggressive! Is it normal for a child to be like that? What can I do?" wailed Miss Lambert, Billy's teacher.

It's probably of very little comfort to Miss Lambert to know that into the life of every teacher comes a Billy at one time or another. Children like Billy exhibit aggressive behavior sufficiently uncontrollable to cause teachers and parents alike to question why and to try to find ways to divert such aggression into more acceptable channels.

First, it is important to look at how we all feel about aggression. In most instances the word has a negative connotation. When we describe a child as being aggressive, we immediately visualize a destructive, hard-to-manage child. Adults also find it difficult to relate in a positive way to a child who "deliberately hurts others." To better understand Billy's behavior, one needs to look more closely at the nature of aggression.

The dictionary definition says that an aggressive person (1) "moves or acts in a hostile fashion" or (2) is "assertive, bold, enterprising." Most of us would ascribe the former definition to Billy's behavior. Yet, in order to be effective with children like Billy, the teacher needs to consider the second definition carefully in light of each child's nature. Oftentimes it is aggressiveness that propels us to learn, to overcome challenging tasks, to invent, and to be creative. The first step in working with an aggressive child is to recognize that aggression is not always bad. When we have students who seem only to show the hostile, destructive side of their nature, we want to know how to help them redirect these tendencies into more socially acceptable behavior.

Children are not born destructive. The way they behave today is very much tied to the way they have been raised up to this point. The way they feel about themselves and others is the result of past experiences, and these experiences are reflected in their behavior. As an infant, Billy was totally self-centered in that his needs for food and physical comfort had to be satisfied. He was completely dependent upon his caretakers to satisfy those needs.

But as he matured, he quickly learned that he didn't always get what he wanted. He entered into a world of "no-nos" and realized that he must conform or be punished. All children must go through this process of progressing from total egocentrism to becoming a socially conforming individual. The process is often painful, rarely smooth, and never without some discomfort on the part of the child and those with whom he lives and learns.

Imagine all the things children learn they "must" or "must not" do from the time they enter the toddler stage until enrollment in nursery school. They must learn not to put some things in their mouths, but it's all right to put other things in their mouths. They're expected to touch the toys we provide for them, but they must not touch other things. They must learn to go potty at a certain time and certain place and not at other times and places. They learn that they are "naughty" for doing things that seem very natural.

To see an example of the frustrations facing a young child, just go into any grocery store and watch a parent shopping with a preschooler. There are all the colorful fruits and cereal boxes just begging to be touched, and what is more natural than for a child to want to reach out and grab something enticing? But the child quickly learns that those are no-nos and are not to be touched. What frustration!

Put yourself in that child's place. You want to touch, to explore, to taste, but you are told "no" and punished or made to feel guilty. How do you feel? Angry? Frustrated? Resentful? Sad? Rebellious? Perhaps all of these.

What happens to these feelings? Given the situation, they certainly seem to be appropriate. But the ways in which parents and children deal with these natural feelings determine, in great part, how the children behave in future situations.

Children now feel guilty, sad, and frustrated *because* of their parents, and they also feel resentful, angry, and hateful *toward* their parents. These feelings are very powerful, and they are usually frightening to the children. They do not understand that it is natural to feel the way they do. They certainly find it difficult to understand why they can't do certain things. Through many such firsthand experiences, their parents gradually "socialize" them to be "civilized" members of society. But in the process of this socialization, the children experience many painful and frightening feelings. They are caught in a dilemma in which they both hate and need (love) their parents. This confusion (ambivalence) of both hating and loving causes inner conflict.

Does this mean we should let children do whatever they want? Not at all. Understanding and accepting feelings does not mean we give in to them. But real understanding provides the adults with a better perspective from which to interact with the children.

Do you remember a time when you were so angry with your parents for punishing you unjustly that you wished they were dead or you fantasized killing yourself? This is common, but young children often confuse thoughts with reality. They do not understand that having these feelings is natural. They feel guilty and believe themselves to be "bad" for entertaining such terrible thoughts. The resolution for most children is that they learn to inhibit these thoughts and accept rules and limits because of their need for and dependence on their parents. During this phase of their lives, you will often hear children repeating to themselves, "That's a no-no. Mustn't touch. Bad." As children mature, their personal standards and values grow out of experiences with people who are important to them. Gradually, these values become more integrated into their total being and they derive their own concepts of right and wrong from inner standards.

If, during this important early learning period, young children are given a lot of love, understanding, and support from their families, they are more likely to learn how to return this love and warmth. How they feel about others depends largely on how they see the world during these formative years. If it is friendly, loving, accepting, and supportive, children are more likely to be willing and able to accept reasonable limits with a minimum of resentment. If, on the other hand, they see the world as an unfriendly, hostile place, they may resist control or limits. This resistance can take many forms: aggressiveness, destructiveness, fearfulness, even passivity. We all have different ways of covering up our true feelings. Children who are "too good" or conforming can be manifesting problems too.

This early learning period, both for children and parents, is crucial to later success in emotional and social growth. The teacher can be a very important person in helping parents to understand the behavior of their youngsters and helping children accept and express their own feelings in a safe environment.

Most parents have had no special training in raising young children. The mere fact of giving birth to a baby does not make the mother an expert on child rearing. Teachers with training in child development will recognize when both parents and children need a more objective third person to interpret the meaning of behavior so parents can get some insight into how young children feel and why they may be behaving in a certain way.

In addition, children need a person who is accepting of their feelings and one who will interpret their behavior for them. "I know you're crying because you're angry. That's OK. Sometimes I cry when I get angry too" (accepting and sharing feelings). "You hit Margie because she took your play dough. How do you feel when she takes your play dough? What do you think you can do about it?" (recognizing and exploring feelings). "I know you're really mad, but I can't let you kick the other children" (acknowledging feelings and setting limits). Teachers can model through their interactions with children the kinds of strategies that "work." They can demonstrate how much more effective they can be by accepting feelings, by making emotional space for others to explore how they feel, by interpreting behavior, and by being firm but loving. Adults may have to repeat these kinds of phrases over and over again during the children's early years, but consistency, patience, and persistence do pay off in healthier children and happier parents.

It is clear that using physical punishment to deter aggressive behavior only tells the children that adults rely on force. Ignoring aggressiveness also seems to be ineffective. This may imply that adults do not care or do not know how to deal with the situation. Many teachers have been told that providing a substitute such as a punching bag is effective for working out aggressive feelings, but recent research does not bear this out.[1] Children who are aggressive, for whatever reasons, need to be told firmly and consistently that their behavior is unacceptable. Adult disapproval should be made very clear.

Changing a child's aggressive behavior is most likely to succeed when the school and family and all the other important people in the child's life agree on using consistent methods. If Billy gets the message that his teacher *and* his neighbors *and* his parents all value the same kinds of things and disapprove of certain others, he is apt to be less confused about what is "good" and "bad." This requires communication and identifying the areas in which parents and teachers have agreement. This agreement is especially important in setting limits for aggressive children. Children learn very early that they can "get away with" certain things with one person and not with another. Many family arguments arise over the lack of support or limits "I told Maggie she had to be in bed by eight o'clock, but her dad let her stay up as a special treat." When disagreements begin to surface, it is time for the family and school to discuss how best to agree upon and cooperate on consistent strategies. (See also Discipline).

1. L. Berkowitz, "Control of Aggression," *Review of Child Development Research,* vol. 3, ed. B. Caldwell and H. Ricciuti (Chicago: University of Chicago Press, 1973).

The following suggestions can be helpful in working with aggressive children:

1. *Set firm limits.* Mean it when you say "no." Otherwise, don't make a rule you can't enforce.

2. *Be fair about limits.* Too many no's are hard to take and set both teachers and children up for failure.

3. *Be supportive.* Don't look upon the aggressive behavior as a deliberate violent act against you. If you see nonconforming behavior as an attack upon your authority, you will be working against the children and forcing your superior will and strength upon them. When this kind of attitude prevails, the relationship breaks down to "you against me" and someone has to win and someone has to lose.

4. *Try to understand the meaning of the aggressive behavior.* Is the child acting out of frustration for having too many rules imposed on him? Is he confused by having too much freedom? Is he unclear about what is important to you? Does he get inconsistent messages? Does he feel neglected, unloved, jealous, overprotected? This is where parents and teachers need to discuss possible causes.

5. *Be prepared to use physical means to restrain an aggressive child.* Teachers are sometimes hesitant to follow through with their warnings ("I can't let you hurt other children") by physically holding and restraining an aggressive child. New teachers report that this kind of physical control makes them feel like they have failed at using more acceptable techniques. They also express concern that the child won't like them anymore.

6. *Anticipate potentially aggressive situations.* Children's play often starts out peacefully but quickly escalates into situations that result in fighting. Experienced teachers will recognize that playing "Monster" or encouraging highly excitable encounters invariably leads to someone getting hurt. Often the young child does not participate in such play with the intention of hurting others. It is the adult's lack of direction and proper intervention that leads to destructive play.

7. *Interpret the meaning of behavior to children.* Adults often assume children "know better" or are able to predict the outcome of their actions. Children need to be told again and again: "When you hit someone, it hurts." "I don't like it when you do that." "*Tell* her what you want. Don't hit her."

8. *Aggressive acts need follow-up.* Stopping the action or intervening while a child is behaving aggressively is necessary, but once the action is stopped the adult needs to follow through to make a learning situation out of the behavior: "The other children threw sand at you because you were hitting them. They don't like to be hit. What do you think you can do so they will let you play with them? I'll help you learn how to play with the other children." Be prepared to give such children the necessary tools to learn social adjustment. Tell them some of the words they might use to gain acceptance. Show them alternative activities. Plan projects that will give them lots of satisfaction. Praise them when they are doing well. Summarize what they did and remind them of the positive things they have done: "I see you shared some of your trains with Mary and now you're both playing nicely together. I like what you did." "That was a good idea when you helped the other children build a bridge. They like to play with you when you work together. See? You are learning how to play with other children. That's really good." Children also need to be reminded of the future consequences of behavior: "What did Johnny do to you the last time you hit him?" "What do you think he will do if you hit him now?" "What else can you do?" "What do you think will happen if you do that?"

9. *Provide opportunities for children to learn responsibility for their own behavior.* Whether the children are rejected or clobbered by others use the situation to point out to them that other people behave this way toward them *because* of their actions. Gradually help them rely on themselves to determine how things will turn out rather than turn to adults to solve problems for them. This takes time, patience, consistency, and support from the adult, but it works!

13

Absences of Parents (Separation Anxieties)

"My five-year-old won't let me out of her sight! We're going to have trouble getting her to stay at school." Every teacher of young children has heard that lament.

Your reassurances that this is normal does little to alleviate the anxious feelings of both parent and child at the moment. In looking back on such experiences, parents often report that when their child clings and cries they feel embarrassed, confused about what to do, ambivalent (both sorry and angry), and guilty for leaving. They also wonder what they might have done wrong in raising such a child when it is obvious that everyone else's child appears to be adjusting easily!

It is especially important that children are handled with confidence during a separation. If parents and teachers can behave and talk in such ways as to let children know that this is OK and reassure them that Mommy or Daddy will be back, children will sense the confidence of the adults.

It is difficult for parents to act confident when in reality they are uncertain. This is a time when the teacher needs to model for the parents by suggesting some useful methods. It does help to begin by telling parents that this happens often and that their child is not the only one who does this. It helps the teacher to know how the child has reacted to similar situations in the past. Has Susan had any traumatic experiences with baby-sitters? Has she been left frequently? The "history" of how the parent-child interaction around separation has taken place can be helpful information for the teacher.

In situations where the parents work and there is no choice but to leave the children, there are some things teachers can recommend to parents to make the separation easier:

1. Always tell children the truth. "Mother has to go to work. She will be back to get you after snack time" (or whatever time based on an activity in the child's schedule).

2. Do not sneak out on children. Tell them you are leaving and reassure them that you will be back rather than disappear without notice. It is better to have a tearful but honest good-bye than to hope children will be distracted and simply forget.

3. Help children look forward to a favorite activity or person who is appealing. Talk about the happy experiences while taking the children to a caretaker or child care center.

4. Remind the children when you come back that you kept your promise. "I am back to get you right after work. Just like I said I would." "I'm going to take you to school every day and I'm going to come back to get you every day." "Mom and Dad go to work and Jimmy goes to school every day."

5. Keep a brief schedule of your child's activities during the day so that conversation can reinforce the good times. One of the least fruitful questions a parent can ask a child is "What did you do today?" The response is usually "Nothing." "Did you make any friends?" "No, nobody played with me."

Based on such questioning the parent often gets a very sad and lonely picture of the child sitting alone with nothing to do. However, given some information about specific kinds of activities provided in the daily routine of the school, a parent might be encouraged to say something like "I wonder what you and your friends had for juice and snack time today?" "Did you get to eat your favorite kind of cracker?" "Was there someone named Margie who sat at your table when you helped to make popcorn?" "The teacher sang some new songs today, didn't she?" "Can you show me how you make your fingers open and shut?"

Parents often request copies of songs or finger plays their children learn in school. Such materials along with the schedule of activities allow the parent to reinforce the teacher's work with the child. Even a quickly printed sign posted at the door announcing the visit of a community worker (e.g., "Fireman Visiting Today") will give the parent some familiar topic to discuss. This kind of information produces a quite different picture of how the child is adjusting to separation from mother and father.

In situations requiring that children be separated from people they know and love, the important thing to remember is that it is very natural and normal for them to feel sad. It is not wrong or abnormal for them to cry and to resist being left in a strange place, and there is no reason to imply that there might be something wrong with them. The adult's attitude in such a situation can convey much to the child about the acceptability of such feelings.

When possible, the adult should plan to stay with the child in any new situation until the child is ready to be left. It is also helpful to give the child small positive doses of being left with new people. Perhaps the parent can make opportunities to leave the child with a relative or a sitter for short periods of time. Planning some special activity such as cooking, doing something the child likes, or reading a favorite story can help make a smooth transition.

Finally, the attitudes of adults go a long way in helping children build self-confidence about matters of separation. If adults can convey that they understand, they can be trusted, and they are confident everything will work out all right, children will be more ready to build on positive experiences in a supportive environment.

14

Bed Wetting

Bed wetting is always a "popular" topic for discussion among parents of preschoolers. Every parent goes through the period of "potty training" with varying degrees of success or failure.

Once accomplished, the frustrations are soon forgotten, but while parents are in the process of trying to "train" children, they wonder if the day will ever come! One mother said in desperation, "The only way I could maintain some degree of patience was to convince myself that Billy would be dry by the time he was eighteen!"

Toilet training and weaning from the breast or bottle seem to be the two areas in which parents tend to do most comparing with others. Sometimes the ages and stages of development are looked upon not as general guidelines, but as goals to be surpassed. "My child threw his bottle away five months before the book said it was time to be weaned." "My child stayed dry the day I bought him a potty seat for his second birthday!" Comments like these do little to enhance a parent's sense of confidence in raising the child who is still wetting the bed at age four and five.

By the time they enter nursery school at age two or three years, children have probably had some "training" to stay dry through the night. Some parents are embarrassed to tell teachers that their children still need help going to the bathroom. Others threaten children that they cannot be "big kids" and go to school unless they learn to stay dry. The area of toilet training is often fraught with strong feelings.

The first child or only child in a family is frequently the focus of concern for parents eager to do what is right. These parents are often reassured by hearing more experienced mothers and fathers share their ideas about toilet training, weaning, talking, walking, etc. Teachers also recognize from experience with many families that it is not at all unusual for a child of three or four or older to wet the bed from time to time.

Some Questions to Consider:

1. Can the bed wetting be related to a recent event such as a new baby in the family, a frightening experience, or the absence of a friend or parent?

2. Is the child tense or anxious about something such as starting school or going on a trip? Or does the child appear to be concerned or anxious or tense about anything in general?

3. Is the child's daily routine comfortable, relaxed, consistent? Or are there many demands to be "good," to perform up to high standards?

4. Are the people around the child relaxed and well adjusted?

5. Has the child had a complete physical recently (within the past six months)? Is the child's physical development sufficiently mature to enable bladder control?

Some Things for Parents to Try:

1. Devise a plan to help the child stay dry. He is not wetting his bed on purpose. It helps if the parent can understand that the child also wants to stay dry. Tell him you will take him to the bathroom sometime during the night, and suggest that he will urinate and go right back to sleep and stay dry. Using positive suggestions can be of help. Praise the child when he stays dry.

2. Limit the amount of liquids a child takes after a certain hour in the day (about four hours before bedtime). It is best not to make a big fuss about no liquids so the child will not feel deprived. Make it a point to offer plenty of liquids earlier in the day and do not serve any before or during dinner.

3. A young child may simply be more comfortable in diapers during the night because staying dry is too much of a hassle for parent and child. If this is the case, do not shame the child for having to stay in diapers.

4. Make it as easy and as comfortable as possible for the child to get up and go to the bathroom at night. Provide a good night light, a clear pathway, and perhaps a potty chair in the bedroom. Take the child through the motions of using the toilet while he is awake, and suggest the routine to follow when he has to get up at night.

5. Be relaxed and matter of fact about occasional wetting. Children need reassurance that this is normal and that the problem will be overcome eventually. Scolding and punishing only create guilt and helplessness.

15

Biting

A child's bite is, in fact, an animal bite. If the skin is broken, the person who has been bitten needs to be certain his or her DPT shots are up to date. Parents and teachers who realize the seriousness of biting will communicate very clearly to the child that biting is not allowed.

The director of a nursery school reported that children were biting adults and other children when she first took over the program. Within two weeks the biting had stopped. When asked how she managed to be so effective, the director replied, "I feel very strongly that biting is not an acceptable way to express feelings. When a child bites another person I get to the situation immediately and let them know through words and actions that this is serious. I tell them that when the skin is broken the other child can get very sick and may have to have a shot. I simply make it clear that *no* biting is allowed. The children get the message. Of course, I suggest other ways that a child can work off frustrations. I also have the parents support my rule so the children get the same message from all the adults. It works!"

Young children often learn through trial and error that biting is a good way to get what they want. Sometimes children who are physically smaller than their playmates find that biting is effective where words or other actions fail. If this is the case, the adult needs to see to it that the child is not rewarded for such behavior and gets satisfaction through other methods. Praise the child for being able to get what he or she wants without biting.

Keep a mental record of the times a child is most likely to resort to biting. Is it when the child is tired, upset, or frightened? Try to avoid the situations which bring on such behavior. Supervise more closely to anticipate when biting might occur and intervene before it happens by distracting or redirecting.

Sometimes very young children do not understand how much it hurts to be bitten. Adults sometimes ask if they should bite back just to show the child how it feels. This kind of behavior simply tells the child that the adult also resorts to biting to show anger and reinforces the use of violence. Letting the child bite on a doll or a teething ring can be an acceptable substitute.

Biting, hitting, and other antisocial acts are symptoms that tell us the child is feeling frustrated and unhappy. A well-adjusted, happy child usually wants to please and to do things that are socially acceptable. Consistently destructive behavior signals that the child needs help.

16

Crying, Whining, Temper Tantrums

All parents know that crying in an infant is natural, normal, and the baby's only means of letting others know of its discomfort. Crying is necessary for survival.

When does crying become unacceptable? During an evening discussion on the topic of crying and whining, some of the parents commented:

"I guess I really hate to hear Janet cry because it embarrasses me. It calls attention to me and I don't want people to think I'm a lousy mother."

A father stated, "Chris shouldn't be crying so much now that he's a big boy of five. I don't want people to think he's a sissy." (The same father said he would not object to his five-year-old daughter crying.)

"Margy knows I can't stand her whining and crying, so I usually give in to her after a lot of threatening."

"Billy gets picked on by all the bigger kids in the neighborhood, so he comes home crying many times during the day. I feel so sorry for the poor little tike that I give him a treat like a cookie and an extra hug."

"Ever since her younger brother started walking and getting into her things, Janie has been crying and complaining until I can't stand her incessant whine! I know her brother bothers her, but he needs space and attention too. I've been losing my patience with her, and that only makes matters worse!"

Crying symbolizes many different things to different people. Some, like Janet's mother, see the child's crying as a reflection of their worthiness as parents. Others, like Chris' dad, feel that boys ought not to cry.

Our ideas and attitudes about children's crying are conditioned through our own early experiences. Some parents in other cultures never allow their children to cry. They will carry them, hold them, comfort them, and maintain constant body contact, feeding or soothing the child at even the slightest whimper. Others believe crying is healthy for the lungs. Most parents learn very early to detect the seriousness of a child's cry. They can tell if the child is mildly uncomfortable, wants attention, or is in dire need.

Some parents can recognize their own discomfort over a child's tears or tantrums. One mother promised a special treat for her little girl if she would stay with the baby-sitter without having a tantrum. Now the child has a tantrum every time she is left with a sitter unless she receives a treat. The special treat served to reinforce the negative behavior. Researchers in behavior modification have found that rewarding a behavior tends to reinforce that behavior. Thus, it is argued that parents should use positive reinforcement such as praise to reward approved behavior, and ignore undesired behavior as effective means of getting the child to behave in acceptable ways.

Other parents look upon whining and crying as deliberate attempts by children to get their own way. These parents are unyielding and completely unsympathetic, even to legitimate cries of a child.

Understanding the reasons for the tantrum or tears is essential to a successful resolution of the problem. Punishment, ignoring, or using negative reinforcers may only treat the symptoms. Parents who complain to teachers about their child's excessive crying need to have the opportunity to discuss the subject thoroughly enough to determine some of the underlying causes of such behavior. The parent may be helped by having the teacher share her observations of the child's patterns of interactions at school—when the child is most easily upset, the time of day, the kind of situation, etc. These clues along with the parent's report of home situations which tend to induce crying can identify a pattern that adults might be able to alter or adjust in order to make life less stressful for the child.

Other useful kinds of information include knowing more about the way important people in the child's life feel and behave in regard to the child's tears. Does the child get sympathy, undue attention, punishment, ridicule, or special privileges as the result of tears? Are there some understandable reasons behind the crying? For example, the young child may find that it is difficult to meet all the demands of growing up and staying babylike is much safer. Or perhaps the whining is a signal that adults are ignoring the child's need for affection and opportunities to increase his or her self-confidence. Tears are often a healthy release for pent-up feelings, and the wise adult will recognize appropriate responses for such incidents.

Teachers report that children sometimes come to school with learned habits of communicating. The little girl who uses a whiny voice when she wants an adult to intervene on her behalf, or the child who immediately reverts to babyish behavior when he sees his mother are children who will learn through experience with others that the kind of behavior that gets them what they want at home may not be successful in other situations.

As children develop self-confidence and find satisfying relationships, they are less likely to continue with crying as a crutch. The school can be of much help in providing the kinds of experiences children need in order to feel important and loved. Children as well as adults need occasional relief from the pressures of family living, and the perceptive teacher will make a special place for the child whose crying signals a need for a warm understanding environment with fewer pressures.

17

Death

Unlike the ordinary, routine problems that arise from day to day, teachers and parents are not accustomed to dealing with the problems related to death and the young child. Generally, young children have their first experience with death when a pet dies. This provides the adult with an opportunity to share beliefs and attitudes with the youngster.

It is important that the teacher is made aware of the family's feelings regarding death so that the child is not confused or given conflicting kinds of information. Some beliefs are based on the family's religious background, and transmittal of this kind of information is best left to the family. However, when an animal dies in the child care center and children want to know what happened, how is teacher to answer? Adults need to clarify their own beliefs about death and be clear about the kind of information the child ought to have.

Some adults tell their children that the pet has "gone to sleep" and will go to heaven. Others prefer to remove the pet and not say anything at all about death. It seems preferable, given the inexperience of the child, to stay with facts and simple information based on what the child does know. Some of these facts (depending on what the child seems to be interested in knowing or able to assimilate) are:

1. Dead means the pet is not able to move, or breathe, or see anymore.
2. It will not be alive again.
3. It cannot feel anymore.
4. It is not the same as being asleep.
5. It will not come back to life.
6. Everything that lives has to die at some time.
7. We do not plan to die in the near future.
8. Death is natural.
9. There is nothing to fear.

These points and others based on facts should be introduced only as the child appears ready to accept and understand them. Giving a "lecture" to be sure to cover all the points is not advisable.

Having a clear idea of your own philosophy of death is important so that you can impart with clarity facts about a natural occurrence. So often, people feel that young children should be protected from the "ugliness of death" when they really need these experiences as part of growing up. Babies are born, grow up, grow old, and die; children need to be exposed to each and every aspect of the cycle of life in the most natural way possible. Adult attitudes carry over to the youngster.

Opportunities to ask questions and get honest answers help determine the kind of healthy outlook a child develops. A more sensitive area is the death of a family member or close friend or relative. Facts similar to those regarding pets should be imparted to the child. Of course, the discussion of feelings of sadness and mourning need to be brought out, shared, and accepted. The child who can see others feeling sad, mourning, and expressing feelings openly will realize that he too can express his feelings without fear or shame. He learns that death is natural, as are sadness and mourning.

Depending on the age and maturity of a child, the adult can use books, articles, and other outlets such as art for self-expression to help integrate the experience more smoothly. Young children profit from opportunities to talk about happenings that may be difficult for them to understand or accept. It helps to let them draw or paint or dictate a story or simply hear again and again what they need to hear. They need calm, self-assured, loving adults who are patient and supportive to reassure them that things will be all right.

Children sometimes relate death to themselves and their loved ones and become frightened that the same thing might happen to them. This is an important time to reassure children that neither they nor you are going to die soon. In some instances when death of a family member is imminent, teachers report that the best thing to do is prepare the child by telling him that this person is very sick and will die soon. Let the child know that he will continue doing all the things he is doing, and attempt to maintain as consistent a daily routine for him as possible. (See p. 164 for an annotated list of storybooks for children on the subject of death.)

18

Discipline

"I try to be firm and consistent with Jamie, but my husband lets him get away with anything he wants to do."

"My mother-in-law says I'm too strict, just because I make Susie stay in her room until everything is picked up."

"The arguments I have with my wife are mostly about the kids. We don't agree on how they should be disciplined, and the kids are suffering from the lack of consistent rules. Our marriage is in trouble!"

How is a teacher—perhaps less experienced than the parents involved—to counsel these parents about such an emotionally loaded topic as discipline?

One of the mistakes friends, neighbors, and relatives often make is to offer well-meaning advice. Rarely does this advice take into consideration the backgrounds of the parents in relation to discipline. Before the parents quoted above can be effective with their children, they must do some in-depth exploring and discussing of their own backgrounds and why they feel the way they do. Some of the insights resulting from such a discussion are:

"I came from a very strict family where we were spanked soundly for misbehaving, and that hasn't hurt me. I think my success today is based largely on the fact that I learned responsibility at an early age."

"I don't like to see my kids 'get away' with unacceptable behavior so easily. Boy, I wouldn't have gotten away with half the stuff they pull."

"Life's too soft for children today. I want them to learn that things don't come easily. They have to make a living some day."

"I think children should have fun while they're young. We're too serious about making rules all the time. I never got to have fun when I was young."

"I come from a big family where we were pretty relaxed about discipline. Everyone pitched in to help. My wife is an only child and her parents were very serious with her, so she doesn't understand how I can be so casual."

Parents and teachers often fall into the trap of having to embrace one extreme or the other with regard to discipline. There are those who feel that children's instincts are antisocial and they need to be reared in a very strict fashion according to adult rules, which they are not to question. On the other hand, some feel that discipline (meaning punishment) weakens children and causes negative feelings about themselves and others, loss of trust in the world around them, and inhibition of their creativity. There are varying degrees between these two extremes, and adults need to arrive at some agreement as to where they stand, why they feel the way they do, and most important, ways to adopt consistent methods to implement their beliefs.

Parents who have raised several children will often reminisce about the "mistakes" they made with the first child. Most will agree that they (the parents) lacked the experience to enforce the proper amount and kind of discipline. "We get more mellow and relaxed with each child, and we can see how tense and anxious we were now that we look back. We were always worried about doing the wrong thing, so I think we were too serious and too strict with the first child."

Teachers who have had years of experience also comment on how they have changed over the years. "I can laugh with a child over something mischievous that is perfectly normal for a preschooler where I would have given him a lecture in my first year of teaching." That does not mean that people necessarily get more lax as they mature. It does mean they are more comfortable about making reasonable rules and sticking by those rules (because they know from experience that they are good rules), and they can see the problem from a larger perspective so that every little infraction does not seem like a major catastrophe or a personal affront.

The inexperienced parent or teacher may have difficulty in knowing how and when to set firm limits. In some cases, the young child simply may not be capable of being as responsible as the adults expect. In others, the expectations may not be high enough. The adult needs to be a caring helper who is confident of his or her more mature knowledge and who understands when a youngster has not had enough experience or is truly old enough to "know better." Combining affection with control is quite different from demanding immediate obedience, even if the expected outcome is the same.

Regardless of the amount or method of discipline, it is helpful for both teacher and parent to keep the following in mind:

1. *Discipline does not necessarily mean withholding love.* Setting firm limits, denying a privilege, and even a whack on the bottom are methods to be used for keeping a child out of trouble, not withholding love.

2. *"Good" discipline always respects the child's need to grow and learn.* Limits are for the safety and well-being of the child and others concerned, not for the inhibition of curiosity or creativity.

3. *Adults (disciplinarians) must not be too proud to learn from their mistakes.* Punishing inappropriately, establishing unworkable rules, and being unreasonable in terms of the child's abilities to obey must be recognized, reevaluated, and changed.

4. *Reward acceptable behavior.* Praising the child for "good" behavior is more effective than punishing for bad behavior. Ignoring undesired behavior tends to extinguish it.

5. *Making the child eventually responsible for his own behavior should be the goal of disciplinary measures.* Rather than "laying down the law," the adult should use every opportunity to help the child understand why rules are necessary.

6. *Flexibility in making changes according to the child's developmental level is important.* What worked last month may not be relevant today because the child's capabilities and maturity level have changed. The perceptive and sensitive adult is willing to give the child more responsibility and more space to make mistakes as the child seems ready.

7. *Learning through firsthand experience with proper guidance and evaluation is worthwhile.* Children need an environment with enough freedom to explore and try out some of their social skills in safety. Adults who never let them make a mistake or who punish them every time they do something wrong do not allow for healthy intellectual or emotional growth.

8. *Many discipline problems can be avoided through proper anticipation.* The teacher or parent who sees potential problem areas will plan the situation or activity to avoid some of the obvious trouble spots. For example, setting up the furniture in a classroom to isolate noisy activities from quiet areas or placing natural barriers in locations to discourage running will help eliminate many disruptions.

9. *Consistency is essential for successful discipline.* Agreement among those people responsible for the child is highly important in carrying out a workable program of discipline. When the school feels one way about discipline, the parents another, and the grandparents still another, the child receives confusing messages about what is important and expected. Under such circumstances it is no surprise that the child learns to manipulate the adults and work one against the other.

10. *The caring disciplinarian is more effective.* Adults who truly care about children and who let them know they love them can be firm and strict by many standards without fear of "messing the child up." Children know when they are loved, and they also sense when a teacher or parent is insincere and uncaring.

11. *Be clear about what is expected of the child.* It is important that adults mean what they say. Perhaps more than any other single suggestion, this one is most important for the inexperienced student teacher or parent to learn. People who are effective in getting children to do as they ask will agree that it is absolutely essential to communicate clear messages and show your intention to follow through. Laurie, a young student teacher, reported in a hopeless tone of voice to the supervisor that she had been trying without success to get one of the children to come inside for juice time. The supervisor went up to the child, got down to his eye level, looked him straight in the eyes, and said firmly, "Glenn, it's juice time and I want you to come in." Glenn squirmed uncomfortably and started to turn away. The supervisor held both his arms and repeated, "I want you to come in now." Glenn walked in with the supervisor. "What did you do?" wailed Laurie. "I tried the same thing, but it didn't work."

It is important to let children know through your tone of voice, your body language, the way you look, and the way you touch them that you are *telling* them what to do—not asking, requesting, imploring, or wishing. Your intentions must be clear and you must really mean what you say; the children have no choice in the matter. This does not mean that you will be cruel to them or punish them or abuse them if they do not obey. But it does mean that you will carry a child in if necessary and that you will do it *every time*. Reasoning with a child ("You'll miss your favorite juice") or threatening ("If you don't come in, we'll lock the door) only communicates your *wish*. This gives the child the choice of postponing an action or choosing the consequences of your threat.

12. *A sense of humor underlies all healthy relationships.* Too often the task of educating and bringing up a child seems so formidable and serious that adults forget how important it is to share a laugh or make light of some incident. As adults we often remember with fondness those people who were loving and strict, who were firm and consistent, but who had a keen sense of humor. Proper discipline is important in the life of a young child, but equally important is the fun of being with and learning from someone you love.

19

Divorce and Single-Parent Families

The notion that Dad goes to work, Mom stays home and bakes cakes, and every family has an average of 2.5 children plus a dog or cat is long past.

Most young children will be living in a society of divorced parents, remarried parents, single parents, unwed parents, and families where parents must work outside the home. Divorce, one-parent households, and numbers of working women are on the increase. Holding to the romantic view of the nuclear family as a norm is no longer useful. This is not to mean that teachers and parents should not have goals and standards about what is desirable, but it does mean that adults need to be realistic in raising children in a society with increasingly fewer traditional family groupings. To criticize this fact or pretend it is not true does a great disservice to the young child who must learn to cope with such situations.

In the past, movies, TV, and books have always shown the "perfect" nuclear family. Many teachers and parents today come from cultures where divorce was a hush-hush affair. Only recently have some children's picture books begun to explore such topics as divorce and working mothers.

There seems to be no doubt among sociologists that the child who comes from a whole family with stable extended family members is at an advantage over a child from a less stable background. As more marriages dissolve and more parents enter the work field, schools and other such institutions will be called upon to carry out the roles formerly held by traditional family members. This presents a challenge as well as a dilemma for the teacher who questions whether he or she can or should be a substitute mother or father.

The necessities of making a living often drain the single parent of much of the energy that would otherwise be devoted to children and the home. Teachers and aides in child care centers need to be very sensitive to the possibility that parents may feel a sense of guilt for "neglecting" their children. And, in a real sense, they may indeed be neglecting their children.

In many instances, young children spend most of their waking hours in a child care center. They are most influenced during those times about values, getting along with others, what their world appears to be, and generally getting some important first impressions that will mold their thinking and the way in which they will relate to others in the future.

Children also bring with them to the center a "history" of their home life and the manner in which this other environment has influenced them. The two worlds can be either in harmony or conflict. Striving for harmony is one of the goals for the school to achieve. Some of the things a teacher can do include:

1. *Plan a well-balanced environment for the child.* Offer an environment in which there are opportunities for satisfying physical and emotional release. Equipment encouraging large-muscle activities such as pounding, jumping, pushing, hitting, running, and rolling around are indispensable. There should also be inviting areas for quiet contemplation and a place to be alone with a minimum of disruption.

2. *Provide as consistent and stable an atmosphere as possible.* Young children need the comfort of knowing that there are predictable events in their lives. Familiarity with a daily routine is important.

3. *Counseling and referral services are important to parents during a divorce or times of stress.* Often the teacher need only provide a sympathetic ear to help relieve some pent-up feelings that need expression. It is best not to take sides, but it is important to keep the welfare of the child uppermost in mind since the school may be able to make some necessary adjustments based on the situation.

4. *Teachers should share their concerns about the child with the parents, either separately or together.* Teachers often see more of the child and can be more sensitive to his or her needs. A genuine concern coupled with helpful suggestions to the parents should be part of the home-school relationship. Often the teacher is reluctant to contact the father in the case of divorce because the mother is usually the parent with whom the teacher is accustomed to talking. However, the teacher would do well to assume that the father is equally interested in his child but may feel it is inappropriate to contact the school. Of course, both parents should be informed of the teacher's intentions, and in the event of custody problems, the teacher must be careful to carry out the wishes of the custodial parent.

5. *Children of divorce are not necessarily "deprived."* True, it would probably be preferable to have a whole family that is happy and well adjusted, but in many cases, divorce may serve to relieve tensions that were detrimental to the family. The teacher should not automatically assume that the child will be suffering or will be worse off because of a divorce. Listening and observing will provide the teacher with clues as to how the child is adjusting to divorce in the family.

6. *Sensitivity to each child's special situation can be carried out in subtle ways throughout the curriculum.* The teacher needs to be conscious of referring to "mommy" and "daddy" during sharing time in such ways as to be certain the child with no mother or father does not feel left out. School activities such as Father's Day or Mother's Day must allow for escape hatches. Gifts for holidays should reflect the special needs of the child. Alternative ways of participating should be planned for those parents who, because of work schedules or other reasons, cannot cooperate in school activities.

7. *Provide an environment in which the child has many role models of all ages and both sexes.* Teen-agers, grandparents, and babies should all be part of a child's world. Through interactions with and feedback from people of different ages and backgrounds, the child will develop a healthy self-image.

8. *Young children are not capable of understanding the complex emotional problems underlying a divorce, but they do sense when things are wrong.* It is important to tell children, within their ability to understand, what is going to happen in relation to their everyday life. "Your father is going away to live at another place, but he will come to visit you and take you to see where he lives." Sometimes parents are so preoccupied with their own immediate problems that they overlook the seemingly innocent child. Honest explanations can serve to avoid later problems.

9. *Discuss the subject as openly as possible with the child.* Give the child plenty of opportunity to ask questions and clarify any misconceptions. One preschooler told his teacher his mother moved away because he was a bad boy. Children often feel they are somehow responsible for something that happens because they have done something "bad."

10. *Don't give the child inaccurate information.* Remarks indicating that the absent parent "has gone bye-bye" are misleading. The child may expect the mother or father to return soon or perhaps believe after awhile that the absent parent is dead. The child is likely to connect "bye-bye" with all kinds of misconceptions.

11. *The child should not have to take sides.* Often even the most intelligent parents find they are unwittingly trying to justify their situation by influencing the child and teacher to "blame" the other parent. It is important for the teacher to remember that the image the child has of a man or woman is greatly influenced by early impressions, and how the child sees mom and dad will affect his or her own self-image and the way in which he or she relates to men and women in the future.

12. *Access to good resources is important.* Knowing where to turn for responsible counseling, familiarity with groups that can provide the needed support and information, having good books for parents and children—all of these resources should be familiar to the good teacher who then can make proper referrals. (See the annotated list of books for children on pp. 164–65.)

20

The Doctor, Dentist, and Hospital

Most of us associate some degree of unpleasantness with a trip to the doctor or dentist. This attitude is conveyed to young children through the anxious behavior of adults. To be sure, we should not lead children to believe that such visits are going to be fun, but neither should we frighten them.

The best course for parents to follow is to prepare children and plan in advance whenever possible. Routine examinations from the time the child is an infant are good experiences on which to build positive associations with the doctor or clinic. The same is true of dentists if the child can be started quite young with painless dental examinations. Familiarity with any routine can dispel much of the fear when a child must undergo some discomfort at a later time. Knowing the doctor or dentist and the nurses as friendly, helpful people will make a real difference during an illness or emergency.

Parents and teachers can also familiarize a child with medical and dental care by providing opportunities for the child to act out the situation. For example, reading a story and sharing a picture book about such an event and then giving the child materials such as a stethoscope, a hypodermic syringe (without the needle), bandages, and a doll to practice on will integrate the experience more clearly for the child. The adult can go through much of the routine with the child and explain what the "doctor" is doing—listening to the heart, taking the blood pressure, taking a blood sample, giving a shot, etc.

If something painful or uncomfortable is to be done, the parent should be honest with the child and tell him "This will hurt for a minute when the doctor does it, but I'll be there with you."

The purpose for giving children honest information is not to make them fearless, but to give them the necessary tools to cope with an uncomfortable and probably frightening situation. Young children are not old enough to understand why something that hurts is good for them. But if they have some idea of what is going to happen and can trust adults not to trick or deceive them, they are more likely to accept the discomfort.

The National Center for Health Statistics reports that almost four million children under the age of fifteen are hospitalized each year.[2] According to a pamphlet issued by the Department of Health, Education and Welfare, young children can get the misguided notion that they are being sent to a hospital to be punished for something they did.[3] Not knowing and understanding the real reasons can lead to distrust of adults. Today, many hospitals and clinics have special preadmission tours in which children and their parents have an opportunity to see the patient rooms, handle some of the objects they will be using, and generally become familiar with a strange environment. Sometimes hospital personnel are assigned to show children some of the routine details involved in planned

2. "Take the Mystery Out of a Child's Visit to the Hospital," *Palo Alto Times,* January 10, 1978, p. 16.

3. *When Your Child Goes to the Hospital* (Publication 014F, Department of HEW), available for 85¢ from the Consumer Information Center, Pueblo, Colo. 81009. (See also the annotated list of books for children at end of this section.)

operations like tonsillectomies and hernia surgery. Some hospitals provide cots or beds to allow at least one parent to stay with the child. The child is even allowed to bring a favorite toy along. It is best to be matter of fact, calm, and confident about an impending visit to the doctor, dentist, or hospital so that anxiety does not build up.

Being afraid, shy, and tearful is natural. We all have these feelings. Insisting that children be brave and hold back their tears may only serve to place a greater strain on them. Understanding, accepting, supportive adults can help the child grow in his ability to handle the discomfort associated with the doctor, dentist, or hospital.

21

Eating Problems

"When Jeremy was a baby he loved to eat anything we put into his mouth. Now he dawdles over his meals and refuses most of his food." Most two to three-year-olds exhibit "eating problems" for several reasons:

1. Growth rates slow down at this age, and the appetite is likely to reflect this phenomenon.

2. The preschooler is beginning to exercise autonomy, and the areas over which he or she has some control (eating, toileting, sleeping) are being tested.

3. The two to three-year-old is more aware of, and sensitive to, surroundings and is more easily influenced by feelings, people, and the physical environment.

Parents who understand this phase of a child's development are less likely to insist that Janie "finish everything on her plate" or that she eat at times of the day that do not coincide with her limited capacity for food intake.

This does not mean the parent must feed only on demand, but it does require some careful planning and some flexibility to avoid unnecessary eating problems. For example, the young child eats best when hungry but not famished, when relaxed but not tired. Small, frequent meals are more likely to be accepted by the child than three large meals. Adults often forget how easily a small person can fill up with what appears to be insignificant amounts of food. That is why it is especially important to see that the child eats only nourishing foods and does not have a chance to fill up with empty calories and carbohydrates and sweets.

A good basic diet should include the following foods every day:

Milk and milk products
Meat, poultry, fish and eggs
Vegetables and fruit
Whole grain bread or cereal
Sugars and starches should be limited.

If snacks are planned around nutritious foods such as raw vegetables, fresh fruits, nuts, and seeds, eating at any time during the day should present fewer problems since the food being ingested is all good for the child. If, however, Janie is told she can't have dessert until she eats all her meal, the message is that the sweet stuff at the end of the meal is "good" and the main part of the meal is not. Parents are often guilty of buying "junk foods" (highly processed foods with little nutritional value) or offering children treats that are appetite depressants and then complaining that they will not eat dinner.

A good basic understanding of nutrition and a firm resolve to offer only healthful foods can go a long way toward establishing good eating habits.

The following suggestions can be helpful to parents in working with a finicky eater:

1. Do not have junk food around the house. Offer only healthful snacks.

2. Have a flexible schedule of feeding based on the child's changing growth patterns.

3. Feed the child separately from the rest of the family if necessary to avoid waiting too long for the meal or being too stimulated by eating with others.

4. Provide a calm, relaxed atmosphere.

5. Let children do as much as they can by themselves. Cut foods or prepare them in such a way that the child can get them to his or her mouth without your help.

6. Serve small portions and offer seconds rather than heap the plate full.

7. Offer a variety of colors, textures, and tastes to make the meal look appealing.

8. Do not insist that the child eat all of one thing as opposed to another. All the foods should be equally healthful.

9. Favoring one food (for example, peanut butter) over all others is not unusual. Continue to offer other good foods.

10. Do not pressure the child unduly about good table manners. You don't need to let the child splatter applesauce on the ceiling, but neither do you want to stress holding the spoon properly or not eating with his or her fingers to the point of making the meal a chore.

11. Resist cries for sweetened cereals, candy, and junk food advertised on TV and colorfully displayed in grocery stores.

12. Give children opportunities to express autonomy by offering them choices of foods that are all good for them and praise them for their efforts at feeding themselves.

13. Be casual and confident about a child's eating. Let children know that you are certain they will not starve, and with all the good foods you have to offer, you are confident they will get all the nourishment they need.

14. The attitudes adults have toward food and eating are extended to children; if you like good foods and enjoy eating, your child will most likely learn by your example.

22

Fears of Young Children

Scott's parents prided themselves on being aware of good child care practices. They read the latest literature on child rearing; they provided a warm, loving, consistent environment, and they were careful to protect Scott from any potentially frightening experiences. Yet sometime around his fourth birthday, Scott refused to go to bed alone and would often awaken during the night crying about the monsters in the dark.

Fears such as Scott's seem to be universal, and even when parents take all kinds of precautions, young children will go through periods of seemingly unreasonable fears. Adults are particularly frustrated by their children's fears when there seems to be no basis for them.

"There's no reason for Scott to be afraid of the dark."

"We've never given Marianne any reason to be afraid of dogs."

"I can't understand why Jody is afraid to go near the water. She certainly enjoys playing in the bathtub."

Children's fears appear to develop out of imaginary as well as real experiences. Causes include:

1. *The child's lack of experience.* A parent will complain that there is "no reason" for the child to be fearful, but to the child who is not mature enough to know that the permanence of an object remains the same in the daylight or in the dark, the dark can be very frightening. As an adult, you know that you will come back when you leave your child with a sitter, but to the young child, you are gone and he or she does not know if you will be back. Telling the child you will be back is helpful but not sufficient. The child must learn through experience and maturation the realities of the situation.

2. *The child's size and helplessness.* It is frightening to have a dog as big or bigger than you come pouncing up. Imagine yourself in such a situation. Words such as "Don't be afraid. He won't bite" are of little comfort at this time.

3. *Lack of control.* Somewhere around the age of two or three children become aware through their experiences with other children that they are not in control of all situations. Very often young children will take to a new nursery school situation with glee, but after a week or so, they cry and cling to their mothers and refuse to be left. During this initial period they have had time to "bump up" against some of their peers who might be less friendly than their parents; they have also had time to observe some disruptions and are able to see or have experienced some potential threats to their safety. This is a time when their emotional dependence on adults is likely to be tested.

4. *Fears from within the child.* Children feel guilty and angry when scolded and disciplined. These feelings are translated into fantasies and wishes ("I wish Mommy would get sick and die"; "I wish the baby would fall out of its high chair"). They do not realize that such thoughts are normal and harmless, so they often feel guilty for having such "naughty" thoughts. Psychologists tell us children will invent scary monsters, boogymen under the bed, or other such things to punish themselves for their guilt. These seemingly unreasonable fears dissipate as children become more secure and less overwhelmed by their feelings.

5. *Fears are contagious.* When children see that others around them are frightened or they hear others discuss things in a frightened manner, they are likely to react in the same way. If the adults around them approach potentially fearful or dangerous situations with caution but optimism, children learn to use the same strategies and realize that fear can be overcome.

6. *Fears based on good causes.* Sometimes a child has had a frightening experience with an animal, or has been given a painful shot at the doctor's office, or has fallen off the slide at nursery school. All these and other such traumatic experiences can frighten the child sufficiently so that he or she will be cautious and fearful of other unknowns.

How can parents and teachers deal with fears of young children?

1. *Be supportive and understanding.* When children fall off a trike and resist riding it again, give them time. Let them know you realize it was scary and that you will help them by holding the trike so it won't tip. Give them useful information about how to avoid falling. Encourage them to try it again, and if they refuse, let them know you will be around to help when they think they would like to try it again. Offer to help them overcome their fear at a later time. Praise them when they show that they have overcome their timidity.

2. *Familiarize children with frightening situations.* If children are afraid of the swimming pool or of an animal, provide small but gradually increasing doses of exposure to the feared object. Let them see you and others swimming or playing with dogs. Don't insist that they participate. Keep reassuring them that things are all right. You know they don't want to go in the water or touch the dog, but neither will it hurt them. Let them know you will hold their hand and stay with them. Be patient.

3. *Build up the child's self-confidence in all areas of life.* Praise children, encourage them, and give them many opportunities to experience success. As they become more confident and secure about themselves, their imaginary fears will also be less dramatic.

4. *Set realistic standards.* Parents' expectations for model behavior can be so high that they are unattainable. Sometimes children will try to be as good as older siblings, and the goals they set for themselves are frustratingly unreal, resulting in anxiety and fearfulness. In such instances, parents and teachers need to impress on children that failing at something is not all that serious. They can try again. Let them know you love them as they are.

5. *Provide outlets for self-expression.* Encourage children to paint or tell a story about their fears. Give them opportunities through dramatic play to relive those incidents that are disturbing to them. Help them talk about their fears by being a good listener and giving them the words they need to express themselves.

6. *Recognize and accept the fact that children's fears are very real to them.* Do not suppress fears. Telling children not to be afraid or making fun of their fears will not help to relieve their anxiety.

7. *Help children learn to distinguish between what is real and what is pretend.* Young children are highly impressionable, and they remember many details of frightening scenes from TV and the movies. Adults should encourage them to talk about their concepts of real and pretend and help clarify any misconceptions.

8. *Prepare children in advance of any potentially frightening experience.* Eliminate as many unknowns as possible from new experiences. This can be done with storybooks, role playing, relating a new experience to something familiar, going through some of the actual routine, and so on.

9. *Be conscious of the way in which you teach children to be cautious.* It is not good to use the threat of death or terrible pain or instill guilt to teach children caution. "If the car hits you, you'll have to go to the hospital and Mommy will be very sad" is a much less effective message than "Do not go out in the street. Cars are big and they can hurt you. I will spank you very hard if you go out in the street." The phrase "be careful" is also much less clear to a child than a specific command such as "stay on the sidewalk" or "hold on with both hands when you climb." (See the annotated list of storybooks for children on pp. 165–66.)

23

Hyperkinesis—Learning Disability

By the ripe old age of five, Johnny D. had been "kicked out" of two nursery schools and one child care center. His destructive behavior was such that none of the teachers could control him, and he constituted an uncontrollable threat to the safety and well-being of other children.

His parents, rightfully concerned about his forthcoming adjustment to kindergarten, were ready to try anything that promised to make their son more acceptable. His older sister, Ginny, was a model child and had never presented any problems in her behavior. Johnny's parents, both well-educated and seemingly sensible people, were discouraged, frustrated, and embarrassed by Johnny. They wavered between a firm resolve to get to the bottom of this abnormal behavior and a complete loss of confidence in themselves as adequate parents.

From the time Johnny was a baby, the mother reported, he was difficult to handle. He seemed to be high-strung, he cried and fussed a lot, and he didn't seem to need much sleep. As a toddler he continued to be very active and exhibited a short attention span and even shorter temper. He suffered from asthma and eczema. When he was three and a half, his teacher at nursery school recommended that Johnny's parents take him to a child psychiatrist after he pushed a child off the top of a slide and deliberately rammed his trike into two other children.

As the result of his visits to the psychiatrist, Johnny was placed on Ritalin and an antihistamine with a tranquilizer. This seemed to calm him down for a while, but his behavior was still erratic and unpredictable, and his learning abilities were far behind those of other children his age. His parents were concerned about overdosing him on drugs—that he would be dependent on them. While under the influence of drugs, he would alternate between high and low moods, and though he was easier to control, he didn't seem normal.

The story of Johnny and others like him has become familiar to many parents and teachers. Some of the classic symptoms of a hyperactive, learning-disabled child are as follows:[4]

1. Marked hyperactivity and fidgetiness
    Rocks
    Jiggles legs
    Dances
    Wiggles hands
    (In infancy this may be manifested by crib rocking or head knocking.)

2. Compulsive aggression
    Disruptive at home and in school

4. Ben F. Feingold, *Why Your Child Is Hyperactive* (New York: Random House, 1975), pp. 49–50.

Compulsively touches everything and everybody
Disturbs other children
Cannot be diverted from an action
Commits acts dangerous to own safety

3. Excitable—impulsive
Behavior is unpredictable
Panics easily with temper tantrums which are usually an expression of frustration

4. Tolerance for failure and frustration is low
Demands must be met immediately
Cries often and easily

5. Short attention span—unable to concentrate
Flits from one project to another
Is unable to sit through a school project
Is unable to sit through a meal
Is unable to sit through a TV program

6. Exceptionally clumsy
Poor muscle coordination
Eyes and hands do not seem to function together
Has trouble buttoning
Difficulty with writing and drawing
Difficulty with playground activities

7. Poor sleep habits
Difficult to get to bed
Hard to get to sleep
Awakes easily

8. Normal or high I.Q. but fails in school

9. Involvement of boys at a ratio of 9:1

10. Rarely more than one child in a family

A few, several, or all of the symptoms can occur in varying degrees and at different times. Because of this wide variability, it is difficult to classify a child as hyperkinetic according to any one set of descriptive behaviors.

Since the 1960s more than one hundred kinds of learning disabilities have been identified. It is no wonder there is so much confusion among parents and educators as to just what the various labels attached to LD children really mean. Such terms as perceptually handicapped, minimal brain dysfunction, dysgraphic, dyslexia, and other equally ominous sounding labels have been attached to the hyperactive, learning-disabled child. Medical researchers themselves are unclear about just exactly what learning disabilities are or what might cause them.

There seems to be agreement, however, on some facts about LD children:

1. Learning disabilities do not stem from mental retardation.

2. LD children come from all socioeconomic levels, and being poor or disadvantaged is not a contributing factor.

3. Learning disabilities are not related to race or intelligence.

4. Boys are more likely to be affected than girls.

The likeliest causes for learning disabilities are suspected to be heredity, viral illnesses, allergies, and possible slight neurological disturbances caused by head injuries or problems during birth and prolonged labor.

Children with learning disabilities, no matter what the label, usually exhibit problems in one or more of the following areas: behavior problems, such as hyperactivity and inattentiveness; reading problems, such as dyslexia; speech and writing problems, such as an inability to copy or sound out words and sentences; conceptual problems, such as an inability to grasp abstract ideas like distinguishing between "many" and "few," or "today" and "tomorrow."

It is estimated that only about half of the LD children in this country are diagnosed and treated. Parents who suspect their child of having a learning disability should consult experts in neurology and child development. A thorough medical testing program is essential to determine the extent of treatment.

There are no quick cures, but a multidisciplinary approach seems to be sensible. That is, educational therapy using special teaching techniques, nutritional therapy in which food additives and artificial colors are eliminated, and possibly drug therapy can be explored.

There is much controversy about the use of amphetamine-type drugs like Ritalin to keep a child quiet. Some doctors feel there is no harm in drug treatment, and others argue that drugs treat only the symptoms rather than the cause. There is also some evidence that drug treatments have harmful side effects such as disruption of the growth hormones. Parents who are advocates of diet therapy report dramatic success when all food colorings, artificial flavorings, additives, and salicylates are eliminated.

The controversy over causes and cures will continue for some time to come. Meanwhile, parents and teachers would do well to seek professional expertise in diagnosing the child who is suspected of being hyperactive or learning disabled.

24

Imaginary Companions

"It's bad enough having to set a place at the table for Jennifer's imaginary friend Archie," complained Mrs. S., "but the other day I had to drive all the way back to the doctor's office so she could retrieve him from the waiting room."

Mrs. S. had read that it is normal for a four-year-old to have pretend friends, but there were times when she wondered if maybe the family was indulging Jennifer too much. When should an adult insist that "Archie" or some other imaginary companion really does not exist? At what point do you simply force the child to abandon his or her "friend"?

The first thing to determine is how the youngster uses the pretend friend. Imaginary companions may be the only acceptable outlet for acting out some inner feelings and conflicts. Projecting "naughty" ideas onto someone else or spanking a companion for daring to do something "bad" may serve a very healthy purpose during a child's preschool years. It's all right for an imaginary dog or tiger to strike out at someone or even bite them, but this is definitely not approved behavior for a little boy or girl. To what extent does a child need to act out aggressions through the identity of some ferocious animal? A child who often feels helpless may learn to rely on such imaginary companions to relieve angry and aggressive feelings.

Adults can use the child's behavior as a clue to what might be more satisfying to her or him outside of a fantasy life. For example, does the child tend to use imaginary friends as scapegoats for all his or her unacceptable behavior? Perhaps demands to "be good" are too difficult to achieve. Adults may need to reassess their rules and expectations. Or does the child retreat from adjusting to real friends because he or she is too young or inexperienced to cope with their more powerful demands? It is a comfort in this instance to have imaginary friends you can dominate. Being able to determine the outcome of any interaction gives one a sense of power, and every youngster can benefit from such an experience, especially if the opportunities are lacking in real life.

The degree of intensity and the length of time imaginary companions exist are the two factors for consideration among parents and teachers. If adults can put themselves in the place of the child, perhaps they can better understand some of the reasons for the child's need for imaginary friends. Also, if the environment can be made less threatening and more enticing, the child is more likely to interact with real people and toys.

Playing along with the child's imaginary companions will tend to reinforce their existence. Teachers report that they will tell a child matter-of-factly that "Archie" is not real and they do not have a place for him. The teacher stresses how eager she is to relate to the real child and lets that child know that there are lots of real playmates and lots of fun things to do at school. When one child bit another child and blamed it on his "tiger," the teacher was very careful to impress upon the biter that he was responsible for the act. It is important for adults to let the child know that they know the difference between real and pretend. If adults play along with the imaginary friend when it is convenient and then expect the child to discard this friend when parents find it inconvenient, the child may become confused.

It is not a good idea to forbid the child to have imaginary companions. Punishing or pressuring will only make matters worse. A casual attitude toward such "friends" and respect for this phase of the child's development will go a long way in helping the child to grow out of the need for imaginary friends.

Imaginary companions do provide outlets for strong feelings. They needn't be of concern to adults unless the child appears to be retreating into an unreal world too much of the time and to such an extent that he or she cannot tell the difference between what is real and what is pretend. In most cases, young children discard their imaginary companions by the time they get to grade school, and parents and children can look back upon this period as just another phase in the child's development.

25

Jealousy

Feelings of jealousy and envy are normal, often upsetting, and seemingly unreasonable. These feelings are common to both adults and children. The difference, however, is that adults have learned to repress or sublimate these "socially unacceptable" feelings, while children tend to act out how they feel in the face of a real or imagined threat to their well-being.

Anything or anyone threatening to alienate the affections of a parent is likely to bring on a jealous reaction from children. Sibling rivalry is most apparent during the preschool years. Young children frequently request that the baby be sent back to the hospital. Regression to more babylike behavior is common. The "displaced" child is also more likely to rely on fantasy, imaginary companions, and sublimated aggressive behavior at this time.

Parents and teachers can do much to help soften the blow of any potentially threatening situation for a young child. For example, children can help with preparations for a new baby. Making them an important part of the plans can go a long way in alleviating jealous feelings. Exposing them to other families with babies can give them a realistic experience of what to expect. There are some very good books covering the subject of a new baby in the family. (See the list on pp. 166–67.)

Parents are fortunate when there are extended family systems of close relatives who can assume substitute nurturing roles. Having several loving adults around who can give undivided attention to the young child as well as relieve the parents of many busy tasks can be a real help. Young children are apt to show signs of jealousy just when the parents have the least time to spend with them. This need for extra time and sensitive interaction can create a stressful period for both parents and children. It is at this time when relatives and close friends can serve to "extend the family" in very real ways.

Teachers who are aware of jealousy problems can make an extra effort to provide the child with positive and satisfying experiences. The young child will benefit from having some extra attention, an added bit of praise, and some opportunities to release feelings of jealousy.

Jealousy does not always stem from having a new baby in the family. Sometimes a young child may feel loss of love for many other causes—real or imagined. Co-op parents in a child care center report that their children started "acting up" and demanding more of their attention than usual when they first started working in the co-op.

Jimmy was always independent until we started attending the child care program together. I was disgusted with the babyish way he was behaving, always clinging to me and crying and tugging at me if some other child happened to sit next to me. It was hard for me to believe that he was really jealous of the other children. He certainly had no reason to be that way!

This mother knew Jimmy was special to her and would always be her child, but Jimmy didn't know that. Apparent as the facts may be to the adults, it is still necessary to reassure the child, both with words and actions, that he or she has not lost favor with the parent. Jimmy's teacher suggested that the mother simply tell the other children, "This is my little boy and he's special to me. Let's make a place where he can sit with me."

The adult may not feel that this is being fair to the other children, but youngsters can generally accept the fact that Jimmy is special and needs special attention, in the same way that they may want to sit next to their own parents. Jimmy's mother also learned to approach Jimmy from time to time when he wasn't near her, just to give him a hug or some reassurance that she loved him and wanted him to know he was her special little boy.

Parents rarely have the opportunity to prepare for such experiences; they need suggestions and permission from the school to be honest about expressing their feelings toward their own children. Some co-op parents feel that in order to do a professional job of assisting in the center, they should not treat their own children any differently from the others. This does not mean they should ignore their own children. Some flexibility on the part of the school and curriculum is necessary to allow parents and children time to work out a comfortable adjustment to the program.

The young child who is jealous needs to accept the fact that there are some situations he or she cannot change, such as getting rid of a new baby. Adults need to be clear about letting the child know very matter-of-factly that they have no intentions of sending the baby back, or dropping out of the co-op center or whatever they are committed to. Some children are confused by the uncertainty of parents, and jealous reactions are prolonged unnecessarily because the child has gotten unclear messages from the adults.

Sometimes adults unwittingly make comparisons without realizing that the young child's security is threatened. A comment such as "Your new baby sister is going to be the prettiest in the family!" may be just enough to make an older child resentful and jealous. Adults sensitive to the inner world of young children will be especially careful to see that children know they are loved and appreciated for what they are.

No child is going to be totally free of jealous or envious feelings while growing up. There always will be the other child who can perform better, the neighbor who has a nicer toy, the baby who gets more attention, the youngster who is better looking or stronger, and so on. No child can or should be protected from such feelings.

Parents and teachers also need to recognize that it is normal for young children to be self-centered. Until they reach a certain level or stage of maturity, they are not able to identify with the feelings of others or to understand a perception different from their own. It is easier to understand and accept jealousy if the adult realizes that the child simply needs to mature and grow out of the more egocentric stage.

As children confront feelings of jealousy and learn how to deal with them in a realistic manner, they also learn about their ability to cope with potentially threatening situations. A sense of self-reliance, independence, and security can result from successful confrontations with moderate amounts of adversity. (See the annotated list of books for children on pp. 164–67.)

26

Lying

Adults need to discriminate between a child's deliberate lies and occasional distortions of the truth based on confusion between fantasy and reality. Young children, particularly those between the ages of two and four, often have difficulty distinguishing what is true from what is false.

Sometimes children will not tell the truth because they are curious to see what will happen. Other times, they merely want to escape punishment. Adults who punish severely tend to encourage lying in children. When children are placed in harsh situations, their only defense is to tell an untruth to try to protect themselves.

Sometimes children have learned that they can feel more important by telling lies, exaggerating, or bragging. The same is true when they use swear words as an indication of being "big" or "smart." If adults can understand the reasons for the child's lying, bragging, or swearing, they can better deal with the problem.

Oftentimes, lying can be the result of a power struggle between adult and child. For example, adults who are insecure in their authority may interpret a child's falsehood as a deliberate and serious threat to their power over the youngster. When this happens, the adults may overreact and the child thus learns to use lying as a weapon against the superiority of the adult.

Children who lie need to learn by examples of adults and through their own experiences that being truthful is more practical than telling lies. Lectures on morality seldom help. They must learn that telling falsehoods gets them nowhere.

Dealing with underlying reasons for lying helps to defuse the problem. In some cases, the child who lies needs more loving attention; another child may need help in building self-confidence and developing a stronger self-concept; yet another may simply be too fearful of the consequences, in which case the punishment needs to be less severe. Adults can try to put themselves in the place of the youngster and ask why the child would need to tell a lie and try to determine how he or she feels.

Branding a child as a liar only closes off opportunities for further communication.

27

Nightmares

"I'm so tired from lack of sleep that I don't know how much longer I can tolerate Jody's nightmares," complained Mrs. D.

"How long have they been going on," asked Jody's teacher, "and can you relate them to any particular incident?"

"No, the whole family has been trying to figure out just why she is so upset and terrified. She started having bad dreams about three weeks ago, and I can't recall that anything unusual or frightening happened before they started."

"What have you done up to now?" asked the teacher.

"What haven't I done! I've tried everything from being patient and staying with her—sometimes for hours—to getting mad and scolding her. I hate to admit it, but I've tried bribing her with a special surprise present if she can sleep through the night. So far, no luck."

Mrs. D's situation is not unusual. Most children have frightening dreams, some more intensely than others. There doesn't seem to be any easy recipe for helping the child get over nightmares, but some suggestions based on experience may be helpful.

First, children who are awakened by scary dreams are truly frightened and have difficulty discerning reality from what was dreamed. The dream episode is experienced in a very real way, both physically and emotionally. The blood pressure may rise, more adrenalin is secreted, breathing becomes heavier, and eyes dilate. Emotional symptoms are obvious: crying, screaming for help, trembling, wetting the bed, running out of the room.

It is difficult to watch children experience nightmares and not be able to comfort and soothe them and simply make those bad dreams go away. Parents feel frustrated and helpless, knowing how frightened the children are and knowing also that there is seemingly little one can do to reassure them that everything is all right.

Understanding the reality of the experience for the child is important in helping to deal with his or her fears. If we make fun of it or scold the child for disturbing our sleep, we are being insensitive to a traumatic experience that calls for understanding and sympathy.

Adults need not make an unnecessary fuss over the dream by carrying the child into the parents' bed or communicating in some way that nightmares are indeed horrible. But parents do need to show sympathetic understanding coupled with firm reassurance that the dream was not real and that the child should go back to sleep. It is best to remain in the child's bedroom and not get into a pattern of taking the child out of the room if at all possible. The point is not to develop rewarding kinds of consequences that can reinforce the child's fearful behavior.

Children who are old enough to verbalize dream experiences can benefit by talking about them with parents and teachers. They learn through words and descriptions how to distinguish reality from a dream. It is helpful to ask children in school if they know what a dream is. Teachers can help children define for themselves what is pretend and what is real by relating these words to firsthand experiences. For example, you might ask what TV programs the children watch. Using those programs as a basis, you might then ask if the characters in cartoons are real. You can correct their mistaken notions as they are verbalized. Sometimes children believe that the animals can talk or that people who are killed can come back to life again because they saw it on TV. It is important to correct those false notions. The perceptive teacher or parent will make opportunities to bring up such discussions because the child's comments will provide important feedback to the adult about the child's mistaken beliefs.

Younger children may not be able to benefit as readily from verbal explanations, nor are they able to tell you clearly just why they are awake and crying. Most children are reluctant to go back to sleep after a nightmare because they fear the nightmare might return again when they are asleep and helpless. Staying awake is a way of protecting themselves against uncertainty. That is why parents need to be patient and be prepared to sit with the child and provide a night light or some other comforting reassurance such as a cuddly toy or special blanket to help ease the child back into relaxing.

Children are more likely to have nightmares if they are especially active just before going to bed. Rough and tumble play or concentrated physical activity of any kind can make it difficult for the young child to relax into a deep sleep. Also, noisy, frightening, active TV shows can start the child's imagination going, and such mental stimulation can prevent restful sleep. If a child is having nightmares, the parents should definitely make it a point to limit exciting physical and mental activities prior to bedtime. Sometimes eating hard-to-digest foods may also be suspected.

Fear of the dark is usually coupled with frightening dreams. In such cases, parents can gradually expose children to pleasant experiences in the dark in order to help them associate something positive with what they fear. For example, exploring in a dark closet with a flashlight can be a fun experience. Eating in the dark by candlelight, hiding under a tent, playing under the bed, or simply relaxing or napping with someone trusted in a dark room can be a reassuring experience that will help build a child's confidence.

Each child needs differing amounts of sleep. Parents should be flexible in gearing the child's bedtime to accommodate his or her needs. Having to go to bed when one isn't sleepy can bring on many negative associations with the bedroom and bedtime. Not getting enough sleep can also cause problems of crankiness and being overtired.

A calm and predictable routine leading up to bedtime is most effective. If children know either by the clock or in relation to other familiar occurrences that it is now time to brush teeth, take a bath, or whatever the routine is before bedtime, they are more likely to adhere to a schedule. These calming influences go a long way toward alleviating the fearful experience of having a nightmare.

28

Sex

"What do I say when a child asks where she came from?"

"Should children be allowed to see naked members of the opposite sex?"

"Should the teacher allow a child to masturbate?"

These comments raise questions as to when and to what degree a child should be told about sex, and how much of this should be the responsibility of the parents and how much the school's.

In the past, sex was not a topic for discussion in school—and probably not in many homes either. Today, along with a greater understanding and awareness of relations between men and women, the ideas about sex education are also changing to include more open and honest discussions with young children. This can present a dilemma to the family and school unless both agree on a mutually compatible philosophy and program to provide sex education for young children.

Suppose the teacher feels that children ought to be encouraged to play in the nude and feels that the notion that the "body is perfect and no one should be ashamed of it" should be incorporated liberally into the curriculum. Suppose, also, a parent is shocked to see three- to six-year-olds curiously inspecting each other's bodies and playing doctor during her visit to school? How is such a problem reconciled? Should the parent determine the sex education or should the school take the responsibility of being better informed and imparting such important information?

Parents who have been interviewed on such matters appear to prefer that sex education take place in the home and that the school reinforce truthful ideas for young children. Both teachers and parents feel it is appropriate to expose children to natural experiences such as seeing how animals procreate and how they are born. They also feel that the school is a good place to provide nature studies of all kinds and that the teachers should have books and information suitable for the child's age and ability to understand. However, many parents feel that encouraging nudity, allowing physical play with one another, and generally teaching a lack of modesty are all in poor taste. They feel a teacher should distract a child who is masturbating by substituting another activity.

Adults need to be prepared to answer questions about sex as they arise, whether in school or at home. Children should learn about the facts of life from trustworthy adults, not from friends who may not be as accurate or as well informed as they should be. When a child's curiosity about sex or any other matter is answered openly, honestly, and matter-of-factly, the curiosity is satisfied and a sound basis is established for future related questions.

An example of a conversation in the children's bathroom shows how a teacher handled a child's questions:

(Three-year-old girl watching a little boy urinate)

Girl: "Teacher, what is that thing?" (pointing to the boy's penis)

Boy: "It's my pee-pee."

Teacher: "That's his penis."

Girl: (Looking down at herself) "I don't have one."

Boy: "No, silly. Only boys have one."

Teacher: "Boys have a penis and girls have a clitoris and vagina."

Girl: (Still looking a little uncertain) "Do you have a penis?"

Teacher: "No. I'm a girl just like you, and I have a clitoris and vagina."

Girl: "Do really big people have it?"

Teacher: "Have what? A penis?"

Girl: "Yes."

Teacher: "No. You see, all boys have a penis and all girls have a clitoris and vagina. That's how boys and girls are different. See, (pointing to another boy) David has a penis because he is a . . . " (waiting for girl to complete)

Girl: "Boy!"

Teacher: "That's right! Now, look at Mary. What is she?

Girl: "She's a girl!"

Teacher: "How do you know?"

Girl: "I don't know. She just is, that's all."

Teacher: "Does Mary have a penis?"

Girl and Mary together: "NO! NO!" (both running out to play)

The lesson in sex differentiation may be a short, informal situation, but the little girl has been given accurate information even though she may not retain much of it at her age. But her curiosity has been satisfied in an open and honest way by the teacher.

Another conversation reported by a parent went as follows:

Mother to four-year-old son: "Mommy is going to have a baby."

Son: "Where is the baby?"

Mother: "Inside my body." (patting her stomach)

Son: "Can we get it out?"

Mother: "It has to grow some more until it is bigger."

Son: "How long?"

Mother: "About three more months—a long time. It will be after your birthday."

The mother reported that her son accepted the news matter-of-factly and went on with his play activities. She was a little disappointed that she could not relate more facts of childbirth to him, but she realized he did not want any more information at this time so she did not force it.

Later the following month when father and mother were making plans for the new baby, their son asked:

"Mommy, is the baby still inside you?"

Mother: "Yes, see I'm getting bigger all the time and that means the baby is growing."

Son: "Yeah. You're fat!"

Mother: "Do you want to hear the baby's heartbeat?"

Father: "See, (putting his ear up to the mother's stomach) you can hear the baby's heart beating."

Son: "No. I want to hear it cry." (puts his mouth up close to stomach and yells) "Hey, can you hear me?" (runs off)

Still later, when mother and son are shopping at the grocery store and mother is busy selecting some vegetables:

Son: "Mommy, how did the baby get inside you?"

Mother: (thinking "What a time to ask me!") "Daddy planted a seed inside my body."

Son: "How did he plant the seed?"

Mother: (hands the child a banana and pushes the cart out of earshot of other shoppers) "Well, Daddy put his penis into Mommy's vagina."

Son: (not to be distracted by the banana, asks loudly) "Mommy, where did Daddy get the seed to plant inside you?"

Mother: "All men have seeds that grow inside them."

Son: "Do I have seeds?"

Mother: "When you get bigger you'll have seeds too."

Son: (loudly) "When I get bigger I'll plant some seeds with my penis too."

Mother: (looking surreptitiously to see if anyone has overheard the conversation) "Yes, son. Eat your banana."

As the humorous report from the mother shows, children seem to ask questions at the most inopportune times, but the curiosity of a young child does not confine itself to times when adults feel it is appropriate. Sometimes it isn't convenient to answer a child's questions, but it is a good idea to satisfy his or her curiosity when it is at its peak. The adult may have to repeat the same answers again and again under many different circumstances before a child is satisfied. Sometimes parents may want to introduce the subject by using stories or drawings in order to encourage the child to ask questions. The goal in sex education with young children is to provide youngsters with honest information geared to their level of understanding when they are ready for it. Full knowledge and a healthy attitude about sex come about as the result of many questions answered honestly over a long period of time. Adults cannot expect to give children one lecture on the facts of life and have them understand the total reproductive process.

The best way to teach facts about sex to young children is to provide them with many natural experiences with plants, animals, and other reproductive systems. In this way, their curiosity is aroused naturally and the information given is easily related to firsthand experiences. Young children have difficulty understanding technical and theoretical facts. They learn best through experiences such as planting seeds and watching flowers bloom, caring for animals and seeing birth and death, being exposed to both sexes in a healthy open atmosphere, and having questions answered in an honest way. These experiences provide the best basis for healthy attitudes about sex.

Some guidelines to remember in the sex education of children are:

1. Always tell the truth.

2. Use correct terminology.

3. Give only as much information as the child can process at one time.

4. Never avoid a question.

5. Let children know by your attitude that they can feel free to ask further questions in the future.

Some simple concepts that can be incorporated into the daily experiences of children are:

1. All babies come from their mothers.

2. All animals (including humans) produce babies of the same kind.

3. There has to be a father and a mother before a baby can be born.

4. Males and females are physically different.

Additional information dealing with specific questions children are apt to ask about sex may be obtained from
The Institute for Family Research and Education
760 Ostrom Ave. Syracuse, NY.

A bibliography of recommended sex education books and pamphlets is available by writing

Planned Parenthood Association of San Mateo
2211 Palm Ave.
San Mateo, CA 94403
Enclose a self-addressed envelope with 30¢ postage. (See the annotated list of books at end of this section.)

29

Selfishness and Sharing

"Janie is so selfish I'm embarrassed to have friends over to play with her," complained her mother. "I know she's only two and a half, but is it normal for a child her age to be so selfish?"

"My Marc is five years old," commented another mother, "and he still has a tantrum when I make him share his toys. Then he sulks and goes off to play by himself!"

Parents want their children to be unselfish, to be friendly and willing to share with others.

"Everyone has to learn to share or they won't have any friends in this world," remarked one parent.

"You can't live with other people, even in your own family, and expect to make a good adjustment unless you learn to share," stated another parent.

What is difficult for adults to recognize sometimes is that we are all selfish and self-centered to certain degrees. This is not abnormal. To insist that children negate feelings of wanting to have the whole pie, of not wanting to give up any of their special toys, or of being threatened when they think they will have less of a parent's love—these are unrealistic demands. This does not mean we let children have everything they want, but it does mean we use an approach that recognizes the child's feelings—natural feelings—about not wanting to share.

"It's time to let Mary hold the doll now. You can help wash the dishes" is much more effective than "You know it isn't nice to be selfish. Now let Mary have a turn with the doll!"

Comments like "That isn't nice" or "You have to share" attach guilt to demands. Most people, children as well as adults, do not react well to such comments. On the other hand, when the person in authority recognizes natural inclinations of the child, he or she will build in options that are equally interesting and acceptable. If this is not possible, then the adult can still let the child know the reason for such a request: "It's time for Johnny to have a turn on the swing. I'll save it for you when it's your turn again."

Distracting a young child with something that seems to be equally satisfying can often work in solving the problem of sharing: "Mary Jo wants to use the rolling pin right now, but look, you can use this cookie cutter." Of course, some people carry having enough toys for everyone to extremes. One school ordered enough tricycles for every child to have one. But they discovered to their disappointment that the children still fought over a "favorite" or simply wanted to have the trike someone else was sitting on.

Situations such as these offer opportunities for young children to learn that (1) they can't always satisfy their selfish needs, (2) other people feel the same way they do, (3) sharing and taking turns help to make life much more pleasant in the long run, and (4) having to share is difficult to learn.

Adults can be the best models for showing children the rewards and satisfactions that come from being unselfish. Instead of insisting or demanding that a child share, the adult can use every opportunity to stress the importance of cooperating and working for the common good. "I'll help you put these blocks away, Joanie, and if Dennis and Bobby give us a hand too, we'll all finish in time for juice."

"That was nice to have so many people help."

"Let's all help wipe the tables so they will be clean for the children who use them tomorrow."

Sharing does not mean simply giving something up. It also means cooperating and participating in an effort that will lead to later or different kinds of gratification. Unfortunately, some young children have been rewarded for going through the superficial motions of being selfless without regard for their true feelings. This overgenerous behavior on the part of a young child can be the result of a lack of self-confidence and should not be taken as "being good."

Adults need to respect the fact that there are certain things a young child simply cannot bear to give up at the moment. The child must learn gradually and through repeated experiences that give-and-take is part of the larger cooperative society in which he or she lives.

Adults may sound like broken records in having to repeat suggestions about sharing, and it may not seem apparent that the children even notice, but children learn by example. When others are considerate and cooperative and share willingly, the child will gradually learn to do the same.

30

Shyness

Some youngsters appear to be naturally more cautious and timid than others. Parents and teachers who recognize and respect this in their nature will avoid pushing shy children into new situations without plenty of opportunity to become more confident beforehand.

Some parents who are concerned about excessive shyness should assess what it is in the child's background that might be causing such behavior. For example, are the adults in the family frightening the child with warnings: "Don't go near the water. You'll fall in and drown." "Better not climb so high. You might get hurt." "Take your dirty fingers out of your mouth. You'll get sick."

Anxious feelings in adults carry over to children. Even when parents think they are careful to conceal their own fears, children are able to sense them. Body language, tone of voice, and facial expressions all carry important messages. When adults approach new situations with confidence, youngsters will learn to follow their example.

One teacher who was clearly squeamish about handling animals reported that the children she worked with avoided the guinea pig cage and reacted in a frightened manner when the guinea pig moved upon being petted. Another teacher who handled the guinea pig firmly and with confidence taught the children how to handle it responsibly and without fear.

Sometimes children are afraid of failing because they feel the standards for behavior are too high. One little boy avoided all art activities because he wanted to draw a dinosaur that his daddy would like and he knew he couldn't draw one good enough; so he simply did not participate in art at all. Some children refuse to try something new because they know they can't ever be as good as a big brother or sister.

In their concern that they might spoil a child parents will withhold well-deserved praise, not recognizing that a big hug and some encouragement help to raise morale and provide the child with the necessary confidence to carry over to other tasks. Easing up on strict rules, establishing more reachable goals, reassuring children that they are fine just the way they are, and introducing a sense of humor and relaxed attitude about achievements can all help to give the assurance children need to overcome shyness.

Gradual exposure to the situation or thing that the child is timid about can be useful. If children are not pushed or rushed into acceptance of a new experience, they are more likely to adjust in a positive way. Shyness with strangers, cautiousness about approaching new activities, unwillingness to do things alone, timidity, and fearfulness all require sympathetic, understanding guidance. Young children's discomfort is very real to them, and insensitive adults who make fun of this shyness only make the situation worse.

Children often cannot tell adults exactly why they are shy or afraid. The real reasons may not be apparent to either adults or to the child, but with patience and careful observation much progress can be made toward better understanding.

It is important to remember that shyness is common and not necessarily a negative trait. Some very famous people who are basically shy have found that the ways in which they express their shyness have been advantageous to them. Although it is necessary and desirable for adults to help children overcome excessive timidity, it is equally important to recognize their natural tendencies and respect them for those traits that are unique to their own personality.

31

The Spoiled Child

Descriptions of a "spoiled" child often include comments like:

"A stubborn, disobedient brat."

"A child who always gets his way."

"A child who insists on having all the attention whenever he or she wants it without regard for others."

"A totally self-centered child who has tantrums if his needs aren't met."

In most cases, the "spoiled" child is one who exhibits behavior that is annoying to adults. The annoying behavior, however, may or may not signal that a child has been spoiled.

Take children who cry and whine for attention, for example. These children may be genuinely in need of some adult love and physical affection. Meeting children's needs is not necessarily spoiling them. Sometimes adults are afraid to "give in" to children's cries for attention because they don't want to spoil them. As a result, parents may ignore some genuine cries for satisfying attention. Children who whine and cling to their parents and act generally unhappy may be children who are deprived of parental love and attention. To some observers such children may seem spoiled.

On the other hand, adults who shower children with attention and try to anticipate their every wish may inhibit their emotional growth. We cannot and should not protect children from every little altercation and potential unhappiness. Wise parents will use common sense in raising their children; they will know when to leave a child alone, when to be firm, and when to "give in" to the child's genuine needs.

Parents don't want children who are called "spoiled brats." Such children reflect on the inability of parents to raise children in a sensible way. These children's behavior says that some of their more basic needs are not being met in spite of the fact that they may have many material things and lots of attention.

Do parents spoil children by giving them lots of toys and material things? Not necessarily. Children who do not have many things can also be spoiled. The important point is that children who get their security from knowing they are loved do not need to rely on material possessions to find happiness. Adults should be cautioned against giving children the false notion that material possessions contribute to their sense of security or feelings of being loved. Using gifts and toys as rewards for being good and as indications that this is the way to show how much you love someone can mislead children into attaching their emotional needs to material things.

There are children who insist on being the center of attention and having their every need satisfied immediately. Depending on the age of such children, the adults around them can use varying degrees of firmness and control in letting them have opportunities to consider the rights of others.

Very young children have a poor concept of time and simply do not understand "You'll have to wait just a minute until we're through talking." How long is a minute? Sometimes taking a few patient moments at the beginning of such an interruption to settle the child onto something interesting may be the best solution.

Young children cannot be as sophisticated as adults would like them to be when interacting with other people. Refusing to share a toy, crying for attention, or hitting out at others may be a child's first clumsy attempts at socialization. The child needs many firsthand experiences to learn how to be more socially acceptable, and such behavior should not be attributed to "being spoiled."

The child who continues to insist on immediate gratification in spite of maturity and experience probably needs two things: (1) firmer and clearer rules about expected behavior, and (2) more appropriate kinds of affection.

"Spoiled" behavior reflects on the methods of discipline and control used by adults. If parents are inconsistent—being strict one time and giving in another—the child is rewarded intermittently. For example, a parent might say "no" the first few times a child asks for a candy bar but give in when he persists. The child learns that he might get what he wants by making a fuss, so he will continue to use that strategy because it gets results. Parents need not be harsh or overly strict, but to be effective, they do need to be firm, consistent, and make rules that are reasonable and understandable.

The need for affection is very strong in all of us. Young children, especially, can feel threatened if they are uncertain about whether or not Mommy and Daddy love them. It is easy for children to confuse being loved with having material things and immediate attention. While adults are teaching young children to learn consideration for others, they must also reinforce expectations for conformity to rules by strong reassurances that the children are loved. Hugging and kissing and showing genuine affection cannot spoil children. In fact, it is unlikely that children can learn to care for others until they have a firm basis of love themselves.

32

Stealing

"My seven-year-old has been sneaking money out of my purse," reports a worried mother.

"My eight-year-old has been shoplifting useless little items from stores," complains a father.

"My four-year-old hid a nursery school toy in his pocket and brought it home," says another parent.

Why do some children steal, even when they seem to have plenty of love, understanding, and just about all the material things they could want? Most parents like the ones in the above examples are puzzled and embarrassed at the "predelinquent" behavior of their young children. They feel these small transgressions may not be serious, but they want help in dealing sensibly with a potentially larger problem.

The motives behind such incidents are not easy to discern. Often the children themselves cannot figure out just why they stole certain things. In some instances, especially where young children are concerned, the need for immediate gratification is too much to deny. A four-year-old who sees a gleaming toy car that he wants desperately, or some enticing object that he has been denied, may simply take advantage of an opportunity to hide it and keep it. Children who are given what they want without having an opportunity to learn delayed gratification may take something simply because they are unaccustomed to doing without. But on the other hand, some children who have had to share everything without ever having something special all to themselves may also be vulnerable to temptation. There is no simple way of knowing.

Sometimes children learn from others around them to equate love with material things and money. They may feel that giving things to their peers will make them popular. This is related to the need for power, control, and a feeling of importance.

Television advertising and store displays are designed to entice people to acquire things. Children are impressionable and can be easily seduced. Even their parents are not immune to such enticements.

The causes for stealing, the age of the child, and the number of occurrences all need to be considered in determining the most effective means of deterring future thefts. Parents need to be careful not to impose forms of punishment that are inappropriate to deal with the true motives. Sometimes having a child return the article along with an explanation of why he or she cannot have it is sufficient. In all cases, children need to know that adults understand their feelings.

More serious cases of long-term stealing may be associated with some forms of anger, frustration, and feelings of helplessness. Parents need to enlist the help of trained professionals in such instances.

33

Stubbornness

Every teacher hears "I won't and you can't make me!" at some time or other, and some common reactions are:

"He's just daring me to make him!"

"I wish I could get her alone."

"Why is she so stubborn?"

There are contributing factors to a child's "stubbornness": (1) age and phase of development, (2) rules and methods of discipline, and (3) natural personality traits. All of these are interdependent, and the perceptive adult will work with a stubborn child keeping all three in mind.

Somewhere around two to four years of age, children discover they are individuals, separate and apart from all other individuals. They are learning independence and autonomy. This realization does not come upon them all at once or even in a smooth continuous line of development. Rather, it is erratic, and they will at one time seem to be "stubborn" and obstinate and other times be quite compliant. However, it is natural for their age and phase of development to exhibit behavior that says they are independent individuals and you simply cannot "make" them do what you ask. They are testing not only you but their own powers. Adults who understand this phase of development may still end up making children obey, but the adult attitude will reflect an understanding of a child's need to test his or her powers of autonomy. A child's stubbornness is not cause for a "showdown" where the adult is challenged to prove his or her greater strength.

Simple comments such as "I know you want to stay on this trike, but I can't let you" or "I know how you feel, but you'll have to stop now. Here, I'll help you," go a long way in preventing "stubborn" behavior. We all know how it feels to get into a battle of wills where no one wins. You feel backed into a situation where your pride will not allow you to "give in." Such situations can be avoided by adults who truly understand that everyone needs to test their independence.

Does this mean that adults should let children have their own way? Sometimes, if the child seems to be genuinely in need of more time or freedom, yes. For example, at one child care center everyone was expected to come in for snacks at 10:00 A.M. The teachers reported that one of the boys always put up a fuss and refused to come in. They learned from observation that he tended to get into a project such as carpentry or sand building and hated to be disturbed. He was called "stubborn" until they made allowances for him to complete a project. When his needs were met, he was no longer "stubborn."

Sometimes adults have to be inconvenienced by allowing more time to children who need it. In cases where this is not possible, children can benefit from "warnings" that they will be expected to finish whatever they are doing in a few minutes. Giving a five- or ten-minute warning about the impending transition and following it up with an offer to help plus some comment relating to the new activity gets the child's mind set for the transition: "We're going to have juice in a few minutes. You won't have time to finish your puzzle, but we can put it up where it's safe and you can finish it after juice. What kind of snack do you think we'll have today?" If the child refuses or ignores you, a suggestion like "Would you like to put two, three, or four more pieces in before we put it away?" provides a definable limit that gives the child some options and a feeling of control.

Rules that are based on an understanding of child development and feelings that are normal for all of us usually work best. Rules that inevitably lead to a power struggle reinforce "stubborn" behavior on the part of the adult as well as the child.

No one is born stubborn. However, just as some people are more predisposed to being allergic or more susceptible to certain diseases, each of us is unique in the sensitivities we display in our personal and emotional development. Some children need to test their autonomy more than others. Depending on the rules and expectations of the home or school, some children will naturally be more compliant than others.

Teachers who complain that little boys are more stubborn than girls may need to assess their own rules and expectations to see why the boys are less compliant. Does the curriculum allow for each child's uniqueness by providing escape hatches for those who are not ready for group conformity? Does the teacher appreciate that everyone does not need to be like everyone else and that a child's apparent stubbornness may simply be normal behavior that is inconvenient to the teacher? A detached, objective observation can often be very helpful in identifying the causes of "stubbornness."

34

Television

Most parents will agree that they probably allow their children to watch TV more than they should. And most will also agree they're not certain how much is enough. It is not unusual for TV to dominate most of the waking hours of a preschooler's time at home. Some children report that they turn on the TV early Saturday morning to watch cartoons and stay in front of the set until late afternoon. In some families the television is on all day long whether or not someone is watching it. The influence TV has on the viewer is important and adults should be more aware of and more responsible for its use.

Let's consider some of the pros and cons of television viewing. The two-dimensional aspects (sight and sound) of TV can be a stimulant to further learning and increased curiosity. Programs designed with the welfare of the child in mind and presented in a responsible manner can do much to enhance a child's intellectual curiosity and mental growth. The ideas to which children are exposed become an important part of their education and can be a positive aspect of their learning environment. Although the positive aspects are questionable for the child, parents have found the TV to be a good baby-sitter. Adults who take time to monitor children's programs, to discuss with the children what they have seen, and to set limits to viewing times will probably find that TV can be beneficial.

Critics of TV watching point to many negatives, and some of them are worth noting. Powerful influences on children are exerted in two areas that have been cause for concern: One is violence; the other, consuming junk foods.

Many research studies have been carried out to determine the effects of television on children. According to a review of recent research, programs directed at young children were particularly violent, and cartoons displayed the highest frequency of violence.[5] While adults may think cartoons reduce the effects of violence because of their unreality, young children appear not to make the distinction between what is real and what is pretend. Studies have demonstrated that even one exposure to a violent cartoon can lead to increased aggression in the child.[6] According to Stein and Friedrich, "Children of both sexes across a wide range of ages and social class backgrounds respond to television violence with aggression. The effects are not limited to males, to the very young, or to the poor, as some people expected."[7]

Preschoolers who are going through the phase of learning how to express strong feelings in socially acceptable ways are probably most susceptible to TV violence. They are at a sensitive, impressionable age

5. Aletha Huston Stein and Lunette Kohn Friedrich, "Impact of Television on Children and Youth," Review of Child Development Research, vol. 5, ed. E. Mavis Hetherington (Chicago: University of Chicago Press, 1975).

6. G. T. Ellis and F. Sekyra, "The Effect of Aggressive Cartoons on the Behavior of First Grade Children," Journal of Psychology 81 (1972): 37—43.

7. Stein and Friedrich, "Impact of Television," p. 224.

and are more likely to emulate what they see. Studies indicate that watching models is very significant in social learning, and excessive exposure to violence can have harmful effects. Adults often forget that cartoons seem harmless to them, but children do not sort out fact from fancy, as indicated in research studies; and violence, even in a cartoon character, can influence a child's behavior.

Studies indicate that bright children tend to watch less TV than those children with lower I.Q.'s. Sitting passively in front of the TV can rob the child of time from more active endeavors, and since young children learn best by doing, those who watch less TV probably have more time to engage in active learning. As children get older, poor TV viewing habits interfere seriously not only with schoolwork but also with leisure time social activities.

Food, drink, and vitamin products are more heavily advertised on TV to children than adults. According to testimony presented to the Subcommittee on the Consumer of the Senate Commerce Committee by Joan Gussow, "out of 388 network commercials run during 29 hours of children's television, 82 percent were for ingestible items—food, drink, candy, gum, or vitamin pills."[8]

According to this testimony, a child who gets up at 8:00 A.M. and watches cartoons for one hour will have been subjected to twenty-seven commercials tempting him to eat the advertiser's products. Most adults do not get up at 8:00 A.M. on a Saturday to watch children's cartoons. They may only be subliminally aware of the degree to which these commercials are antinutrition.

Healthful eating habits are learned early and are difficult to change, as witnessed by the many popular diet fads in magazines for adults. With so many tempting-looking foods offered to us through the media, adults have trouble resisting empty calories. How can we expect children to know how to choose a balanced and nutritious diet?

Parents not only have to eliminate their own biases toward junk foods but also have to offset the more seductive and powerful commercials to which their children are constantly subjected. Young children often cannot discern the difference between a commercial and the cartoon, especially when advertising companies use the cartoon characters to sell their products.

Since preschoolers do not do the shopping, how do TV commercials affect their eating habits? A study by Dr. Scott Ward at the Harvard Graduate School of Business Administration shows that attention to

8. Joan Gussow, "Counternutritional Messages of TV Ads Aimed at Children," *Journal of Nutritional Education* 4 (1972): 49.

commercials was greatest among the youngest children. A table prepared by Dr. Ward involving five-to-seven year-old children appears below:

"Percent of Mothers 'Usually' Yielding to Child's Purchase Influence Attempts"*

Breakfast cereals	88%
Snack foods	52%
Candy	40%
Soft drinks	38%

*S. Ward and D. B. Wackman, "Television Advertising and Intra-family Influence: Children's Purchase Influence Attempts and Parental Yielding," June, 1971.

By the time children were eight to ten years old, 91 percent of the mothers were yielding to their children's influence on which cereal to purchase.

What can parents and teachers do to offset the negative effects of TV on good nutrition?

1. The home *and* school must cooperate to offset the negative effects of TV by talking and working together on common goals.

2. Children are more likely to accept limits if both the teacher and their parents reinforce them.

3. Children need to be taught the difference between the main part of the program and the commercials.

4. Children should be taught what a commercial is—someone trying to sell you something. They need to learn to be wary of, or at least discerning of, the motives of the seller.

5. Parents and teachers should emphasize good nutrition and tell the children what foods are good for them and what foods are bad for them. There is little reason to serve children foods with high sugar content, food additives, artificial colorings, and lots of empty calories when they can learn to enjoy fresh fruit, colorful vegetables, and high-protein foods.

6. Adults should read labels for contents and teach children to do likewise.

7. Cooking projects, both at home and at school, should concentrate on serving fresh rather than processed foods.

8. Parents and teachers should write to TV stations to protest undesirable programs showing violence and commercials that are misleading.

9. Adults need to be firm and confident about limiting the programs children are allowed to watch. Just as you would not knowingly put bad food in a child's stomach, you should not put bad ideas in a child's head.

There is no doubt that television has become an important part of the lives of many families. Parents complain that they fight a losing battle in trying to compete with the seductiveness of TV programs. Many are concerned not only about the negative effects of cartoons and commercials but also about their children becoming so accustomed to sitting passively in front of the TV that school learning will be a disappointment to them.

Educators point out that parents need not consider their problem insurmountable, but they do need the determination to do something about it. The most effective action parents can take is to limit viewing, especially in the early years. They simply need to be firm and consistent, even at the risk of upsetting the child, and turn the TV off. Another thing parents must continue to do is let children know how they, the parents, feel about violence and aggression and junk food. If this verbal disapproval is combined with healthy child-rearing practices, children are more likely to learn the values their parents convey. Adults may think they sound like a broken record at times, repeating rules and beliefs, but they should take a lesson from TV commercials: To be effective, use repetition.

Another technique parents have used in limiting TV is sitting down with the children and selecting programs they can watch a day or two in advance of showing. That way, the children can anticipate beforehand the amount of time they will be allowed to watch TV. Also, parents will have input into selection of acceptable shows. This helps to avoid a battle about censorship after the child is "hooked" by a show he or she has already started to watch.

But what of educational programs for children? It appears that young children learn many useful skills from well-planned programs. Children who watched "Misterrogers' Neighborhood," for example, demonstrated increased cooperation, better understanding of feelings, and greater empathy for others.[9] Two years of extensive evaluations by the Educational

---

9. Stein and Friedrich, "Impact of Television."

Testing Service show impressive gains in cognitive skills and school-related tasks by children who watched "Sesame Street."[10] Some educators, however, have been critical of the show for using fast-paced, commercialized techniques to reach the children. Parents and teachers need to recognize that the program was not designed as a substitute for formal education. "The Electric Company," designed to teach reading, showed positive results only on children who watched the program in school. There was no appreciable improvement in reading skills for children who viewed the program at home.[11]

Television has many worthwhile experiences to offer the viewing audience. Our lives have been enhanced by educational programs, documentaries, worldwide coverage of news events, and the like. Watching a close-up of a famous ballet performer, an underwater scene with Jacques Cousteau, or scenes of animals caring for their young all add to our greater awareness and appreciation of the world around us. Adults need not be helpless in surrendering their values to TV programs of questionable taste; instead, they can enlist the positive effects of TV to enhance the teaching of values and good taste to their young children.

For publications, listing of most violent programs, and other useful information about TV, write:

Children's Committee on TV, Inc.
1511 Masonic Ave.
San Francisco, CA 94117
(415) 863-9434

National Citizens Committee for Broadcasting (NCCB)
1028 Connecticut Avenue, N.W.
Washington, D.C. 20036

35

Thumb Sucking

All babies are born with the instinctive need to suck. During the first year and a half of children's lives, much of their development is dependent on their ability to ingest food through their normal sucking tendency. Very

10. S. Ball and G. A. Bogatz, *The First Year of "Sesame Street": An Evaluation* (Princeton, N.J.: Educational Testing Service, 1970).

11. S. Ball and G. A. Bogatz, *Reading with Television: An Evaluation of "The Electric Company"* (Princeton, N.J.: Educational Testing Service, 1973).

early in their development, babies may find their thumbs and discover how satisfying it can be to suck on them.

Some doctors believe that slow-feeding babies who are allowed to breast feed or suck on a bottle for longer periods of time are less likely to suck their thumbs, blankets, or other objects.

Parents need not be concerned about babies who suck their thumbs. It is quite natural. But some parents are worried that their children will have difficulty breaking the habit as they get older. Pacifiers are good substitutes if offered before the children get used to their thumbs or blankets. It is a good idea to have a clean supply handy. Many children continue to suck on their thumbs or pacifiers until the age of four, five, or even six. Most drop the habit when they are sufficiently preoccupied with toys, rattles, and other distractors, but it is common to see preschoolers pop their thumbs into their mouths during periods of stress.

Adults should recognize that the security object, whether it be the thumb, blanket, stuffed animal, or what-have-you, represents a safe retreat for the child. Interfering with the normal comforting and pleasurable activity of the child can result in stuttering, shyness, and other emotional upsets. If adults refrain from making a big fuss about thumb sucking, the child will gradually grow out of the habit.

"But what about my child's teeth?" asks a mother who is concerned about her five-year-old. Some dentists are concerned about the teeth growing out of line, but others feel there is no evidence to indicate that thumb sucking is the cause of malocclusion.

The parents of older children who continue to suck their thumbs should observe when such children are most likely to revert to their habit. Are they more likely to do it when they are tired, frustrated, bored, or afraid? What need does thumb sucking satisfy? Are these children still acting dependent and "babyish," perhaps jealous of time parents may be spending away from them? Even when adults appear casual about this habit, children learn that thumb sucking is an effective way to get attention.

Teachers and parents should also note when such children do not suck their thumbs. What are they doing at the time? In what activities do they participate that seem to give them sufficient satisfaction to replace the need for their thumbs? Increase the children's exposure to more of these satisfying activities to discourage reliance on thumb sucking.

The most ineffective solution is punishment. As with masturbating, nail biting, and stuttering, punishing children may make them stop out of fear, but the consequences can be unfortunate. Emotional disturbances in later life can often be traced back to the use of severe punishment to interfere with normal, satisfying activity. Everyone needs an acceptable form of release and retreat from daily pressures, and to deny children by making them feel bad or guilty for wanting to be more comfortable can be damaging.

All children who suck their thumbs are not necessarily upset or unhappy. As long as the adults around them can accept their need and treat it casually, being careful to assess any possible causes for stress, the children are likely to discard the habit.

Normal children crave for and benefit from play with others their own age in environments designed for their level of development. Given the enticements of play groups and interesting equipment, young children will gradually rely less and less on their thumbs for gratification.

36

Toilet Training (See also Bed Wetting)

In some families toilet training can be achieved smoothly and with a minimum of conflict, while in others the transition from diapers to potty becomes a traumatic battleground between parent and child. How and why does that happen? Is it natural for some children to wet their beds until they're into grade school or to withhold their bowel movements and remain constipated for weeks?

Teachers and doctors who have heard complaints from parents going through difficult toilet training procedures with their youngsters can visualize the grim faces of the adults and equally adamant expressions of their children. When the problem has gone as far as the child's fifth or sixth year, something had indeed gone wrong, and both parents and child are in need of help.

It is necessary first to go back to the child's early years to determine what constitutes more routine kinds of "ages and stages" in the process of toilet training. In the old days, parents were taught to take their one-year-old to the potty and sit him there routinely until he learned to go by himself. Later, child developmentalists pointed out that until a youngster is sufficiently mature physically, toilet training is useless. The general consensus now is that the optimal age to begin toilet training is around two and a half years. At this age children are able to (1) perceive signals from their bodies that tell them they have to urinate or defecate, (2) hold the process back long enough to tell someone or get to the toilet themselves, and (3) control their sphincter muscles sufficiently to relax them at the appropriate time.

Until the child is capable of all three, parents will have difficulty keeping the child dry. Children differ as to the ages when they arrive at the optimal developmental level, and the recommended age of two and a half is not to be taken literally. Doctors report that generally girls seem to be able to control their sphincter muscles earlier than boys. Also, children usually learn to stay dry during their waking hours long before they stop wetting the bed at night. And bowel control is usually reached before control of urination.

Even when children are physically capable of being trained, they are going to have many "accidents" due to circumstances beyond their control. It is not unusual for preschoolers to wet their pants occasionally (or even quite frequently), and adults should not shame children or lead them to believe that they're "too big" to wet their pants since they're in school. Sometimes parents tell their children they cannot start school until they are toilet trained. In some instances this may be true, but most child care centers recognize that most children between ages two and five cannot be expected to be completely trained. Parents would do well to inquire about such policies, and the school should make this information readily available to enrolling families so that the home and school can agree on acceptable procedures to follow.

Sometimes parents expect the teacher to remember to keep the child dry and inflict their disappointment on the teacher when their child has an accident. If expectations are made clear during orientation and enrollment, many of these parent-teacher-child conflicts can be avoided. If the teacher's schedule is such that the parents' expectations cannot be fulfilled, the teacher should be candid about it at the beginning. In some instances parents may unwittingly transfer onto the teacher the training problems they have been having with their child, and teachers understandably do not want to accept a role with hostile or negative connotations to the child. In such cases, teachers should tell the parents honestly how they feel about wanting to build their own relationships with the child and say that they do not mind changing the child's pants (or diapers) in the event of an "accident." A teacher's own philosophy about the child's readiness must be considered and shared with the parent. Otherwise, feelings of disappointment and failure will result.

Some suggestions for helping children during the toilet-training period are:

1. Provide children with a small potty chair that they can sit on when they want to. It is difficult and uncomfortable to climb up onto the adult-size toilet. Adults often do not realize how awkward it feels, but look at a two-year-old clinging for dear life to the sides of the toilet seat with feet dangling! Some are fearful of falling in, and others dislike the loud noise of flushing. Children may not be able to verbalize their fears, but perceptive adults will try to avoid all the potentially threatening aspects of toileting to help children make the transition as easily as possible.

2. Recognize that children sometimes simply cannot bear to leave an engrossing activity to run to the toilet. Schools should try to design their facilities so toilets are child-size and easily accessible from the playground as well as the indoors. If children have to run a long distance to get to the bathroom, they are more likely to misjudge the time they need or simply forget the whole matter and soil themselves. It is not at all unusual to see a nursery school youngster who is deeply engrossed in play stopping occasionally to press both legs together, knees knocked, pained expression on his face, but fighting the need to leave what he is doing. It is no wonder that little boys will simply do what is most convenient under such circumstances and urinate on the playground. Though most teachers do not encourage this practice, it needn't be treated as such a naughty thing to do. "The next time you have to urinate, I want you to use the toilet. Let me show you where it is." Sometimes the child resists saying he already knows where it is. It is still a good idea to take the child to the toilet so that he gets the message clearly and realizes that he still loses time from his play even if he urinates outdoors.

3. Strange places can discourage youngsters from using the toilet. Some institutional-type rooms are sterile and forbidding, and it is not unusual for children to balk at going into a cold, large room seemingly removed from all humanity or perhaps overcrowded with other children who are likely to make fun of them. Friendly, understanding adults should take time to help children adjust by staying with them and reassuring them until they gradually become accustomed to the new surroundings. Let them know they can come to ask you or some other adult to take them to the bathroom when necessary.

4. After an illness or new birth or some unusual occurrence, children are more likely to revert to bed wetting or soiling their pants. Again, adults need to allow for such backsliding. The transition from diapers to staying dry is not smooth and even. It is more likely to reach plateaus and reversals before the child is completely trained.

5. Avoid comparisons with other children. Some youngsters simply learn to stay dry more readily than others. Parents who are casual about toilet training seem to have more success than those who are tense and "uptight" about staying clean and enforcing their rigidity on children before they are ready.

Getting back to the question posed at the beginning of this topic, what about the "older" child—the child of five, six, or seven—who is still suffering from enuresis (involuntary urination) and withholding bowel movements? Assuming that the child has had a physical examination and is found to be normal, the approach calls for counseling and more help than the teacher might be able to give.

It is probably safe to assume that the conflict over toilet training is so deep and serious that usual strategies will not work. One mother informed the teacher that she had to take her five-year-old daughter to the hospital for enemas every week because she was so constipated she cried from the pain. No laxative seemed to do any good.

A father was so ashamed of his seven-year-old son "purposely holding his B.M.'s and then standing in a corner to do them in his pants" that he refused to take the child along with the rest of the family on a vacation. He later reported that he was finally successful in getting the child to use the toilet by bribing him with trading stamps. Every time the child used the toilet he would earn a page of stamps, and when he filled his book he could trade it for a special toy.

This is not to recommend the same procedure for other parents, but when older, physically normal children have toileting problems, the adults who work with them must recognize some deeper needs and concentrate on finding the causes and satisfying those needs rather than relying on punishment and shame. The children are undoubtedly feeling ashamed and guilty already, but the need to withhold a movement may be a reflection of their anger and hatred toward someone or something in their environment, or their continued bed wetting may be an indication of a deeply felt, unsatisfied need for more security and love. Both the parents and the children need professional counseling at this point, and the wise teacher will be supportive and understanding of the painful conflicts of such families at this time.

Parents and teachers would do well to remember that toilet training is one of the first learning experiences a young child encounters. If it is positive, the relationship the child has with adults in regard to future learning is further strengthened. Staying dry and learning to use the toilet need not be so serious and frightening for the child that adults lose sight of long-term goals. Positive early learning experiences lay the solid groundwork for enthusiasm in later education.

Annotated Readings

The following books cover topics that may be helpful to parents and teachers who want further resources for dealing with child-rearing problems. A list of books suitable for children is also included.

Ames, Louise Bates, and Ilg, Frances L.
Your Two Year Old. New York: Delacorte Press, 1976.
This is one of a series of three books covering the growth and development of young children in easy to read style. Covers normal growth and problems associated with each year. Also *Your Three Year Old* and *Your Four Year Old.*

Biller, Henry B.
Father, Child, and Sex Role. Lexington, Mass. Lexington Books, 1971.
Discusses the father's influence on the development of boys and girls. Research on father absence, fathering and female personality development, etc. is covered.

De Rosis, Helen
Parent Power, Child Power. Indianapolis, Ind.: Bobbs-Merrill Company, Inc., 1974.
What do you do when your fifteen-year-old stops talking to you, or your three-year-old refuses to go to bed, or your seven-year-old still wets his bed? These questions are covered in helping parents detect and solve problems with children.

Dodson, Fitzhugh
How to Father. New York: Signet Books, 1974.
A survival kit for fathers of children from infancy to teens.

Dodson, Fitzhugh
How to Parent. New York: Signet Books, 1970.
Covers stages of development from infancy to primary school. Topics include teaching self-discipline and selecting toys, books, and records.

Dreikurs, Rudolf
Coping with Children's Misbehavior. New York: Hawthorne Books, Inc., 1972.
A parent's guide to understanding and dealing with problems common to children. The same author also has a book on *Discipline without Tears* (1974).

Feingold, Ben E.
Why Your Child Is Hyperactive. New York: Random House, 1975.
A controversial but increasingly accepted theory attributing hyperactivity to food additives. Includes Feingold's special diet.

Fraiberg, Selma H.
The Magic Years. New York: Charles Scribner's Sons, 1959.
A popular book covering theories of early childhood from birth to six years. Easy to read and full of practical insights into the world of childhood.

Gordon, Thomas
P.E.T. Parent Effectiveness Training. New York: New American Library, 1975.
Teaches an approach emphasizing both the rights of the parents and the rights of children to be themselves. Enhances dignity and worth of the individual in personal relations.

Grant, Wilson W.
From Parent to Child about Sex. Kentwood, Mich.: Zondervan Publishing House, 1975.
A look at sexuality, how to explain it to children, what difficulties may arise, and how to deal with them.

Grollman, Earl A., ed.
Explaining Death to Children. Boston: Beacon Press, 1967.
Brings together the best thinking of specialists from psychology, education, and religion and others.

Grollman, Earl A., ed.
Explaining Divorce to Children. Boston: Beacon Press, 1969.
A book of essays by psychologists, educators, religious leaders, parents, and children on the topic of divorce.

Jackson, Edgar N.
Telling a Child about Death. New York: Hawthorne Books, Inc., 1965.
A helpful book for adults in understanding the nature of children's grief. Includes suggestions about when and how to talk with a child about death.

Kübler-Ross, Elisabeth
On Death and Dying. New York: Macmillan Publishing Co., Inc., 1969.
Discusses fears and attitudes surrounding death. Includes some interviews with terminally ill patients.

Ostrovsky, Everett
Sibling Rivalry. New York: Cornerstone Library, 1970.

Discusses sibling rivalry in terms of how to discipline, and covers such topics as belligerency and marital discord.

Phillips, E. Lakin
Children's Reactions to Separation and Divorce. Arlington, Va.: Document Reproduction Service, Computer Microfilm International Corp.
A fourteen-page report presenting three aspects of children's reactions to divorce, factual research summaries on the influence of divorce on children, and some proposed remedies.

Redl, Fritz, and Weiman, David
Controls from Within. Techniques for the Treatment of the Aggressive Child. New York: The Free Press, 1952.
Discusses how a child's environment can be designed to contribute to sound development. Suggests opportunities for emotional expression through play and games. Psychiatrically oriented.

Renshaw, Domeena C.
The Hyperactive Child. Boston: Little, Brown and Company, 1974.
Discusses diagnosis, management, medication, prognosis, and prevention of hyperactivity.

Rowan, Robert L.
Bedwetting: A Guide for Parents. New York: St. Martin's Press, Inc., 1974.
An analysis of emotional, psychological, and sexual factors as underlying causes for bed wetting. Explains how to recognize and handle bedwetting problems.

Salk, Lee
What Every Child Would Like His Parents to Know. New York: Warner Books, 1977.
How to help children with problem solving. Ideas on how to tell your child about death, divorce, illness, and other topics.

Uslander, Arlene S.; Weiss, Caroline; and Telman, Judith
Sex Education for Today's Child. New York: Association Press, 1977.
Deals with most often asked questions and how to answer them from early childhood to puberty. Covers such topics as homosexuality and parent nudity.

Wolfgang, Charles H.
Helping Aggressive and Passive Preschoolers through Play. Columbus, Ohio: Charles E. Merrill Publishing Co., 1977.
An explicit, well-defined, systematic approach to handling problem preschoolers. Describes intervention techniques the teacher can use in the classroom with aggressive and passive children.

Books for Children

Death

de Paola, Tomie
Nana Upstairs & Nana Downstairs. New York: G.P. Putnam's Sons, 1973.
A touching story about Tommy's visits to his grandmother and great-grandmother. One day Nana Upstairs died, and Tommy's sadness points out the warm and special relationship a young child can have with the very old.

Fassler, Joan
My Grandpa Died Today. New York: Behavioral Publications, 1971.
A young boy's close relationship with his grandfather and his adjustment to the old man's death.

Viorst, Judith
The Tenth Good Thing about Barney. New York: Atheneum, 1971.
After Barney the cat dies, a young boy tries to remember ten good things to tell about Barney at the funeral.

Divorce, Separation, Single Parent

Adams, Florence
Mushy Eggs. New York: G.P. Putnam's Sons, 1973.
Mom has to work every day and the children can only visit Dad on weekends, so Fanny, the baby-sitter, becomes a very special person in their lives. One day Fanny tells them she is returning to Italy, and the children must learn to deal with terrible feelings of sadness and loss.

Goff, Beth
Where Is Daddy? Boston: Beacon Press, 1969.
A book written by a psychiatric social worker in simple terms to help the young child understand divorce.

Lexau, Joan M.
Me Day. New York: Dial Press, 1971.
Rafer's parents are divorced and he's disappointed because he hasn't heard from his Dad yet on his birthday. Then his mother sends him on a mysterious errand. Good for discussion of feeling. Written in black dialect. Appropriate for K–3.

Zolotow, Charlotte
A Father Like That. New York: Harper & Row, 1972.
A sensitive and touching story about a young boy's imaginary family where he wished he had a father, but his father went away.

Doctor, Dentist, Hospital

Berger, Knute, et al.
A Visit to the Doctor. New York: Grossett & Dunlap, 1960.
A detailed, factual account of a child's physical examination. Realistic illustrations. Appropriate for all ages.

Chase, Francine
A Visit to the Hospital. New York: Grossett & Dunlap, 1957.
A boy goes to the hospital to have his tonsils removed.

Collier, James Lincoln
Danny Goes to the Hospital. New York: W.W. Norton, 1970.
Actual photographs of a boy who has an operation to repair a damaged eye muscle.

Garn, Bernard J.
A Visit to the Dentist. New York: Grossett & Dunlap, 1959.
Many details and factual information about a boy who has a checkup at the dentist.

Paullin, Ellen
No More Tonsils! Boston: Beacon Press, 1958.
Photographs of a girl who goes to the hospital to have her tonsils removed.

Shay, Arthur
What Happens When You Go to the Hospital? Chicago: Reilly & Less, 1969.
A black girl has her tonsils removed. Photographs show routine procedures.

Fears and Other Feelings

Babbitt, Natalie
The Something. New York: Farrar, Straus, & Giroux, 1970.
A pretend story of a monster named Mylo who is afraid of The Something until his mother gives him some clay to make a likeness of the thing he fears.

Showers, Paul
A Book of Scary Things. Garden City, N.Y.: Doubleday & Co., 1977.
Humorous glimpses of real and imaginary fears of children and adults.

Watson, Jane Werner, et al.
New York: Western, 1971.
These authors have written a series of books dealing with feelings for parents and children to read together. Some of the titles include *Sometimes I Get Angry, Sometimes I'm Afraid,* and *Sometimes I Get Jealous.*

Sex Education

Gruenberg, Sidonie Matsner
The Wonderful Story of How You Were Born. New York: Doubleday, 1970.
Excellent illustrations showing sperm, ovum, fetus. Appropriate for K–3.

Manushkin, Fran
Baby. New York: Harper & Row, 1972.
Humorously illustrated story showing the various positions and facial expressions of a baby inside Mommy and its reactions to other family members waiting for it to be born.

Sheffield, Margaret
Where Do Babies Come From? New York: Alfred A. Knopf, 1973.
By far the most explicitly illustrated book showing conception, reproduction, and the life cycle. Appropriate for all ages.

Showers, Paul, and Showers, Kay Sperry
Before You Were a Baby. New York: Thomas Y. Crowell, 1968.
Simply illustrated book appropriate for preschoolers.

Sibling Rivalry, Jealousy

Arnstein, Helene S.
Billy and Our New Baby. New York: Behavioral Publications, 1973.
Billy shows his jealousy of the new baby by being aggressive, by crying, and by regressing to bottle feeding. He learns that it is all right to have these feelings. The book includes a helpful guide with information about sibling rivalry.

Hoban, Russell
A Baby Sister for Frances. New York: Harper & Row, 1964.
Frances, the badger, is jealous when a new baby comes to the house.

Keats, Ezra Jack
Peter's Chair. New York: Harper & Row, 1967.
Peter decides to take his little blue chair and run away from home because he is angry about having to give up his cradle, crib, and high chair to his new baby sister.

Schlein, Miriam
Laurie's New Brother. London: Abelard-Schuman, 1961.
Laurie resents her new brother because she wants Mommy and Daddy all to herself.

Appendix of Resources

Over the years, every teacher collects and stores away printed materials and resources that "might come in handy some day." In the following section I have pulled together what I consider to be the best, or most helpful, materials and resources from my collection.

Most of the resources gathered here are probably familiar to teachers. They consist of an assortment of sample evaluations—questionnaires, checklists, suggestions—all intended to help sort out and identify ways of assessing various areas and people in an educational program. The sample forms are organized to assist the teacher in evaluating (more efficiently, hopefully) the physical aspects of the program, the parents, the children, and the teachers. These samples are intended only to provide a basis for further revisions of evaluations more suited to each teacher's unique situation.

A select list of films, their cost, how to order them, and a short description of each is included to provide teachers and parents with ideas for group meetings. There are addresses of film companies that can provide additional listings.

Although most local libraries and community service agencies can provide schools with information about referral sources, the teacher may find it helpful to use the annotated list of associations. They are categorized under education, social services, health services, and legal services. The addresses and phone numbers are for national offices where further information can be obtained.

Evaluations

We all want to know what others think about us, but we are often afraid to be evaluated. Why?

"Because I'm afraid I'll be criticized and my feelings will be hurt," comments one teacher.

"I'm already aware of my faults," says another, "but I'm hoping they aren't apparent to others."

"It hurts my ego to think that some people might not like me."

All evaluations, however, do not have to be threatening. We can obtain useful information and maximize the positive aspects of evaluations. When parents and teachers work together to determine the needs served by evaluations, the threatening aspects are diminished. For example, both parents and teachers can usually commit themselves to improvement of various aspects of the program. If the decision is to "engage more of the children in music activities," the need to evaluate teachers, participating parents, and children makes sense. Methods of evaluation should be determined in advance and should be acceptable to all involved. No individual should be singled out to accept responsibility or blame for program components.

Parents and teachers first need to decide what they want to evaluate. Refer to the table on planning parent programs (p. 67) and review needs, objectives, methods, and evaluation procedures. Once the needs of the group are identified, methods of evaluation can be decided upon.

Some impersonal areas requiring evaluation are:

Physical facilities, such as spatial arrangements, maintenance of equipment, design of new equipment to meet changing needs, rearranging rooms to encourage more quiet and solitary play, and eliminating hazardous and useless toys.

Program areas, such as the dramatic play corner, the cognitive area, and the storytelling area. Do these serve the purpose for which they were designed? Observations and checklists by parents and teachers are a way to evaluate effectiveness of program areas.

Use of community resources, such as field trips, visits by community workers, use of referral agencies, and social services. Doing a systematic evaluation of the actual number of times resources have been used and assessing the school's needs for such resources can lead to a better use of agencies in the program.

Personal evaluations can include the following:

Parent involvement in a program should be assessed. Are the present families and teachers satisfied with the way parents are participating? How can more parents be involved, and should they be involved? What elements should be revised or omitted from parent regulations? Improvement of this aspect of the program requires evaluation of the people involved, and both parents and teachers should have input into the methods acceptable to judge how well the adults have done in accordance with the goals and objectives specified by those same adults. In some cases an outside consultant familiar with parent-teacher groups might be helpful.

Teachers, staff, and other paid professionals benefit from objective evaluations related to their effectiveness in helping meet the needs of the program, the parents, and the children. Sometimes, publicly funded programs have required forms and evaluations that must be followed. These do not preclude a school designing its own forms to better assess its performance. Informal evaluations such as comments by parents or feedback from the children give a teacher some notion from day to day about the quality of her performance, but more formal procedures can be found at the end of this section.

In-service training and parent education aspects need to be revised from time to time in order to meet the needs of changing families. Some adults are more sophisticated and experienced than others in certain areas of the program. New parents will want other kinds of topics and educational opportunities. Keeping up with latest developments in the field requires constant monitoring and frequent changes in program offerings.

Children are evaluated in many different ways. Teachers' reports and observations are useful, but many schools may want to have pretests and posttests of actual performance gains. Parents may also want to know if their children are ready for the next step in education. There are some suggested tests at the end of this section.

Effective evaluation is essential to the success of a parent-teacher program. When someone asks what your school is doing and are you successful in carrying out your objectives, your evaluations should answer these questions for you. Moreover, you should also have a clear idea of exactly where and how the program is being improved. Good programs do not leave such things to chance.

Evaluation of Programs

Much can be done by teachers to "set the stage" for positive evaluations. You can build in success or failure by the way you approach program planning with parents. Teachers and parents often assume that everyone is in agreement as to what a good program is all about. That kind of assumption leads to disappointment.

Much has been written about different philosophies of education. Student teachers have all read about open classrooms, behavior modification, child-centered versus teacher-oriented education, cognitive versus affective learning, content versus process, planned instruction versus self-discovery, etc. During their training, they may have embraced one or two models as being the best (usually based on the lab school where they were trained). But parents are not as familiar with various philosophies and may not be as supportive of the ones you like.

Even when the school district or funding agency spells out clearly what philosophies underly their programs, you must be aware of what the parents want and start at that point. For example, a survey might show that most of the families feel school achievement is important and they want their children to learn their letters and numbers. Your plans for an informal child-centered program of self-discovery will undoubtedly rate poor evaluations. Even if you are convinced your ideas are for the good of the children, you must have parental support to succeed in carrying them out.

Creating a climate of goodwill, establishing trusting relationships with the parents, and relating positively to the children all help to make it possible for you to "sell" your ideas more successfully. You simply cannot carry the program in spite of, or without the help of, your parents. Also, the needs of the parents must be incorporated into the curriculum. If they want more cognitive-type activities, they probably have good reason. The underlying causes of their concerns should be considered when you introduce techniques and methods that are unfamiliar to them. If you can convince a mother how free play can help her child succeed in school, she is more likely to support your suggestions.

There is no one best philosophy for all early childhood programs. Each group of families must custom design a program that best fits their needs and goals. That is why a needs assessment has to be made and methods determined to reach objectives. These methods might borrow from a variety of techniques designed to serve many differing philosophies.

A look at some differing viewpoints might be helpful in providing some ideas for parents and teachers to consider in establishing program philosophies to be evaluated.

Some "traditional" preschools are oriented toward free play organized around a loosely structured program of activities such as art, music, cooking, science, cognitive table toys, and indoor and outdoor play. The child is free to move around as he or she pleases, and no special attempts are made by the teacher to require that the child engage in any particular task.

The structured classroom is oriented more toward planned activities requiring group participation and teacher-directed tasks. Expectations and rules are generally spelled out clearly, and activities are organized around definite routines.

The Traditional versus the Structured Classroom

	Traditional	Structured
Philosophy	Oriented toward free play, creative expression, social skills, and individual growth. Each child learns at his or her own pace.	Oriented toward group and teacher-directed activities, education of the senses, formation of habits, and learning school-related skills.
Activities	Major concern is for individual differences, original expression, and well-rounded personality.	Group and teacher directed. Major concern is for the welfare of the group.
Curriculum Planning	Themes and work are organized with the development and motivation of the child in mind. Based on interest and curiosity of the child.	Work and materials set up by the teacher around an organized and structured program. There are specific outcomes or products expected.
Rules	Rules tend to be flexible. Teachers show a greater tolerance for testing rules.	Firmly established rules. Usually more of them than in traditional school.
Children	Children encouraged to interact with each other. Independence is encouraged.	More dependence on the teacher. Relates to tasks and activities and the group.
Discipline	Attempt to understand and channel feelings.	Greater control over impulses and expression of feelings expected of child.

It is a mistake for people to take sides over which philosophy might be better. Most programs are combinations of a variety of approaches. It is important, however, to specify very clearly just what parents and teachers want so that program evaluations can be carried out successfully.

Following are some suggested lists for parents and teachers to use in evaluating the physical and programmatic aspects of a nursery school, child care center, or early elementary program. You can use these as a basis for designing your own evaluation check sheets.

Safety Checklist

To be used when evaluating the child care center, classroom, and/or home as a safe environment for children to be in.

_____ Traffic patterns and stairways free of clutter with guard rails on stairs.

_____ Floors free of tripping hazards (electric cords, throw rugs, toys, etc.).

_____ Screens and windows in good repair.

_____ Fence in good condition. Absence of protruding nails, wires, or loose boards. Gate latched securely.

_____ Garbage area clean and enclosed, separate from play area. Tools are safely stored.

_____ Check the yard daily for hazards such as broken glass, sharp objects, toadstools, and animal droppings.

_____ Decals on glass doors and windows at children's eye levels.

_____ Matches, lighters, candles, and other tempting fire hazards locked up out of reach of children.

_____ Keep flammable liquids, such as gasoline and paint thinner, outdoors in appropriate, tightly capped metal containers and locked up out of reach of children. _Keep in original containers._

_____ Develop a fire drill and/or emergency exit plan for your child care center.

_____ Have a fire extinguisher in a convenient location. (A one-pound can of baking soda, properly labeled, may be kept on premises also.)

_____ Know how to shut off the gas, electricity, and water in case of emergency.

_____ All caustics, poisons, household cleaners, or aerosol sprays stored in locked cupboards out of reach of children. _Keep in original container._

_____ Store all medicines and razor blades locked up out of reach of children, especially prescription drugs, aspirin, wintergreen oil, alcohol, antihistamines, iron pills, and vitamins.
Keep all medicine in original container.
Do not refer to medicine as candy.

_____ Safety plugs installed in electrical outlets.

_____ Keep hot foods and electric cords out of reach of children.

_____ Have a first aid kit in a convenient location and check supplies at least weekly for amount of supplies.
Carry a second kit on all field trips.

_____ Check play area (inside and outside) for poisonous plants. Examples: Dieffenbachia, monkshood, foxglove, nicotiania, rhubarb and potato leaves, atropa belladonna, jessamine, daphne, laurel, azaleas, rhododendrons, castor beans, lantana, oleander, yew, chinaberry tree, jimsonweed, nightshade, and pyracantha.

_____ Do not allow children to eat berries, leaves, stems, flowers, or bulbs of any plant.

_____ Wading pools should be emptied at least daily. Pool should be emptied and stored in appropriate place when not in use (day off, weekends, holidays, off season).*

_____ Pool area should be well supervised at _all_ times by responsible adult. Stationary pools must meet requirements for sanitation.

_____ Have toys, furniture, and play equipment in good repair.
Absence of small removable parts, chips, splinters, and broken, sharp edges. Paint toys and all furniture with lead-free paint. Cribs to comply with federal standards (slat widths, mattress size, locking rails, etc.)
Thin plastic should not be used to cover mattress.

_____ Help children practice careful, thorough handwashing:
Before eating
After toileting
If they are dirty after indoor/outdoor play

_____ Children should sit while eating.

_____ Avoid foods that are likely to cause choking, like popcorn, peanuts, and raw carrots.

_____ Do not leave plastic bags lying around.

*Schools should check with local and state licensing agencies to determine regulations governing the use of pools. Some health departments will not allow the use of pools at all.
Source: From Community Coordinated Child Development Council of Santa Clara County, Inc.

It is helpful to have the parent or teacher aide spend some time observing before participating. A simple checklist similar to the following can be used to provide some framework and to help the observer focus on various aspects of the teacher-child relationship. The teacher should shorten or adapt these questions to suit the situation.

Observation Check Sheet

Name of Observer: _____   Date: _____

Instructions: Please sit down in an unobtrusive place where you can see most of the classroom. In order to observe objectively, it is best to limit your interactions with the children. If they should approach you and talk with you, answer them, but do not encourage a lengthy conversation. If they want you to do something with them, refer them to the teacher.

Give yourself time to take in the total environment. Absorb the general atmosphere, look all around the room, listen to the sounds, and generally acquaint yourself with the surroundings and the people. When you are comfortable, begin to focus on more specific aspects of the curriculum.

In this classroom we want to:

1. Increase the Child's Awareness and Knowledge About the Physical World.

Check

Does the program encourage the development of curiosity through materials and displays that lead a child to explore?   _____

Do you hear children asking questions?   _____

Do the teachers encourage children to ask questions?   _____

Are the children free to touch and explore and actively experiment with materials in the classroom?   _____

Do the teachers foster a child's interest in new things?   _____

Are there opportunities for freedom of choice in a variety of learning activities?   _____

2. Develop Language Abilities.

Are the children encouraged to express themselves verbally?   _____

Are there a variety of language-motivating materials available to the child? (Records, books, puppets, dramatic play materials?)   _____

Do you hear children expressing ideas and feelings?   _____

Do the activities encourage verbal interaction between and among the children?   _____

Do the teachers introduce new concepts and terminology?   _____

Do the teachers name objects and verbalize clearly about procedures to the children?   _____

3. Foster Mental and Emotional Health.

Do the children appear comfortable in the classroom?   _____

Do the children seem self-confident?   _____

Are the teachers respectful of the child who is different?   _____

Do the children seem secure in the routines and methods used by the teachers?   _____

Are disciplinary methods fair and reasonable?   _____

Are the teachers sufficiently firm and flexible?   _____

Do you see examples of building a child's strong self-concept?   _____

Do teachers value individual children?   _____

Are children learning responsibility for their actions and choices?   _____

Are children learning to care for others?   _____

4. Teach Cognitive Skills.

Are there materials designed to teach children concepts like large and small, geometric shapes, numbers, colors, letters?   _____

Are there small group and individual instruction times set aside during the day?   _____

Is plenty of time allotted for working with learning materials?   _____

Do the children get immediate feedback about the correctness of the concepts they are learning? _____

Are children allowed to learn at their own pace? _____

Do teachers use praise to encourage children? _____

5. Encourage Creative Expression.

Are there many art materials and opportunities for creative expression available? _____

Are there opportunities for dramatic play and imaginative involvement? _____

Are there music and creative movement activities? _____

Are children encouraged to use their imaginations? _____

Is the individual child given space and time to daydream or simply to be alone? _____

This observation form is intended to provide a framework for looking more closely at various aspects of the curriculum. You can expand on these as you work with us in our program. We value your comments and invite your suggestions.

Comments and Suggestions:

What to Look For When Visiting a School

1. Physical Aspects

Check

Ample indoor and outdoor space? (A minimum of thirty-five square feet indoors and fifty square feet per child outdoors.) _____

Space for running and plenty of large-muscle activities? _____

Variety of physical activities encouraged through good design? _____

178   Appendix of Resources

Isolation quarters? _____

Place for quiet contemplation? _____

Supervision taken into account in overall design? Can children be easily seen and supervised, or are there many areas not easily covered at all times? _____

Hygenic conditions? (Clean sinks, toilets, safe conditions, heating facilities, drafts, fire extinguishers well located, well lighted, children appear healthy?) _____

2. Equipment

Sterile equipment leads to limited and sterile responses. Are children able to get many different ideas in use of materials, and are they free to explore and question and work out their curiosity? Can most equipment be used in many ways? _____

Is there enough equipment and materials to go around? _____

Is all equipment in good condition? (Painted, sanded, no sharp or broken edges?) Do puzzles have all pieces? Are books in good repair? Is most equipment readily available for children? _____

3. People

Do you get the feeling the school is friendly? _____

Is it too quiet or too hectic?

Do you hear lots of "No, No"? _____

Do the teachers seem interested, relaxed, but busy? _____

Are the needs of children cared for, or are there some who seem left out and ignored?

What is the ratio of adults to children? (Recommended minimum of one adult to ten children. A better ratio is one to five or six depending on age of children.) _____

Are visitors apparently welcome at any time, or is it necessary to make an appointment? _____

Are children free to express themselves verbally and explore physically without constant direction from adults? _____

Does there appear to be a mutual trust and respect among staff and children? _____

Do the teachers have plenty of physical contact (hugging, holding) with children? Or do they seem to be too busy setting up and cleaning up? _____

4. Program

Does the daily routine offer a comfortable balance between free play and organized activities? Does it allow for flexibility within an organized routine? _____

Do the various areas show adequate preplanning? _____

Are the areas inviting and appealing to children? _____

May children move freely within well-supervised areas? Or do they have to all do the same things at the same time? _____

Are there "escape hatches" for those who do not want to participate with the group? _____

Do art work and "creative play" areas seem stereotyped? That is, are materials precut; are children required to all make the same thing to take home; are some activities "special" and not always available whenever children want them? _____

Is there a good variety of small- and large-muscle activities available—music, stories, nature studies? Do tools and materials (such as carpentry) provide for success experiences rather than frustration and failure? _____

Are there well-planned, cognitively oriented activities with appropriate teaching guidance by an adult? _____

Are there many self-help, self-correcting tasks to engage the children so they can learn at their own pace? _____

Parents and volunteers function more efficiently when they have some idea of the overall program each day. A very general outline such as the following schedule from a children's center provides a helpful guide to orient the assistant to the various activities. The same kind of basic schedule can be designed for the nursery or elementary school.

Basic Daily Schedule—Children's Center

6:45– 9:00 A.M.	Children arrive. Individual indoor and outdoor activities (weather permitting)
8:15– 9:15	Brunch
9:15–10:30	Small group activities; age and ability groupings
10:30–11:30	Outdoor play
11:30–12:00	Story time
12:00–12:30	Lunch
12:30–12:45	Brush teeth, prepare for nap
12:45– 2:30	Nap
2:30– 3:00	Wake up—free play
3:00– 3:30	Snack
3:30– 6:00	Individual and small group activities indoors and out, depending on weather

The sample schedule is merely a skeletal outline suggesting possibilities for designing work areas. One or more can be assigned to each area depending on the number of people available.

One person is assigned to each area. These jobs can be rotated once a week to enable each person to have a variety of experiences in different areas of the school. The parent who follows the schedule for Area I, for example, will be responsible for Area II the next time.

Sample Work Schedules For Half-Day Program

Area I (Kitchen and Cooking Project)

    8:30 A.M. Prepare trays of juice and crackers. Follow directions posted in kitchen.

9:00	Cooking project with children.
9:45	Clean up; send children to bathroom to wash for juice.
10:00	Serve juice and crackers.
10:20	Clean up after juice. Clean children's sinks, water fountain, flush toilets.
11:00	Help supervise in art area as needed.
11:30	Help children at going-home time.

Area II (Outdoors by Swings and Sand Area)

8:30 A.M.	Put wheel toys out; rake sand; check area for safety hazards.
9:00	Supervise play. Station yourself where you can see the whole play area.
9:50	Send children in to clean up for juice time.
10:00	Sit at a table to serve juice.
10:20	Clean up juice table while children are at stories and music.
11:00	Return to outside area.
11:30	Put all outdoor equipment away; lock shed.

Area III (Indoors, Art Area)

8:30 A.M.	Line easels and trays with newspaper and set up paints.
9:00	Mix play dough at art table with children's help. Supervise art area; plan special project as needed.
9:50	Clean up; send children to bathroom to wash for juice.
10:00	Serve juice at a table.
10:20	Clean table and put new art activities out while children are at stories and music.
11:00	Supervise art activities. Put dry paintings and other art projects into children's lockers to be ready for going-home time.
11:20	Clean up with help of children.
11:30	Help children with their art at going-home time.

Area IV (Outdoors, Animals, Carpentry)

8:30 A.M.	Clean animal cages and set up carpentry with help of children.

9:00	Supervise with one or two other assistants at carpentry and surrounding area.
9:50	Put materials away and send children in to wash up for juice.
10:00	Serve juice at a table.
10:20	Clean juice table. Set up outdoor projects while children are at stories and music.
11:00	Feed animals, check water.
11:20	Put projects away.
11:30	Help with going-home time.

These schedules are very general. The teacher responsible for setting up and planning routines can add details to the basic outline. Also, where there are more staff helpers, other duties can be added, such as helping with group activities like music, stories, etc. It is best to have one adult to no more than five or six children. Someone should be available at the story corner and puzzle and small table activities to help children or to read with them as needed. Special projects such as cooking and carpentry may require more than one adult supervisor.

Schedules for K–3 classrooms can reflect the various learning activities where parents are needed to work more closely with children on a one-to-one basis. For example, an area can be set aside for a parent to tutor a child in working on conceptual skills. Another parent might be assigned to help a child practice reading or writing. The teacher must demonstrate effective techniques and give the parent an opportunity to "practice" with some assistance before being assigned to an area.

Copies of printed schedules should be made available to staff so each person can see what is expected in the area routine and thus be able to plan ahead. Parent-teacher discussions can be included at the end of the work day by revising the timing and having one of the teachers do a group activity with the children while the other adults meet together.

A well-balanced curriculum should offer a variety of activities including the following:

art
music and creative movement
language
science
caring for animals

block play
dramatic plays
large-muscle activities
small-muscle activities
nutritious foods and cooking
balance between rest and activity
balance between individual and group activities

Evaluations of Parents

Those responsible for involving parents in a program need to assess, from time to time, whether progress is being made toward reaching their goals. A checklist of questions to be used by the teacher can help focus attention on areas that may need strengthening.

Evaluating the Paren Involvement Component

Check

1. Have orientation sessions been planned and conducted for all new parents, explaining goals, their rights, and responsibilities? _____

2. Is there in-service training for staff, parents, and volunteers? _____

3. Are staff and parents informed of current and planned programs through newsletters, bulletins, etc.? _____

4. Are other community resources made known to staff and parents? _____

5. Are home visits and conferences being carried out and evaluated? _____

6. Are you actively recruiting parents as volunteers? _____

7. Are there opportunities for parents to make suggestions for school activities? _____

8. Have you made note of potential leaders among parent groups and set up training sessions for them? _____

9. Have you found out about special skills and interests of parents? _____

10. Are there educational workshops for parents? _____

11. Are parents involved in curriculum planning and evaluation? _____

12. Are parents involved in policy making? _____

13. Is there money available for parent activities? _____

14. Do parent policy groups have functioning committees? _____

15. Are parents welcome at any time in the school as visitors as well as volunteers? _____

16. Are there arrangements made for transportation and baby-sitting when parents are expected to participate? _____

17. Are there plenty of new and useful materials available to parents on the news racks, in the library, in the parent classroom? _____

18. Have parents been given many opportunities to talk with teachers about their children's progress and adjustment? _____

19. Have you and parents attended any training programs in the last six months? _____

20. Can personal contact between parents and staff be increased? _____

Source: Adapted from "More Specific Questions Can Be Raised in Evaluating the Parent Involvement Component" (Community Coordinated Child Development Council of Santa Clara County, Inc.)

When parents and teachers share common goals, program objectives are more likely to be achieved. The following survey of values can be helpful in assessing the priorities of the adults in a program. Results can be used for further discussion and planning. If, for example, the survey reveals that the majority of parents are troubled about the apparent lack of respect for authority among the children, but the teachers are not concerned, there is an obvious area needing reevaluation. Since many of the questions are only general in nature, participants should be encouraged to write in comments and use results for further discussion.

Values Survey for Parents and Teachers

For each situation select one choice which is of *most* importance to you and write the corresponding letter under *most imp*. Then select the choice of *least* importance and put that letter under *least imp*. Make two choices for each item—*most imp*. and *least imp*.

	Most Imp.	Least Imp.

1. You have fifty dollars to spend for children's books. You would   1. _____   _____

    a. select books teaching numbers and letters
    b. select books on family and friends
    c. select books with pictures and words to stir the imagination.

2. In selecting wheel toys you prefer   2. _____   _____
    a. sturdy tricycles and wagons
    b. fire engines, trucks, cars
    c. enough for everyone to ride at one time.

3. In planning preschool room arrangement you would   3. _____   _____
    a. consider the most efficient setup for the teacher
    b. consider on-the-spot ideas and interests of the children
    c. analyze conditions of the room and plan interest centers dealing with special developmental tasks.

4. Which of the following would influence you most/least in selecting art projects?   4. _____   _____
    a. Does it develop a special skill?
    b. Is it attractive and pleasing to parents?
    c. Is it creative, reflecting child's choice?

5. Which would you prefer to study?   5. _____   _____
    a. Ways to control child behavior
    b. Different creative teaching techniques
    c. Developmental tasks to prepare children for school

6. The last time you were dissatisfied with a preschool classroom it was because it was   6. _____   _____
    a. too academic; too much like elementary school
    b. too confusing; too much disorder
    c. too strict; all children doing same thing.

7. The thing that troubles you most when
working with children is   7. _____   _____
    a. lack of respect for authority
    b. messiness (e.g., art work, juice time, cooking)
    c. short attention span of children.

8. You would like most to be remembered
as a person   8. _____   _____
    a. who developed creative activities for children
    b. who handled an entire class with complete control
    c. who helped an individual child achieve a skill.

9. You most often discipline children by   9. _____   _____
    a. directing attention to another activity
    b. isolating child
    c. having child perform task.

10. You most admire the kind of child who is   10. _____   _____
    a. bright for his age
    b. self-motivated, individualistic
    c. well behaved.

Key For Choices Representing Values

	Behavior Control	Creativity	Acquisition of Skills
1.	b	c	a
2.	c	a	b
3.	a	b	c
4.	b	c	a
5.	a	b	c
6.	c	a	b
7.	a	b	c
8.	b	a	c
9.	b	a	c
10.	c	b	a

Formal written evaluations of parents can be a very threatening procedure. Most parents probably shy away from programs that might judge
them or evaluate the quality of their work. Yet there are informal judgments being made all the time. The following evaluation was used with

high school volunteers in a work experience program where supervisors and counselors needed some formal assessment of the student's work. Teachers who need to evaluate volunteers, parents, or student assistants might want to refer to some of the criteria for the purpose of developing their own check sheet or merely using them as a basis for discussion. All such evaluations must be used judiciously.

Evaluation of Program Participants

Participant's Name: _____   Evaluated by: _____

Dates He/She Assisted: _____

1. Performance

Proficient in all areas	Adequate	Needs improvement	Unable to display any useful skills
Imaginative and resourceful	Adequate	Needs improvement	Unimaginative
Learns quickly	Adequate	Needs improvement	Slow to learn

2. Attitude

Responds well to suggestions	Adequate	Needs improvement	Resents authority
Happy, warm personality	Adequate	Needs improvement	Unhappy, cold toward others
Eager and interested	Adequate	Needs improvement	Disinterested

Sympathetic and sensitive	Adequate	Needs improvement	Lacks sensitivity
Relates well to adults	Adequate	Needs improvement	Relates poorly to adults
Relates well to children	Adequate	Needs improvement	Relates poorly to children

3. General Appearance

Neat and properly dressed	Adequate	Needs improvement	Untidy
Arrives on time, often early	Arrives on time	Sometimes late	Very often late or absent

4. Additional Comments:

Information gleaned from parent surveys can be very helpful in planning and revising curriculum content. Written forms such as the following provide an opportunity for parents to express some of their expectations. Some questions may also suggest ideas that parents had not thought about. Some schools ask parents to complete questionnaires while they are visiting or waiting for their children. Others adapt portions as needed. The following is a lengthy survey which was designed and used by a group of experienced teachers in a variety of child care settings. Results of all the schools were summarized and made available to participants for further discussion.

Before using any family information forms, be certain to clear them with your school district and parent board to determine if any of the questions might constitute an invasion of privacy. Some parents object to questionnaires requiring personal information.

Parent Survey of Expectations of the School

In the areas of social development and hygiene, which of the following would you like the school to encourage:

Personal Hygiene

	Yes	No	Don't Know
1. Toilet training	____	____	____
2. Washing hands before and after eating	____	____	____
3. Finishing food	____	____	____
4. Taking a nap	____	____	____
5. Playing outdoors everyday	____	____	____
with warm clothing on cold days	____	____	____
with water play on warm days	____	____	____
barefoot	____	____	____
6. Attending school three days after a cold even if coughing and nose is runny	____	____	____

In the areas of health and hygiene—such as reminding the children to put on or take off their jackets, going to the toilet, washing hands, eating, etc.—I believe the teachers are: (check along the continuum)

Too casual	Conscientious	Expected to do too much (parents should do this)

Social Development

	Yes	No	Don't Know
1. Developing respect for authority	____	____	____

	Yes	No	Don't Know
2. Calling teacher by first name	___	___	___
3. Learning to stand up for own rights	___	___	___
by speaking out	___	___	___
by fighting	___	___	___
4. Learning good manners	___	___	___
5. Developing self-reliance	___	___	___

1. If your child is using swear words, how important is it for the teacher to stop him?

   Very important ___ Not very important ___ Not important at all ___

2. How important is it for the teacher to encourage your child to use his or her right hand instead of left?

   Very important ___ Not very important ___ Not important at all ___

3. Is it all right for teachers to spank?

           Yes ___ No ___ Don't Know ___

4. If your son prefers to play with girls, play with dolls, and play dress-up and housekeeping, do you wish the teacher to redirect him?

           Yes ___ No ___ Doesn't matter ___

5. If your daughter prefers to play with boys, do carpentry, and do rough and tumble games, do you wish the teacher to redirect her?

           Yes ___ No ___ Doesn't matter ___

Which of the following do you feel are important for your child to learn by the time he or she leaves nursery school or the center?

	Important	Good but not essential	Not important
1. Printing own name	___	___	___

	Important	Good but not essential	Not important
2. Recognizing/naming colors	____	____	____
3. Recognizing/counting numbers	____	____	____
4. Reading simple books	____	____	____
5. Recognizing/naming shapes	____	____	____
6. Understanding concepts like big/little, tall/short, etc.	____	____	____
7. Using correct grammar	____	____	____
8. Learning to speak English	____	____	____

In teaching things like reading, writing, arithmetic, and language, I believe: (check any number)

The teacher should be responsible for most of this ____

The parent should be responsible for most of this ____

The teacher should involve the parents in helping to reinforce these teachings in

the home ____

In teaching manners—how to behave and what is right and wrong—who should have the main responsibility?

The school ____   Home ____   Both ____   Other ____

Which of the following acitivities do you feel the school should have?

	Important	Good but not essential	Not important
1. Painting at easels	____	____	____
2. Finger painting	____	____	____
3. Cutting and pasting	____	____	____
4. Coloring neatly within lines	____	____	____

	Important	Good but not essential	Not important
5. Using play dough and clay	_____	_____	_____
6. Learning to sing	_____	_____	_____
7. Learning to dance	_____	_____	_____
8. Listening to music	_____	_____	_____
9. Listening to stories	_____	_____	_____
10. Dramatic play—dress-ups, make believe	_____	_____	_____
11. Climbing outdoors	_____	_____	_____
12. Riding wheel toys	_____	_____	_____
13. Cooking	_____	_____	_____
14. Sewing	_____	_____	_____
15. Science projects	_____	_____	_____
16. Field trips	_____	_____	_____
17. Bringing examples of work home	_____	_____	_____

Different schools have different policies about parent participation. Which policy (or policies) do you prefer?

1. Parents required to help teach _____

2. Parents prohibited from participating _____

3. Parents and teachers have equal responsibility in classroom _____

4. Teachers have major responsibility with parents as assistants _____

5. Parent help welcomed but not required _____

If your child were to attend a school where parents are encouraged to partici-pate, check the statements that apply to you:

Evaluations   193

1. I would like to participate but don't have the time. _____

2. I prefer not to work with children. _____

3. Parents ought to be in the classroom. _____

4. Parents don't belong in a classroom. _____

5. I would participate if the teacher told me exactly what to do. _____

6. I would work if the teacher left me alone. _____

7. The only reason I participate is because I'm required to. _____

8. I think I'm a good assistant and the teacher appreciates me. _____

Other _____

What do you think helps to make a good teacher of young children?

	Important	Good but not essential	Not important
1. Dressing neatly	_____	_____	_____
2. Patience	_____	_____	_____
3. College education	_____	_____	_____
4. Sense of humor	_____	_____	_____
5. Being aware of latest developments in the field of education	_____	_____	_____
6. Intelligence	_____	_____	_____
7. Being friendly to parents	_____	_____	_____
8. Being outgoing	_____	_____	_____

List other qualities:

Sometimes teachers do not know what parents expect. Think about the "good" teachers you know and the things they do and say that impress you as good qualities. List these:

What are some of the negative or ineffective qualities that teachers should avoid?

If you had to attend two meetings a year at your child's school, what would you want to do at these meetings?

1. Have a potluck dinner _____ have school supply dinner _____

2. Listen to a speaker _____ on what subject?

3. Look at films or slides of your children _____

4. Have a workshop to learn art techniques _____, storytelling _____,

teaching reading _____, teaching writing _____, music _____, other _____

5. Discuss adult problems _____ on what subject? _____

6. Others:

What would you like your child to be when he or she is an adult?

How do you think teachers can help you reach this goal?

How many of your children are attending a nursery school or child care

center? _____ Ages and sex: _____

How many hours each day does each child attend? _____

Why is the child (or children) attending a center or school? _____

_____

Do you think there is too much _____, not enough _____, or adequate _____ structure in the program of the school?

Are you satisfied with the discipline? Yes _____ No _____ Comments:

Family Information:

Ethnic/racial background (e.g., Black, Chinese, Chicano, Caucasian, etc.)

_____

Religious background (e.g., Catholic, Protestant, Buddhist, Atheist, etc.)

_____

Marital status of parents or guardian: Married _____ Divorced _____

Separated _____ Widowed _____ Single _____ Other (Explain) _____

Age of parents or guardians: Male _____ Female _____

Number of people living in home: _____

Number of children in home: _____ Ages and sex:

Primary language spoken in home: _____

Occupation of mother _____ father _____

What are some of the things you like about your child's school?

What do you think needs improvement?

Examples of Questionnaires Used with Chinese Families

The following can be adapted for use with other bilingual and ethnic minorities.

Sample Questionnaire

Mother   Father   (circle one)   Name of child: _____

Place of birth: _____   Sex: _____

How long in U.S.: _____   Age: _____

1. When your child grows up, what kind of adult do you want him or her to be? What kind of job? Living where? What kind of friends? Speaking mostly Chinese or English? Married to a Chinese?

2. What do you think we should be teaching your child in school?

3. What are the most important things we can teach your child that you can't?

4. What things do you teach your child at home that you want us to reinforce?

5. What values do you want your child to retain, even if they are different from those of the American culture?

Sample Questionnaire

Please number the following items according to your order of preference—for instance, #1 for the item you like best, and #5 for the item you like least.

_____ a. Language class (Classes will be provided for small groups of parents interested in conversational English or conversational Chinese.)

_____ b. Cooking, nutrition, and health classes

_____ c. Lending library of books, games, and bilingual materials to parents

_____ d. Training program for parents interested in volunteering and substituting in the classroom or teaching their children at home

_____ e. Center newsletter (This letter will enable board, parents, and staff to communicate about child care news, children's progress, board structure, etc.)

_____ f. American culture/Chinese culture (Class will be provided for parents interested in learning about the customs and ways of another culture.)

_____ g. Field trips (Going to different places in the city with the children.)

_____ h. Handicrafts

_____ i. More frequent parent meetings with teachers, either in small groups or individually. There may be specialized learning groups such as single parents, English classes, child health classes, child care legislation group, etc.

_____ j. Parent visits to other child care centers.

Sample Questionnaire

Parent Program

1. I would like to be trained in the classroom as a volunteer or a substitute.

_____ A.M.   _____ P.M.   _____ full day

2. I would like to come and observe the center.

_____ yes   _____ no

3. I am interested in visiting other child care centers.

_____ yes   _____ no

4. I would like to hold our monthly parent meeting in

_____ a small group   _____ a large group   _____ alternately

5. I would like to hear discussions on

_____ health   _____ nutrition   _____ curriculum

_____ community involvement   _____ Asian American History

_____ child development   _____ discipline   _____ comparison of

Chinese and American educational philosophies and methods

6. I would like to participate on the board and learn about policy making.

_____ yes   _____ no

7. I would like to be informed about the center and child care news and legislation through a newsletter.

_____ yes   _____ no

8. I would like to be kept informed on community events.

_____ yes   _____ no

9. I would like to participate in the community events that are related to child care.

_____ yes   _____ no

Sample Questionnaire

Center—Curriculum

1. I would like my child to learn more

    _____ Chinese _____ English _____ Chinese culture

    _____ American culture

2. I would like my child to be aware of the values of good and bad, feelings of happy and unhappy things.

    _____ yes _____ no

3. I would like my child to know how to treat others:

    _____ to coöperate _____ to share _____ to love

    _____ to help

4. I feel that the following qualities are important for the growth of my child:

    _____ creativity _____ adaptability _____ imagination

    _____ spontaneity _____ independence

    _____ observation-perceptiveness

    _____ sense of responsibility _____ filial piety

    _____ honesty _____ morality _____ respect

5. I would like my child to learn how to

    _____ fight for himself _____ defend himself

6. I want my child to play with weapons or war games.

    _____ yes _____ no

7. I want my child to be aware of the surroundings—i.e., neighborhood— through field trips.

    _____ yes _____ no

8. I want my child to take field trips outside of Chinatown to different neighborhoods and see how other people live.

_____ yes _____ no

9. I want my child to take field trips to places of nature in order to have a better understanding of our natural environment.

_____ yes _____ no

10. I want my child to participate in the following activities regardless of lack of personal interest:

_____ cooking _____ music _____ reading

_____ drawing _____ exercise _____ games

_____ creative movement _____ science _____ math

11. I would like my child to call the teacher by his or her

_____ first name _____ last name _____ either

12. I would like my child to try finger painting and other messy art activities even if it means getting dirty.

_____ yes _____ no

13. I would like my child to play with water under the supervision of a teacher.

_____ yes _____ no

14. I would like my child to learn to express himself or herself freely and openly even if this is very different from the Chinese way.

_____ yes _____ no

Evaluating Children

Certain areas of a child's development are more easily measured than others. For example, social and emotional growth are probably most accurately assessed by people who have been able to work closely with the child over a period of time. These evaluations are more subjective (relying on personal judgments) than tests where there are right and wrong answers. Both kinds of evaluations must be taken into account, however, in appraising the child's overall development. In most cases, the evaluations in this section are designed for teacher use, but any of them can be shared with parents. Some of the items can be answered more accurately with input from the parents. In some instances when a mother or father indicates an interest in evaluating his or her child, the teacher should feel free to share these checklists and forms.

Parents often want more information about the kinds of things their children are expected to know before starting grade school. Both parents and teachers can work with children on all of the following school-related skills:

Number concepts. Simply knowing how to count does not mean that a child truly understands numerical concepts. Young children will often rattle off their numbers in the same way they recite a rhyme. When asked to count out groups of four, or assign a number to a specific object, they clearly do not understand what numbers symbolize. In order to increase numerical understanding, parents and teachers can ask the child to set the table and count the correct number of forks, spoons, plates, napkins, etc. Playing games that require making a certain number of moves, counting objects, or making change all teach number concepts. Using and explaining words such as *bigger, smaller, more, less, taller,* and *shorter* all help the child relate his experiences to quantitative terms.

Form discrimination. Learning to read requires the ability to discriminate between different forms. Children must be able to see that *o* and *a* and *b* and *d* are not the same. Learning to see differences is based on experience in making fine discriminations. Activities requiring sorting skills are good exercises for enhancing skills in discrimination. For example, have the children sort coins, buttons, nuts and bolts, and other small objects. Another good game is blindfolding the children or having them close their eyes while reaching into a bag and pulling out a specified object from among several familiar things. Or let them name the objects they think they feel. Card games, tracing shapes, copying letters, and art experiences all help children learn to distinguish forms.

Naming colors. Children see many colors in their environment but they have to be taught to name or label these colors. Begin with primary colors and make a game of asking them to point to colors and name them. Praise them when they are correct. Help them practice color naming by referring to clothing, toys, crayons, and other common objects. Make learning a natural part of their daily activities.

Visual memory and visual perception. These two skills are essential to learning how to read. When children learn to read the word *dog,* they will have to be able to remember the shapes of that particular group of letters and recognize the configuration as *dog* when they see it again. Matching objects according to shape, size, and color all teach visual perception.

Play games where you set out three different colors, cover them, and have children reproduce the same sequence from memory. Do the same with shapes, playing cards, etc.

Speaking vocabulary. School success is closely related to verbal skills. Children must be able to communicate their thoughts and ideas to others. The best way to help children develop verbal skills is to listen to them attentively, ask questions, and encourage them to talk. Use words in your own speech to help them learn new phrases and new labels. Make a game of naming things. Carry on discussions; use complete sentences; praise them for being verbally expressive.

Listening vocabulary. Listening skills are necessary to understand what others say. A child who talks all the time, but does not listen is not likely to do well in school. Books and reading are excellent sources for developing good listening in young children. Finger plays, stories, puppet shows, and group interactions all entice young children to listen.

General knowledge. The more firsthand experiences children have with their environment and with other people, the more likely they are to have a broader, richer background of general knowledge. Field trips, nursery school experiences, opportunities to do many things with many people all serve to enhance knowledge and serve as a broad base for later learning.

Child Evaluation Form

The physical, emotional, social, and intellectual areas of a child's development form the basis for teacher-parent discussions and observations. There are many forms available in child development books and classes in observation. The following suggested items to explore under each category are simply to aid the adult in determining the important characteristics to concentrate on. In making up your own evaluation of a child, it is helpful to go over these topics to be sure you are covering all aspects of the child's development. It is also helpful to review this list before a parent or home conference.

Child's Physical Development

1. Activity level: Is the child characteristically active, slow moving, etc.?

2. Energy level: Does the child tire readily? Is the child energetic, able to make good use of his natural level of energy in relation to his abilities? Is the child easily overstimulated or slow to work up to energetic activities?

3. Large-muscle skills/small-muscle coordination: Does the child show an obvious preference for one over the other? Does the child handle activities requiring use of both large- and small-muscle coordination well? Are there areas in which help is needed?

4. Health: Are the child's physical health, rate of growth, vision, and hearing satisfactory?

Child's Emotional Development

1. How does the child typically deal with frustrations—express feelings openly, repress them, deal with them in socially acceptable ways? Does the child use effective methods of control? Does she rely on herself or others to relieve frustrations and tensions? Does she have self-confidence?

2. Is the child's observed emotional development consistent between home and school? Do the people who know the child best agree on his level of emotional maturity? In what areas of interaction does the child appear to need help in emotional growth? How can school and home work toward reducing frustration and planning more rewarding experiences for the child?

3. Can the child understand and respond to adult acceptance of feelings but not behavior? Can she verbalize and redirect her anger and negative feelings into positive channels? Is she developing normally and are her emotions appropriate for a child her age?

Child's Social Development

1. Child's relationship with adults; peers. Is he well liked? Does he prefer one or two close friends? Is he selective about playmates? Is he consistent from day to day? Is he able to share toys as well as friends? Is his focus of social interaction objects—like toys, blocks, books, etc.—or other people—running, jumping, talking?

2. Is the child self-directed, getting into and out of social situations independently? Is the child skilled in initiating play situations? Does he depend on others to lead?

3. Can the child interchange leadership and subordinate roles comfortably? How do other children relate to him?

4. Does the child express her individuality, assert her ideas with adults? With peers? Does she extend her self-awareness to being a member of a group? Where is she obviously comfortable or uncomfortable in her social relations?

Child's Intellectual Development

1. Level of language expression: Can the child verbalize accurately and effectively? Does he talk about his experiences and ideas?

2. Concentration span: Does she attend to tasks? Stories? Directions? Is she interested and engaged in projects and carrying out ideas to a conclusion? Can she defer gratification?

3. Can he distinguish between reality and pretending? Does he have a sense of humor? Does he relate stories and ideas in proper sequence?

4. Is he able to do school-related tasks (numbers, letters, concepts) as well as other children his age? Does he enjoy the challenge of learning new things? Does he learn quickly? Give up easily? Depend on others to tell him what to do?

5. Is he able to accept limits and show through his behavior that he has internalized many of the "rules" of his environment?

6. Are her intellectual goals too high? Too low? Is she under pressure, from herself or others, to achieve? To excel? To compete?

Developmental Tasks

The following checklist, adapted from the Santa Clara County Inventory of Developmental Tasks, can be used by parents and teachers to determine the level of development of children four to six years of age. Additional tasks can be designed to strengthen areas that need more work.

Ratings: 0 – Cannot accomplish   1 – Awkward   2 – Smooth

Name of Child: _____ Date: _____

Large-Muscle Motor Skills	0	1	2
1. Child walks up stairs alternating feet.	___	___	___
2. Child runs and stops on signal from teacher.	___	___	___

	0	1	2

3. Child stands with both feet together and jumps forward as far as possible. _____ _____ _____

4. Child hops on one foot for a distance of ten feet, then turns and hops back using alternate foot. _____ _____ _____

5. Child balances on one foot for five seconds, then repeats with other foot. _____ _____ _____

6. Balance beam: Child can walk forward on beam. _____ _____ _____

7. Balance beam: Child can walk beam backward. _____ _____ _____

8. Say to child, "Throw the ball up in the air and catch it." _____ _____ _____

9. Child can skip a distance of twenty feet. _____ _____ _____

Small-Muscle Motor Skills (Visual Motor)

10. Child strings five beads in two minutes or less. _____ _____ _____

11. Child makes two copies of a circle. _____ _____ _____

12. Child makes two copies of a cross. _____ _____ _____

13. Child makes two copies of a square. _____ _____ _____

14. Child makes two copies of a triangle. _____ _____ _____

15. Child makes two copies of a diamond. _____ _____ _____

16. Child can cut with scissors. _____ _____ _____

17. Child can cut on line with scissors. _____ _____ _____

18. Child can lace shoes. _____ _____ _____

19. Child can tie shoes. _____ _____ _____

20. Child can copy letters of name. _____ _____ _____

21. Child can print name by self. _____ _____ _____

22. Note left or right hand dominance. _____ _____ _____

Visual Perception

0   1   2

23. Matching colors
    Materials: three squares each, red, yellow, blue, orange, and green
    Say, "See these colors. Find all the ones that are this color (pick up one)." Proceed with others. _____ _____ _____

24. Matching shapes
    Materials: three shapes each (same color) square, triangle, rectangle, and diamond
    Say, "See all these shapes. Point to another one just like this one." _____ _____ _____

25. Matching size
    Materials: eight squares four different sizes
    Say, "See all these squares. Point to another square the same size as this one." _____ _____ _____

Auditory Memory

25. Child can perform three commands.
    Say, "I am going to ask you to do some things. Listen carefully, wait until I am through talking, then do what I say."
    Give the child three commands, such as "Place your hands on your head, then turn around, then touch the door." _____ _____ _____

26. Child can repeat a tapping sequence.
    Teacher claps hands in rhythmic pattern and child repeats pattern.
    a. •   •   • _____ _____ _____

    b. • •   •   • _____ _____ _____

    c. •   • •   • • _____ _____ _____

    d. • • • •   • _____ _____ _____

27. Child can repeat four numbers.
    Say, "Listen carefully. I'm going to say some numbers and when I'm through you say them right after me." (Speed: one per second)

    6 - 2 - 9 - 7   8 - 3 - 1 - 6 _____ _____ _____

Note: An excellent inexpensive School Readiness Survey booklet by Jordan and Massey that parents and teachers can use to test their four- to six-year-old children can be purchased from Consulting Psychologists Press, Inc., 577 College Ave., Palo Alto, Calif. 94306.

Language Development Guides

The following language development guides for children ages one through six developed by the Palo Alto Unified School District Speech and Language Department should be helpful to parents and teachers who wish to evaluate children's progress.

Age: 1–2 years

Expressive Language
Vocabulary:

(12 mo.)

Note: Active vocabulary may be slower due to motor development.

1–3 words
labeling:
objects: ball, cup, bed
animals: dog, cat
people: mama, dada
names: 1–3 pictures

(15 mo.)

10–15 words
may include: bye-bye, go, hi, no, yes

(18 mo.)

15–50 words
Combines 2 different words;
uses 50 percent nouns;
adjectives and some adverbs

extensive vocabulary
and echoing

Uses verbs but usually not correctly
Refers to name of self; and may
use few names of people
Can ask for simple needs intelligently:
one-fourth of the time

Receptive Language

Understands 120–275 words, including many verbs: eat, cook, play, want, etc.

Follows simple directions (2 or more): "Give it to me," "come here," "stand up," "sit down," "get the chair," "put the block on the chair"

Understands simple questions, i.e., "Where is Mommy?" "Where is the bathroom? Ball?" etc.

(Comprehension may be greater than expression)

Looks at pictures in book selectively, identifying 1–5 objects

Identifies 1–2 or more body parts on doll, i.e., mouth, eyes, feet, nose, ears

Can act or react to gestures

Knows names of acquaintances

Age: 2–3 years

Expressive Language

Vocabulary: can be 50 to over 500 words

(Growth the greatest)

Gives full name upon request (2–3 years)

Refers to self by pronoun but may confuse "I" and "me," and may use name (i.e., "Jimmy do it.")

May repeat "I" frequently and/or first syllable of first words

Beginning to use 2–4 word sentences

Sentence length (mean): 1.8 words   simple phrases, noun-verb combinations: "good (girl, boy)," "car go," "me play ball"

   Verbalizes toilet needs
   Asks: "What's this (or that)?"
   Enjoys matching words with objects

Phonemes: many consonant substitutions, i.e., *a/r, t/f, th/s* (lisping), *t/s*

Generally *from 2.6 years:*

Tells sex: "Are you a boy or girl?"
Uses 3-word sentence (mean length: 2.3–3.1 words)
Uses plurals, pronouns, adjectives, adverbs "more" (indicating another)
Repetition of nursery rhymes begins
Intelligibility—can be understood half of the time (depends on child)

Receptive Language

Identifies 2–7 pictures named; i.e., book, cat, house, chair, candy

Identifies 4–6 doll or body parts (pointing or naming)

Follows directions (4): "Put the car (or block) on the table." "Give me the cup and spoon."

Understands: "Give me one."
   Size comparisons (big, little)
   Prepositions (2 or more): in, under, on . . .
   Descriptive words (1–3), i.e., fast, old, hard

Discriminates between "my" and "your"

Environmental object experience (2–4)
   "Show me what we use to comb hair, drink milk, cook on . . ."

Performs baby games or pantomimes on command.

Age: 3–4 years

Expressive Language

Vocabulary: 400–600–1000+ words; 1200 at 3.6 years.
   nouns–19 percent

Gives full name

Counts to 3; (3.6 years: answers "how many" up to 3)

Names 3–4 primary colors (red, blue, yellow . . .)

Expresses desire for "my turn"

Uses 4–6 word sentences: frequent words—I want, is, it, you, me, that, a, do, this, not

Sentence length: 3.4–3.5 words, 3½ years: 4.3 words

Continues to use pronouns, prepositions, adjectives, adverbs, plurals

Subject and predicate (together) *often* missing: "a little chair," "there a boy," "takes shoes off".

Samples of parts of grammar the child may be using:
(Structural feature underlined)
Daddy worked (past verb)
Boy going (verb + ing)
Get ball (verb + noun)
Come here (verb + adverb)
Eat at home (verb + preposition)
Eat it up (verb + particle)
We go (noun + verb agreement)
he works/ they work (verb forms)

Talks to self in monologue: asks himself questions and answers; i.e., "What's that? A bathtub, that's what it is."

Learns to whisper

Will provide answers for questions; i.e.,
   a. Physical needs: What do you do when you are sleepy? hungry? cold?
   b. Function: What is a book (key, stove) for? (answers one or more)
   c. "when," "what": When you go to bed, what do you wear?
   d. "if": If you fell down, what would you do? If you wanted a cookie . . . ?
   e. "who," "where": "Who is he?" "Where is the cat?"

May sing a simple song.

Tells experiences and describes activities (attempting adult sentence structure).

Receptive Language

Understands 400–800 words

Recognizes two or more different kinds of (picture) action; i.e., "Where are the children running?" eating? jumping?

Environmental object experience (4 or more)
   Which one combs hair?
   Which one . . . put on our feet?

Distinguishes part and whole (2)
　　Where are the wheels of the car?
　　Where is the tail of the horse?

Follows 2-part command (3 years) in sequence, 3-part command (3.6 years)
　　Give me the ball, open the door . . . and come and sit down.

Understands 3–4 or more prepositions (in, on, under, out, etc.) and demonstrates with object, i.e., Put the doll <u>under</u> the chair.

Understands taking turns

Understanding of abstractions: Show me a "happy" face; "sad" face.

Categorizes objects (2 or more): Show me or find all, i.e., animals, things we eat, toys . . .

Responds to big, little, fast, slow, soft, hard; compares size—long, short. (3.6 years)

Recognizes time in pictures (one or more)—Which one is nighttime? Which one is daytime?

Responds to 1–4 nursery rhymes, stories (5–15 minutes)
　　Understands story order
　　Watches TV cartoons

Additional grammar comprehension (the child understands when the following are heard):
　　a. up/down
　　b. who/what
　　c. verb tenses: i.e., will ride (future), is riding (present), rode (past)
　　d. The baby <u>is</u> crying. The baby <u>is not</u> crying (negative). The baby <u>isn't</u> crying (contraction).
　　e. he/she/they (3rd person, singular and plural) her, him/them (masculine and feminine)
　　f. The <u>boy</u> pushes the <u>girl</u> (active doer, receiver). The <u>girl</u> pushes the <u>boy</u>.

Age: 4–5 years

Expressive Language

Vocabulary: 600–1500+ words

Gives age and birthday

Responds to physical needs (three or more)
   What do you do when you are sleepy? hungry? cold?

Can tell opposites (two or more)
   Brother is a boy, sister is a

   Father is a man, mother is a _____.

   In daytime it is light, at night it is _____.

Counts to 10 or more (rote)

Comprehends and responds to senses (one or more)
(4.5 years) What do you do with your eyes? What do you do with your ears?

Comprehends and responds to remote events (one or more)
(4.5 years) What do you do when you have lost something? What do you do
before you cross the street?

Asks meanings of words and can define 4 words by use (4.5 years)

Names penny, nickel, dime; names at least 6 colors (4.5 years)

Sentence length (mean): 4 years: 4.4–4.6 words
                        4.6 years: 4.5–4.9 words
   Uses subject and predicate, but may be defective: "The boy gonna go town."
   "The mommy taking a bath now."
   May omit words (articles, parts of verb, etc.) "Dog eat bone." "That a truck."
   Expresses thought mainly in present time; past may be in present: "The horsie
   fall down." "The man come in."
   Still uses some gestures for talking
   Talks while drawing; playing
   Verbalizes much self-praise
   Listens to and tells long stories—may confuse fact and fiction
   Reads and tells a familiar story by way of pictures

   Intelligibility—can be understood almost all the time.

Additional grammar—child may use:
   a. Compound nouns: teakettle, ballgame
   b. that boy, girl, etc.
   c. Other pronouns: one, anyone, etc.
   d. Possession: that's mine. Joey's ball
   e. Contractions
   f. Negatives

g. Verb tense forms:
   He <u>goes/went</u>
   I've <u>got</u> a dog.
   I like <u>to</u> play.
   <u>Do</u> you/<u>does</u> he go?

Receptive Language

Understands 800–1500 words

Follows 3–4 action commands in sequence: "Put the ball in the box, give me the box, sit down."

Demonstrates meaning of abstract words by pantomime: happy, sad, mad (same as 3–4 years)

Understands use (5–7)—show or find one that: swims in the water, tells time, we write with, we read, we cut with, we eat at,

Understands 4–6 prepositions: on, in, under, by, between, in front of, etc.

Differentiates texture: smooth, rough

Understands number concept of 3; understands "pair"
   (4.6 years) may respond to requests with 4–10 items

Differentiation of both sides of body—i.e., can touch left thumb against right thumb

Can remember and say a nursery rhyme in sequence

Gets information from children's TV programs

Grammar comprehension (what the child understands when heard)
   a. his/her; their
   b. is/are (singular and plural verbs)
   c. when/where questions
   d. "er"—paint/painter; farm/farmer
   e. two adjectives—a large red ball; a small blue bus
   f. either/or—(i.e.) *Either* open the door *or* the window.

Age: 5–6 years

Expressive Language

Vocabulary: 1400–2200 words
            2500 words (5.6–6.6 years)

Can tell full name, age, birthday (same as 4.6 years)

Class grouping—names 6 or more animals upon request

Comprehends and responds to senses (2 or more): What do you do with your eyes? ears? nose?

Uses time sense words: morning, afternoon, night. (5.6 years) yesterday, tomorrow, next week

Can name days of week (5.6 years)

Can name: penny, nickel, dime, and now quarter

Asks for word meanings: gives own definitions by usage, description, and/or by categorization of the object.

Gives description and explanation of a picture

Relates experiences—may have mixture of real and unreal

Sentence length (mean): 5.0–5.7 words
        –5.8+ words (5.6 years)

Can organize thoughts into complete sentences: "The dog is in the yard." "There was a fish in that bowl."

Most statements in the present, but also uses past and future verbs: "I think trucks can go fast." "Two boys were eating." "The girl got in the bathtub."

Will evaluate his/her abilities: "I don't think I can do that." "I can't do too good."

Speech is often fully intelligible:
Corrects own errors in learning to pronounce new words
Correct usage of all parts of speech; i.e., nouns, adjectives, pronouns, verbs, noun and verb agreement, etc.

Receptive Language

Understands 1500–2000+ words

Can recognize or point to higher level vocabulary, i.e., signal, freckle

Follows 3, 4, or 5 action commands in sequence (5.6 years) "Give me the cat, close the door, pick up the ball, and put it in the box, . . . and go take a nap."

Distinguishes weight differences (4 or more). Show me which is heavier, a bird or cow? bed or chair? boot or shoe? car or truck? rock or leaf?

Knows most common opposites:

(5.6 years)

big, small	up, down
hot, cold	in, out
dark, light	on, off

Knows body parts (8 or more): head, arm, hand, knee, heel, eyebrow, little finger, elbow, chin, palm

Can name 5 or more colors: red, blue, green, yellow, purple, brown, black, orange

Comprehends right (right hand)
(5.6 years) right and left

Understands number or relative quantity:
   a. Number concepts, 4–9 or more
   b. Some, many, middle

Comprehends and remembers longer stories and then can retell

Additional:

Grammar comprehension:
   a. verb-noun agreement: The boys jump. The man jumps.
   b. adjective contrasts: faster/slower, tall/taller, tall/short,
      verb and noun: catch/catcher
   c. demonstratives: these/those, that/this
   d. clauses beginning with: if ("If you are a boy, show me the car."), because, why
   e. passive doer, receiver: "The boy is chased by the dog."

Teacher Evaluations

Regardless of a person's job, everyone benefits from taking a look at what he is doing and how well he is doing at any appointed task. It seems particularly essential when that job is one in which success or the outcome is heavily dependent on interpersonal interaction and growth of self-knowledge.

Teachers who work with parents must constantly assess how well they are communicating, directing, involving, sharing, teaching, and cooperating with others. Unless the teacher takes time to evaluate what he or she is doing, there is no systematic way of knowing where the strengths and weaknesses of a program lie.

The purposes for teacher evaluations are the same as for other areas and people in the school: to identify areas where improvement is needed, revise methods, and learn more about yourself. Teachers who are confident about their abilities welcome the opportunity to use reliable feedback for professional growth.

When teachers have adequate input into the design of the evaluation instrument, and when they know the results are not going to be used against them, they are more likely to see the positive aspects of such an assessment. Unless you know yourself, and unless you develop self-awareness and insight, you cannot grow and mature in your job. There is less room for improvement if you aren't aware of the problems. Also, you cannot build on your strengths unless you get some feedback from others regarding their perceptions of your strengths and weaknesses.

The best kind of teacher evaluation form is one that is designed by the teacher. The work of having to identify teaching strengths and weaknesses is an exercise in self-evaluation. Most teachers agree that by the time they have finished making up an evaluation questionnaire about themselves, they already have a good idea of where they need to improve.

The beginning teacher is more likely to feel on trial before coworkers and supervisors. The beginner is also more susceptible to self-blame and self-criticism. Unfortunately, job security is often closely tied in with evaluations, so it is no wonder that the new teacher is anxious about the outcome of such measurements.

Teachers ought to know what the evaluations look like, how they are to be used, and have an opportunity to discuss them with the evaluators. The most helpful results accrue when the teacher is given the information to use in his or her own way.

As teachers become more experienced and more confident, they realize that evaluations are only one source of feedback about their performance. The main resource for gaining satisfaction lies not in the outer academic world, but in the inner and personal aspects of the teacher's life. This does not mean teachers ignore the perceptions of others, but personal standards based on experience begin to take on greater importance. Teacher's are better able to judge the value of others' impressions and weigh these against self-knowledge. They can be more objective about reading their evaluations, and the changes they make will be more compatible with their self-assessments.

Growth in self-understanding comes about through many years of hard work and determination to know yourself. There are many self-evaluation techniques that teachers can use to sharpen their abilities to assess themselves.

One of the ways to practice evaluating yourself is to imagine what others might say under certain circumstances. For example, a group of teachers wrote down what they thought a particular group of parents might want and not want from a co-op school. Here are some of their guesses:

"What I think the parents want from a co-op school:"

1. To get to see what their children are doing.

2. To see if the teachers are doing a good job.

"What I think the parents do not want from a co-op school:"

1. They don't want to have to spend so much time working at the school.

2. They don't want to be embarrassed by their child or their inability to work as a teacher.

The same teachers were asked to write down what they (the teachers) wanted the parents to do in school and also what they did not want the parents to do. Here are examples of some of their responses:

"What I want parents to do in school:"

1. Help relieve me of some of my work.

2. Learn more about good teaching methods to use at home.

"What I do not want parents to do at school:"

1. Pay too much attention to their own children.

2. Disagree with the way I work and use methods that are contradictory to mine.

Parents were asked to do the same thing by imagining what the teachers would say. Many were surprised to compare responses (names were not used), and these results were used as a basis for discussing expectations and growth in self-awareness.

Teachers need to be clear about all the roles they fill during the day. At times they are authority figures who make decisions about the children and parents. During these times, the expectation is that others will be subordinate to their superior knowledge or experience. It may be a simple situation like taking the lead in doing an art project. Many times during the day, routine tasks in the curriculum make it appropriate for someone, usually the teacher, to assume a leadership role.

Other times, teachers are casual friends who chat with parents about activities which may or may not be related to the school. These incidental exchanges are a necessary part of relationships with parents and they serve to redefine roles. At other times teachers may be reinforcers, giving support to parents; or, teachers may be information seekers or givers.

Both teachers and parents need to be conscious of these role changes because evaluations of teachers can be based unfairly on one role expectation when in reality the teacher was not carrying out that particular role responsibility.

When several groups of co-op parents were interviewed and asked to share things they liked and didn't like, along with suggestions for improvement of the parent-teacher relationship in the classroom, some of the responses were as follows:

What Parents Liked or Didn't Like about Teachers

1. *Parents liked the teacher who* greeted each child by name and got down to the child's eye level; spoke to all parents by name; planned routines well; asked parents if things were O.K.; was willing to help; seemed always to be in control and confident; did a lot of the dirty, messy work, like cleaning animal cages and changing children's pants instead of asking someone else to do it; was friendly and warm; offered to take over a job so the parent could join in on other projects for a while; was willing to be firm with the parents who needed direction; praised parents when they did a good job; was familiar with everyone else's job; did not criticize.

2. *Parents didn't like the teacher who* was poorly organized; didn't answer questions; talked with only one or two parents and ignored the others; didn't offer to help when help was clearly needed; avoided real work by looking busy with schedules; needed to smile more; was too bossy; didn't give others credit for knowing what to do; didn't seem to care what each parent was doing; when asked a question, would say, "Do whatever you think is best"; did not check with others to help coordinate work; was detached and disinterested; contradicted parents in front of others; had a tense, hurried manner; did not give any feedback.

3. *Some suggestions:* Improve the daily program by planning a theme and talking in advance with the other parents; give feedback and provide closure to the day with some short evaluation of what happened and how well each did; remind each parent of the next day's duties and things to bring; ask for new ideas; take responsibility for suggesting or planning some unusual projects that require extra work; make some extra efforts to lead the team by making suggestions and offering to do more than is expected of the rest of the staff; have discussions at the end of the day and make comments and suggestions based on observations; be responsible for seeing that people who are goofing off get straightened out; inject some humor into the day and help everyone relax!

Self-Evaluation Sheets

Self-evaluation is a necessary and important tool for the parent or teacher who wishes to improve and continue to grow professionally and personally. The following checklist is based on criteria suggested by experienced parents and teachers. Self-evaluations need not be shared with anyone else; the person taking such a "test" can be honest about the responses without fear of being embarrassed. Results can be used privately or can be shared.

What People Mean When They Say, "This Is a Good Teacher!"

Body Language	I am like this	Something I can learn
1. Body relaxed and comfortable, yet alert	_____	_____
2. Movements efficient but unhurried, no stiffness or tenseness	_____	_____
3. Often gets down to child's eye level	_____	_____

	I am like this	Something I can learn

4. Arms and hands relaxed, ready for holding, touching, or hugging rather than close to body or crossed _____ _____

5. Erect posture, poised carriage _____ _____

6. Walking blends appropriately and rhythmically projecting a happy, relaxed, yet efficient mood _____ _____

7. Positions self naturally in strategic spots _____ _____

Voice

1. Well modulated, gentle, quiet, calm, firm _____ _____

2. Never shouts or yells across room or on playground, especially at a child _____ _____

3. Can use voice to involve children in a story or conversation by varying pitch and tone; uses silence and quiet voice effectively _____ _____

4. Speaks efficiently; does not talk "at" children when they are not listening; does not interrupt unnecessarily; doesn't talk, talk, talk, TALK _____ _____

5. Tone sincere and unaffected whether praising or enforcing rules _____ _____

6. Natural; does not use special voice for children _____ _____

Facial Expression

1. Relaxed, happy, cheerful _____ _____

2. Alert eye movements, attentive _____ _____

3. Frequently smiles spontaneously _____ _____

	I am like this	Something I can learn
4. Looks you in the eyes when communicating	_____	_____
5. Clean, healthy appearance	_____	_____

Use of Senses

1. Listens carefully	_____	_____
2. Filters and sorts out significant sounds	_____	_____
3. Considers sounds of whole area and is aware of happy sounds as well as those signaling danger	_____	_____
4. High tolerance for variety of noise and movement; doesn't expect order every moment	_____	_____
5. Touches children often with movements that soothe, guide, redirect, reassure, reinforce	_____	_____

Teaching Style and Strategies

1. Aware of each child's needs	_____	_____
2. Knows and uses children's names	_____	_____
3. Relates to each child's personality	_____	_____
4. Avoids being center of attention	_____	_____
5. Follows child's lead; does not rush child	_____	_____
6. Sensitive to children's feelings; shares in both joys and sorrows	_____	_____
7. Uses positive statements rather than "Don't"	_____	_____
8. Interprets feelings as expressed by behavior rather than just by words	_____	_____
9. Not threatened by visitors or supervisors	_____	_____
10. Aware of clock but not ruled by it	_____	_____

222 Appendix of Resources

Relationship to Other Teachers

	I am like this	Something I can learn
1. Polite, friendly, but no time spent "visiting" to exclusion of children	_____	_____
2. Willing to seek assistance	_____	_____
3. Willing to listen to suggestions and other ideas but not just a "yes" person	_____	_____
4. Aware of other teachers' needs in classroom and prepared to "take over" when necessary	_____	_____
5. Slow about making judgments or expressing uncomplimentary opinions	_____	_____

Personal Appearance

1. Wears clothing appropriate to the day's work and conforming to school standards; no tight-fitting, dirty, or sloppy clothes; none that restrict ability to move quickly or that can't be touched by children's fingers	_____	_____
2. Clean, neat appearance that reflects pride in oneself and consideration for taste of parents and supervisors	_____	_____
3. Little or no jewelry—none that jangles or gets in the way	_____	_____
4. Weight which reflects good health rather than malnutrition or overeating	_____	_____

Source: From Doreen J. Croft, *Be Honest with Yourself: A Self-Evaluation Handbook for Early Education Teachers* (Belmont, Calif.: Wadsworth Publishing Co., Inc., 1976), pp. 118–119. Other supervisor and parent evaluation forms can be found in the same book.

Some helpful questions you can ask in evaluating your effectiveness as a teacher in working with parents are:

1. Have I defined my roles clearly in relation to children, other teachers, parents, assistants, and authorities? Am I clear about role expectations when I am a teacher, a friend, a surrogate parent, confidante, etc.?

2. Am I able to identify those roles and responsibilities I like most and least? (Jot down some of the things you really like and don't like about your job. This will help you define aspects of your role responsibilities that need work.)

3. In what ways can I optimize my relationships with parents, teachers, children, and others?

4. Am I successfully meeting my own expectations in all areas of my job? Specify areas needing improvement.

5. Identify the strong and weak areas of your program. How do you contribute to these? Suggest changes and ways to implement them.

6. Am I satisfied with myself as a teacher? Will I still want to be doing the same things two years from now? How can I gain more satisfaction from my job?

Films

Some free films (all from Modern Talking Picture Service, Inc.*) that have been well accepted by parent groups are:

Four Children, MTP #9056
The story of four Head Start children, so alike as human beings but so different as people. An intimate look at the children and the homes that influence them.

Jenny Is a Good Thing, MTP #9273
Shows how a nutrition program plays a major role in the daily activities of a Head Start center. Narrated by Burt Lancaster with original music score by Noel Stookey of Peter, Paul, and Mary fame.

Discipline and Self-Control, MTP #9055
This film shows how a teacher can establish control in a friendly climate and prevent disciplinary problems; discusses adequate supervision and the dangers of over and under control, and shows how to help a child accept control. Spanish translation available. A discussion guide and program manual elaborating on the principles of preventing and dealing

*Modern Talking Picture films are available on a free loan basis from their libraries throughout the U.S. Write Modern Talking Picture Service, Inc., 16 Spear St., San Francisco, CA 94105, or 2323 New Hyde Park Road, New Hyde Park, NY 11040 for a list of addresses and additional films.

with discipline in the classroom is available through the Office of Child Development, HEW, Washington, D.C. 20201

Parents Are Teachers Too, MTP #9058
Parents perceive the crucial importance of their role as the child's first teacher—and his most continuous teacher. The film's school situation presents ideas for parents to use in encouraging a child's mental and emotional growth through play. Discussion guides available in bulk quantities upon request to Head Start, 1200 19th St. N.W., Washington, D.C. 20505.

Other sources for purchasing or renting films follow:

Arts and Crafts for Children
A series of six short films showing techniques for using crayons, colored chalk, tempera, print making, and water colors. The films rent for $7.50 to $12.50 and run for 6 to 13 minutes each.
Association Instructional Materials
866 Third Avenue
New York, NY 10022

My Art Is Me
This appealing film shows sequences of four- and five-year-olds working with a variety of materials—painting, drawing, sewing, mixing play dough, manipulating clay, constructing wood scrap sculptures—all accompanied by children's songs and brief commentaries by a teacher. Good ideas showing how to encourage creativity by providing a conducive environment, freedom, and support rather than specific direction.
21 minutes, color, rental $21, purchase $270
Film Sales
University of California Extension Media Center
Berkeley, CA 94720

Don't Give Up On Me
Child abuse is a tragedy, of course, but not only for the child. Behind this desperate, out-of-control act lies another wounded childhood . . . that of the abuser herself. Almost always deprived of love and affection in her own formative years, frequently beaten or ignored or even given away by her parents, the girl grows up in spite of it all and becomes a woman and parent herself. And once there, emotionally bruised, immature, smothered by feelings of worthlessness and rejection, she finds herself unable to cope with the dependencies of her own small children. The result: a battered child, born out of a battered parent.

Recreated scenes from an adapted case history about an abusing mother and her case worker. Useful for teachers and parent groups concerned about child abuse.
28½ minutes, color, rental $50, purchase $375 (available for preview)
Motorola Teleprograms, Inc.
4825 N. Scott Street
Schiller Park, Illinois 60176

Sexual Abuse: The Family
Incest is a difficult subject to bring into the open, but many young children are victims. Unlike rape by a stranger, sexual coercion or seduction of a child by a loved parent or relative creates a complex dilemma. This film deals with the topic of incest in a forthright and responsible manner. Teachers and parents will benefit from watching the methods doctors, counselors, and police use to deal with incest.
28 minutes, color, free
Office of Child Development, H.E.W.
Washington, D.C. 20201

Learning to Look
A series of eight short films recommended for preschoolers through third grade designed to encourage children to look at familiar things in a new way. The films cover topics such as "Let's Find Some Faces," "Learning to Look at Hands," "On Your Way to School."
Films vary in length from 7 to 9 minutes, all are in color, rental prices range from $12 to $15 and purchase prices are from $127 to $163 (available for preview).
McGraw-Hill Films
Dept. BF
1221 Avenue of the Americas
New York, NY 10020

Looking for Me
Based on techniques for the use of movement with normal as well as psychotic and handicapped children as an important means of communication. The film shows a young dance therapist working with normal and emotionally disturbed children and also with a group of therapists and teachers. Perhaps the most powerful sequence shows her working individually with two girls, aged two and five, who have lived in complete autistic isolation. The teacher believes that in our overintellectualized society we tend to forget that our first sense of the world was a body sense, and that the more we can reduce the conflict

between body language and verbal language, the more honest we can be with ourselves and others.
29 minutes, black and white, rental $12.50, purchase $175
University of California Extension Media Center
Berkeley, CA 94720

School Is for Children
(Special Education)
This film involves special education for exceptional preschool children, showing how young children learn to interact with one another in specially designed group activities.
17 minutes, color, rental $20, purchase $210
Teacher/parent version, Code No. 1336; children's version to prepare the child for his first trip to school, Code No. 1337. Both versions are also available in Spanish (available for preview).
AIMS Instructional Media Services, Inc.
P.O. Box 1010
Hollywood, CA 90028

Nobody Took the Time
(Special Education)
This film is directed toward the ghetto child handicapped with learning disabilities, the one most often labeled MR. A variety of highly structured classroom and playground techniques help these children learn there is order to everything, develop language, and gain an awareness of their surroundings. A child's basic trust in himself is fostered through loving care and understanding. Parent involvement is encouraged.
26 minutes, black and white, rental $30, purchase $175 (available for preview)
Other films in special education covering reading failure, visual perception, language learning, and physical activities for mentally handicapped children are also available from the same company.
AIMS Instructional Media Services, Inc.
P.O. Box 1010
Hollywood, CA 90028

The Step Behind Series
A series of three films designed to teach adults how to train mentally retarded children in basic skills. The first in the series is *Genesis*, showing step-by-step procedures in teaching dressing, eating, and toileting through the use of behavior modification techniques.
The second is titled *Ask Just for Little Things* and deals with ambulation,

personal hygiene, and attending. The third, *I'll Promise You a Tomorrow,* covers teaching communication, direction following, and group participation.
20–25 minutes, color, rental $25, purchase $250
Hallmark Films and Recordings, Inc.
1511 East North Avenue
Baltimore, MD 21213

What Color Is the Wind?
A study of four-year-old twin boys, one of them blind. The viewers see the story of courageous parents who try to deliver to the blind boy a sense of the visual beauty of life, and both children learn to share the worlds of darkness and light in a touchingly sensitive film. Many film and TV awards.
27 minutes, color, rental $35, purchase $375 (available for preview)
Allan Grant Productions
P.O. Box 49244
Los Angeles, CA 90049

Safety Films
A series of films for children with adults in mind. Some of the titles most suited for preschoolers include *All about Fire, Animals Can Bite, Walk Safe! Young America.* Others deal with bicycle safety, skateboard safety, and healthy heart functions.
10–19 minutes, color, rental $20–$30, purchase $200–300
Pyramid Films
Box 1048
Santa Monica, CA 90406

Kittens Are Born
An intelligent and gentle treatment of the birth process. A beautifully photographed film showing the actual birth of three kittens. There is no narration, only a lilting guitar accompaniment.

Kittens Grow Up
Growth, socialization, and expanding awareness are the themes in this sequel. We see the newborn kittens progress from crawling to walking, from weaning to drinking alone. A simple ballad describes what is happening as the kittens advance from infancy to independence.
12 minutes, color, rental $17, purchase $175 (available for preview)
McGraw-Hill Films
1221 Avenue of the Americas
New York, NY 10020

I Feel . . . Series
Three films in this series deal with love, anger, and fear. In *I Feel Loving,* the young viewer learns that love includes helping each other and also gives you pleasure. This film encourages children to feel, admit, and express love. *I Feel Angry* helps children accept the emotion of anger positively and openly. It answers in a most affirmative way the often unvoiced question, "I'm angry. Do you still love me?" It indicates that though we often cannot control our feelings, we can control our behavior. *I Feel Scared* shows the child that everyone has fears, but fear does not make you weak. It explores reasonable and unreasonable fears and shows how some fears can be overcome or controlled when identified.
10–15 minutes, color, rental $20–$30, purchase $150–$175
Long Island Film Studios
P.O. Box P
Brightwaters, NY 11718

Bubble Bubble Toys and Trouble
A bumbling witch attempts to stir up "the world's worst toy" by dropping into the kettle toys having the worst hazards. Adults who supervise children need to be alert to the seven toy dangers. This film should be used as an aid to discussion on toy safety. A pamphlet, "Think Toy Safety," is also available to special interest groups.
9 minutes, color, free
Modern Talking Pictures
2323 New Hyde Park Road
New Hyde Park, NY 11040
To obtain more information about toy safety, write:
U.S. Consumer Product Safety Commission
Bureau of Information and Education
Washington, D.C. 20207

The Child
A series of child development films covering infancy to two years. *The Child: Part I; Jamie, Ethan and Marlon, The First Two Months* follows three infants immediately following birth to eight weeks. A narrator elaborates briefly on the developmental changes occurring.
The Child: Part II; Jamie, Ethan and Keir, 2–14 Months traces the world of unfolding, learning, and change. We watch the children attempt to learn basic skills of eating, walking, and communicating. By the end of fourteen months, each has begun to develop a distinct personality.

The Child: Part III; Debbie and Robert, 12–24 Months records the development of two children mastering physical skills, learning language, and showing clear signs of developing social skills. Other child development films cover prenatal development, reward and punishment, language development, and infancy.
Each film 29 minutes, color, rental $20, purchase $425 (available for preview)
CRM/McGraw-Hill Films
Del Mar, CA 92014

Sex Role Development
This film examines some specific sex role stereotypes, tracing their transmission to children via the socialization process. Alternate approaches, which are allowing preschoolers to grow up outside of traditional stereotypes, are also explored.
23 minutes, color, rental $35, purchase $295 (available for preview)
CRM/McGraw-Hill Films
Del Mar, CA 92014

Reward and Punishment
Dr. James Gardner presents specific applications of instrumental learning theory to the management of children. Various uses of rewards and punishment are illustrated, and evaluations of results follow.
14 minutes, color, rental $25, purchase $225 (available for preview)
CRM/McGraw-Hill Films
Del Mar, CA 92014

Films for Special Education
The CRM McGraw-Hill Films Company has produced several films dealing with learning disabilities, educably retarded, blind, and cerebral palsy. Each is in color and runs about half an hour. Rentals vary from $25 to $38 each. Previews are available.
CRM McGraw-Hill Films
110 15th Street
Del Mar, CA 92014

Films about Families and Living
Polymorph films produce a series covering marriage, childbirth, parenting, day care, stepparenting, death, divorce, and other family-related topics. Films are in color and are available for rental or purchase. Previews are booked subject to availability.
Polymorph Films
331 Newbury Street
Boston, MA 02115

Film Companies

Other films and filmstrips for children and parent-teacher groups cover such topics as fantasy classics, poetry, learning concepts, family relationships, children's literature, toy safety, and poison prevention.

Write for catalogs:

Education Development Center, Inc.
55 Chapel Street
Newton, MA 02160

Film Associates
11559 Santa Monica Blvd.
Los Angeles, CA 90025

International Film Bureau
332 S. Michigan Avenue
Chicago, IL 60604

Institute for Developmental Studies
Available from:
Anti-Defamation League of B'nai B'rith
315 Lexington Avenue
New York, NY 10016

National Film Board of Canada
680 Fifth Avenue
New York, NY 10019

Parents' Magazine Films, Inc.
Sound and Color Filmstrips
Dept. 16 C
52 Vanderbilt Avenue
New York, NY 10017

U.S. Consumer Product Safety Commission
100 Pine Street, Suite 500
San Francisco, CA 94111
or call toll free
(800) 638-2666

Walt Disney Educational Media Company
Early Childhood Education
800 Sonora Avenue
Glendale, CA 91201

Washington Montessori Institute
2119 S Street, N.W.
Washington, D.C. 20008

Your Multimedia Invitation to the
World of Children's Literature
Weston Woods
Weston, CT 06880

Referral Agencies

A list of emergency phone numbers and other referral agencies should be available for easy reference in every school. Parents and teachers should look up phone numbers and identify contact people so referrals can be made quickly when the need arises.

The numbers for each of the listed agencies can be found under the city or county, in the yellow pages, or under the specific heading in the phone book. The library often has directories compiled with information about local area referral services. The county health department, civic league, chamber of commerce, and service agencies such as the city or county departments of social services are all good sources to consult.

Following are suggested lists of numbers under various headings. Look up the numbers and names where applicable and add your own as needed.

Emergency Referrals and Local Resources

Emergency

Fire _____

Police _____

Medic or Paramedic _____

Ambulance Service _____

Hospital _____

Doctor _____

Poison Control Center _____

Parental Stress Hotline _____

Suicide Prevention _____

Rape Center (Women Against Rape) _____

Abuse (Juvenile Probation; Protective Services) _____

Alcoholics Anonymous _____

Drug Abuse _____

National Runaway Switchboard _____ (800) 621-4000
    (24-hour, toll free, confidential information center for runaway youth
    needing social service information or contact with their families).

Others _____

Legal

Legal Aid _____

American Civil Liberties Union _____

The Divorce Center _____

Friends Outside (support for prisoners' families) _____

Social Welfare Services

Red Cross (blood bank, first aid training, emergency translations, disaster
relief) _____

Family Service Association (counseling, family therapy) _____

Public Health Department (low-cost or free medical services, VD tests,
clinics) _____

Planned Parenthood (health education, family planning) _____

County Department of Social Services (Medi-Cal, food stamps, aid to
families with dependent children) _____

County Welfare Department (general assistance, eligibility screening for
financial aid) _____

Mental Health Services (list local agencies and names of resource
people) _____

Other useful numbers to have available might include agencies serving
the handicapped, parents without partners, consumer affairs, senior citizens, employment training, housing, and rental information.

National Associations

Education (Adult, child, special for handicapped or gifted children)

Adult Education Association of the U.S.A.
810 18th St., N.W.
Washington, D.C. 20006
(202) 347-9574
Provides career information and referral services.

American Association for Gifted Children
15 Gramercy Park
New York, NY 10003
(212) 472-4266
Works with community and professional groups to find gifted children and help them use their abilities for their own satisfaction and the benefit of others.

Association for Childhood Education International
3615 Wisconsin Ave., N.W.
Washington, D.C. 20016
(202) 363-6963
Conducts workshops, maintains information service and library. Publishes books, bulletins, and portfolios.

Association for Children with Learning Disabilities
4156 Library Rd.
Pittsburgh, PA 15234
(412) 881-1191 or (412) 341-1515
Runs schools, camps, recreation programs, parent education, and information services, and publishes books.

Council for Exceptional Children
1920 Association Dr.
Reston, VA 22091
(703) 620-3660
Concerned with children who need special education: mentally gifted, mentally retarded; visually, aurally, or physically handicapped; children with behavioral disorders, learning disabilities, or speech defects.

National Association for Visually Handicapped
305 E. 24th St.
New York, NY 10010
(212) 889-3141

Offers guidance to children and adults, organizes youth activities, publishes and distributes large-print books. Clearinghouse for all public and private services available to the partially seeing.

National Blindness Information Center
1346 Connecticut Ave., N.W.
Suite 212
Washington, D.C. 20036
(800) 424-9770 (toll free)
National hotline for information and referral service for blindness.

The Orton Society, Inc.
8415 Bellona Lane
Towson, MD 21204
Information on dyslexia and learning and reading disorders.

Social Services (Family planning, counseling and guidance, general information, especially for women and parents)

American Association of Marriage and Family Counselors
225 Yale Avenue
Claremont, CA 91711
(714) 621-4749
Provides nationwide marriage and family counseling. Runs a referral service from the national office.

Big Brothers of America
220 Suburban Station Building
Philadelphia, PA 19103
(215) 567-2748
Provides guidance through friendship on an individual basis to boys in "father-absent" homes.

Big Sisters, Inc.
135 E. 22nd St.
New York, NY 10010
(212) 675-1920
Casework, counseling, psychiatric consultation for girls sixteen and under, and their families.

Family Service Association of America
44 E. 23rd St.
New York, NY 10010
(212) 674-6100
Provides family counseling services in over two hundred communities in the U.S.

Information Center for the National Easter Seal Society
2023 W. Ogden Ave.
Chicago, IL 60612
A list of publications on child development and health is available for twenty-five cents.

National Association for Divorced Women
200 Park Ave., Pan Am Building
New York, NY 10017
(212) 344-8407
Offers legal, employment, and financial counseling as well as child guidance and banking information to divorced women.

National Council of Organizations for Children and Youth
1910 K St., N.W.
Washington, D.C. 20006
(202) 785-4180
Clearinghouse for information about any developments relating to children.

National Family Planning Council
1800 N. Highland Ave., Suite 120
Los Angeles, CA 90028
(213) 461-4951
Birth control clinic, and abortion, vasectomy, and contraceptive counseling.

Parents Anonymous
2810 Artesia Blvd., Suite F
Redondo Beach, CA 90278
(213) 371-3501
For adults who have abused their children. Aim is to rehabilitate abusers and insure well-being of the children.

Parents Without Partners
7910 Woodmont Ave., Suite 1000
Washington, D.C. 20014
(301) 654-8850
Goal is to promote the study of single-parent problems, as well as to help alleviate them.

Health Services (Alcoholism, maternity, safety, mental health, nutrition, development)

Al-Anon Family Group Headquarters
115 E. 23rd St.
New York, NY 10010

(212) 475-6110
For relatives and friends of persons with an alcohol problem.

La Leche International
9616 Minneapolis
Franklin Park, IL 60131
(312) 455-7730
Supplies information for women interested in breast feeding of infants.

National Child Safety Council
4065 Page Ave.
P. O. Box 280
Jackson, MI 49203
(517) 764-6070
Organization interested in furthering the safety education of children. Furnishes child safety manuals, posters, brochures and films.

National Consortium for Child Mental Health Services
1800 R St., N W , Suite 904
Washington, D.C. 20009
(202) 462-3755
Serves as a forum for exchange of information on child mental health services.

National Council on Alcoholism
Two Park Ave.
New York, NY 10016
(212) 889-3160
Sponsors educational programs, community services, and alcoholism research. Maintains a library.

National Nutrition Consortium
9650 Rockville Pike
Bethesda, MD 20014
(301) 530-7110
Provides information to the public on nutrition, food, and health.

New York Institute for Child Development
205 Lexington Ave.
New York, NY 10016
(212) 686-3630
Center for medical diagnosis and treatment of learning disabled children.

Society for the Protection of the Unborn Through Nutrition
17 N. Wabash, Suite 603
Chicago, IL 60602
(312) 332-2334

Establishes nutrition centers in metropolitan areas of the U.S. to help pregnant women with nutritional information. Conducts seminars and maintains a speaker bureau.

Legal Services (Children's rights, child abuse, legislation)

American Parent's Committee
1346 Connecticut Ave., N.W.
Washington, D.C. 20036
(202) 785-3169
Persons interested in federal legislation for the welfare and better education of the nation's children.

Children's Rights, Inc.
3443 17th St., N.W.
Washington, D.C. 20010
(202) 462-7573
Clearinghouse of information on legislation concerning children's welfare. Maintains a speaker bureau.

National Center on Child Abuse and Neglect
U.S. Children's Bureau
P.O. Box 1182
Washington, D.C. 20013
Provides help for parents.

National Committee for Prevention of Child Abuse
111 E. Wacker, Suite 510
Chicago, IL 60601
(312) 565-1100
Seeks to stimulate greater public awareness of the incidence, origins, nature, and effects of child abuse.

Other Resources

The following organizations and agencies publish or disseminate information about young children:

American Association for Elementary-Kindergarten-Nursery Educators
1201 16th Street, N.W.
Washington, D.C. 20036

American Montessori Society
150 Fifth Avenue
New York, NY 10111

American Public Welfare Association, Inc.
1313 East 60 Street
Chicago, IL 60637

Association for Childhood Education International (ACEI)
3615 Wisconsin Ave., N.W.
Washington, D.C. 20016

Bank Street College of Education
69 Bank Street
New York, NY 10111

Black Child Development Educational Center
1028 Connecticut Avenue, N.W., Suite 306
Washington, D.C. 20036

Child Development Associate Consortium, Inc. (CDA)
7315 Wisconsin Ave., East, Suite 601
Washington, D.C. 20014

Child Study Association of America
50 Madison Avenue
New York, NY 10010

Child Welfare League of America, Inc.
67 Irving Place
New York, NY 10003

Children's Defense Fund of the Washington Research Project, Inc.
1520 New Hampshire Ave., N.W.
Washington, D.C. 20036

Council for Exceptional Children
1411 Jefferson Davis Highway
Arlington, VA 22202

Early Childhood Education Council of New York City (ECEC)
220 Waverly Place
New York, NY 10014

Education Development Center (EDC)
55 Chapel Street
Newton, MA 02106

ERIC/ECE, Educational Resources Information Center
Early Childhood Education
University of Illinois at Urbana, Champaign
805 West Pennsylvania Avenue
Urbana, IL 61801

National Advisory Council on the Education of Disadvantaged Children
1717 H Street, N.W.
Washington, D.C. 20009

National Association for the Education of Young Children
1834 Connecticut Ave., N.W.
Washington, D.C. 20009

National Association for Mental Health
10 Columbus Circle
New York, NY 10019

National Association of Social Workers, Inc.
2 Park Avenue
New York, NY 12202

National Committee on Education of Migrant Children
145 E. 32nd Street
New York, NY 10016

National Congress of Parents and Teachers
700 North Rush Street
Chicago, IL 60611

National Council on Family Relations
1219 University Ave., S.E.
Minneapolis, MN 55414

National Council of Jewish Women
1 West 47th Street
New York, NY 10036

Office of Child Development
U.S. Department of Health, Education, and Welfare
Washington, D.C. 20201

Office of Economic Opportunity
U.S. Department of Health, Education, and Welfare
1200 19th St., N.W.
Washington, D.C. 20500

Society for Research in Child Development, Inc.
University of Chicago Press
Chicago, IL 60637

UNESCO Publications Center
317 East 34th Street
New York, NY 10016

U.S. Department of Health, Education, and Welfare
Publishes bulletins pertaining to children. List of publications free from
U.S. Government Printing Office
Supt. of Documents
Washington, D.C. 20402

United States National Committee for Early Childhood Education
Member of World Organization for Early Childhood Education (OMEP)
81 Irving Place
New York, NY 10003

Index

Lastly

To the owner of this book   We hope you have enjoyed reading *Parents and Teachers* and will find it a handy reference in the years ahead. We'd like to have your opinions regarding the particular strengths of the book, as well as the things that need improvement. Could you let us know by filling out this page and returning it to us? In turn, your evaluation will be studied in preparing the second edition of *Parents and Teachers*.

1. What was the most useful part of the book? Why?

2. What was the least useful part of the book? Why?

3. Was any part of the book hard to read or understand?

4. Should anything be added to any section of the book? Why?

5. Should anything be deleted? Why?

6. What did you think of Part 3 on Guidance for Parents? If you are an instructor, would you like to have an expanded version of this part published as a separate book? How long should the book be? In which course would you adopt it and require it of your students?

Your name _____Date_____

May Wadsworth and I quote you in the promotion of *Parents and Teachers?*

Yes_____No_____

Thanks and best wishes,

Doreen J. Croft

Fold Here

Fold Here

FIRST CLASS
PERMIT NO. 34
BELMONT, CA

BUSINESS REPLY MAIL
No Postage Necessary if Mailed in United States

Ms. Doreen J. Croft
Wadsworth Publishing Company, Inc.
10 Davis Drive
Belmont, California 94002

Attn: Roger S. Peterson
Education & Family Studies Editor